The Story of a Life

Volume 2: Liberty Regained

SIMONE M. KLECKNER

Translation by Theodor Massim

PAGE PUBLISHING, INC.
New York, NY

First originally published by Page Publishing, Inc. 2016

ISBN 978-1-68348-340-3 (pbk)
ISBN 978-1-68348-341-0 (digital)

Cover Painting by Gil Nicolescu

Printed in the United States of America

To my families and friends in two beloved countries—
Romania, where I was born, and the USA, where I
experienced liberty, rights, and a happy life

Acknowledgments

First and foremost, I have to thank my many friends for their encouragement to write my memoirs based on the idea that there are things and former events that have to be brought to light for the benefit of future generations.

I am grateful to Iren and Grigore Arsene, owners of Curtea Veche (the Old Yard Publishing House) and their staff for publishing my story in two volumes in 2013–2014 in the Romanian language. Also, I am very thankful to my good friend Maria Lungu for her suggestions.

As for the English version, my gratitude is wholeheartedly extended to my great friend Theodor Massim, who was very kind not only to translate these volumes from the Romanian original but also to give me meaningful advice. Further, his work was a labor of love and patience, enriching the original with educated and comprehensive footnotes that are instrumental for the English-speaking public to understand certain references in this book. In addition, I extend my appreciation to Mr. Edward Claflin for his editorial work on the English manuscript and some of his recommendations.

The writing and publishing of a book is impossible without the help of friends and family. Therefore, I want to mention with gratitude Viorica Belcic and especially Andrei Ungureanu for their interest shown to publish the English version of my memoirs in the USA.

Of course, special thanks go to my husband, Rudi Kleckner, my first reader, the one who created the right ambience at home without which my story would not have seen daylight.

And last, but not least, I want to acknowledge *Page Publishing Inc.* and its editorial board for accepting the story of my life in two volumes. My gratitude goes to Kathryn Koller for her effort and expertise regarding the printing of both volumes: *Liberty Lost* (under communism) and *Liberty Regained* (under capitalist-democracy).

Contents

Foreword

I am happy to write a foreword to Simone Kleckner's *The Story of a Life, Volume 2: Liberty Regained,* a companion volume to her earlier *The Story of a Life, Volume 1: Liberty Lost.* Simone Kleckner is a remarkable woman who has lived the American dream after leaving Communist Romania under much persecution. She understands the difference between communist tyranny and democratic freedom and has proven that one can achieve great things when given the opportunity in a free society.

Mrs. Kleckner has understood from her real-life experience living under communist totalitarianism during the first part of her life that life in a free country is worth fighting for. She has never forgotten the dramatic differences between a free democratic society and an unfree communist dictatorship.

Having written about the misteaching of communism in US universities in the late 1960s, I especially appreciate her observation of the insidious political ideology permeating much of the academia in the United States and the naïveté of those students and professors who don't have firsthand experience or knowledge of the reality of life in the communist world.

Kleckner is a brilliant and accomplished legal scholar who is blessed with a gracious and supportive husband.

She gives a fascinating account of the travails and successes of coming to America and working her way up the ladder of success. Arriving in a new country with a different culture, she rapidly attained a master's degree in library science from Columbia University and a master's degree in international public law from New York University, to add to the Juris Diploma she had earned at the University of Bucharest School of Law.

Her story is an example of overcoming the odds and working hard to achieve the American dream. Through dogged determination, grit, and knowledge, Kleckner has made a positive impact in the annals of US-Romanian relations and in the legal system of the newly democratic Romania. Whether it was earning master's degrees from Columbia and NYU, working as a law librarian at the United Nations, serving as advisor to Romania's first post-communist democratic president, or tirelessly working as president of the Ad Hoc Committee for the Organization of Democracy in Romania (ACORD), Kleckner has left a significant mark and made a difference for good. It is my sincere hope that her work will be widely read and utilized in teaching Americans to understand and appreciate (before it is too late) the blessings of freedom in a country built by people of faith and knowledge of world history.

David B. Funderburk, PhD

Former US Ambassador to Romania
and US Congressman

What Made Me Write My Memoirs
Volume 2: Liberty Regained

As mentioned in my first volume, the events of World War II cast a deep shadow over Europe and changed the course of events in Eastern Europe. My urge to write my memoirs stemmed from the strong desire to give an assessment of what happened then to my country, to my family, and to myself under the influence of the Soviet social-communist regime that goes against human nature. What happened in Romania was typical of what happened in all the other Soviet-dominated countries behind the Iron Curtain, although Romania experienced a harsher regime because of our geographical proximity to Russia.

I thought it was my duty to share with others my experience since very little has been written about communist crimes. Besides, with the exception of a few intellectuals, Americans would not relate to communist stories, which were of little or no interest to them.

However, as it turns out, the ongoing Russian crisis since 2014 in Eastern Ukraine and Russian presence since 2015 in Syria are proof that exposing Russian influence or expansionism is still a topical subject.

While I wrote the first volume from the strong desire to denounce the crimes of communism, the second volume was born from the equally strong desire to show the blessings that I discovered in America when we arrived on April 27, 1966. The contrasting experiences were a dividing point in my life because in the United States, as opposed to social-communism, I had the luxury to make my choices freely and fulfill whatever I set my mind to. I did attend universities, chose and practiced my profession, and freely practiced my religion.

Since I no longer had, as in my first volume, sentimental problems to recount, my main interest focused on the progress of my studies and career in the academic environment at New York University, as international civil servant at the United Nations, and as federal civil servant at the United States Court of International Trade. All of that was intertwined with such personal experiences as the visits of our family and friends to us and our trips abroad.

In addition, because politics have totally changed my life, I believe that they are the most important factor that affects us all, and as a result I could not resist expressing my opinions about the American presidents and their administrations. Although I am a strong believer in the benefits of democracy and the capitalist market economy, however, the reader must take into consideration that my viewpoints are those of a person who has experienced social-communism, and therefore, my opinions will sometimes be somehow different from usual American thinking.

Equally important for me was the 1989 end of the Cold War. As a result, my interests and activities were immediately focused on the issues of neocommunism in Eastern Europe, including Romania. This gave me the opportunity to act against Russia's influence and in favor of democratic institutions, a market economy, respect for private property, as well as Romania's admission into NATO and the European Union. Consequently, from exile I lobbied the American authorities to urge the Romanian authorities to pass the necessary reforms. I did this under the umbrella of an Ad Hoc Committee for Democracy in Romania—in short, ACORD.

Regarding the organization of volume 2, it is divided into seven chapters in accordance with the positions I held, except for the last one when, being retired, I also spent time in Romania.

While writing, I relied mostly on my memory, on the documentation regarding my studies, and my job performance evaluation with the pertinent correspondence. Also, very handy were my twenty photo albums for remembering the sequence of my trips and the visits of relatives, old and new friends, whether Americans or Romanians.

I find myself fifty years in the United States, and thank God that this blessed land adopted us—Rudi, my husband, and I. We both hope for a strong America standing tall for world stability.

October 7, 2015

C H A P T E R 1

Steinberg-Kass, April 1966–December 1967

On Sunday, April 27, 1966, our flight from Rome landed at New York City's JFK Airport at 2:00 p.m. As I firmly set foot on American soil, I had big hopes and many dreams. Making our way to the end of long series of corridors, Rudi and I finally reached the special immigration window where we handed over our documents to the border officer. He examined them carefully before jotting down some cryptic notes and, with his left hand, giving them an official stamp of approval. (Seeing him use his left hand was a first for me. Back in Romania's primary school system, you were forced to write with the right hand regardless of whether you happened to be left-handed.)

Once the officer had finished checking our documents, he returned them and welcomed us to the United States with a broad smile. These brief border formalities were simple, expeditious, and conducted in a friendly manner. What a contrast to the border formalities at the Bucharest airport, where armed military and secret service personnel maintained an intimidating presence at all times!

After picking up our two suitcases in the baggage claim area, we headed toward the exit where "Uncle" Henry and his brother Harry, whom we had not met before, were waiting for us. They gave us a warm hug, and Henry took the opportunity to proudly take credit for our coming to the States, because it had been his visit to Bucharest that actually precipitated and facilitated our emigration.

In the car Henry told us that his sister Aida firmly believed that we were better off coming to the States rather than going to Israel. He said that when she received a note from our friend Sandu Missirliu saying that we had managed to leave Romania and were in Naples en route to Israel, she had been instrumental in convincing her son Norman to sponsor us by sending $500 for us to the HIAS organization in Rome. During that ride from the airport, Rudi was in the front passenger seat alongside Harry, who provided explanations about the areas we crossed on our way to Aunt Aida's house in the Bronx.

Aunt Aida offered to take us into her house since the bedrooms her children vacated when they moved out were available. So Wallace Avenue was our first permanent address in the States.

Crossing the imposing Queensboro Bridge, we saw the Manhattan skyline spread out before us. Henry pointed to several landmark skyscrapers, including the UN building to our left. It was then that, all of a sudden, an idea crossed my mind—that I would like to work for the UN and find out if anything could be done to help rescue Eastern Europe from the communist spell. I could hardly believe myself that such an idea occurred to me less than one hour after setting foot on American soil. I had already determined a future objective. Obviously, at the time I did not have the slightest idea whether I would ever achieve such a dream, but as always, I guess, I was counting on God's help.

Entering Manhattan by car allowed us to take a close-up look at the city that Rudi had been dreaming about for so long. Driving through the streets made us feel as if we were at the bottom of a canyon comprised of tall buildings. We were only able to see small patches of sky. People of all races were on the sidewalks, and all seemed to have a pretty relaxed demeanor. The image of them did not at all fit the stereotypes of communist propaganda, which always portrayed the woes of the rotting capitalist system. Somehow, those first impressions made me feel good about our future, while the fantasy about working for the UN continued to linger at the back of my mind.

When we reached the house of *Tante*[1] Aida (or Ida, as I shall call her henceforth), I began to awake from my reveries. Both Tante Ida and Sam received us with open arms and expressed satisfaction that their desire to bring us to the States had materialized. On the dining room wall they had hung a sign with the words "Welcome Home" written in multiple colors, and they had set a festive table in our honor. We were kind of tired, due to jet lag, and we would have very much preferred to take a nap rather than sit down and eat. But as the French say, "Noblesse oblige." In other words, we had to oblige. So we went to our designated bedroom, left our suitcases, and washed our faces in cold water. Now more invigorated, we felt prepared to get to know our extended family.

Lots of them came. All were anxious to meet their "cousins" about whom Ida, Sam, and Henry had spoken so highly. There to welcome us were Norman, their son; his wife, Sandra, a beautiful, smartly dressed Canadian; and their children—a son, two twins, and an infant daughter. From what Henry had told us, we gathered that Norman was fairly well-to-do. Following Ida's advice, and with the aid of financial assistance provided by his parents (who tapped into their savings), he had been able to get into the garment industry business. It was apparent that Norman was entirely up to the task, and he had become the "success story" of the family.

Norman's sister Corine came with her husband and their three children—two girls, Janice and Stacy, and a little boy, Paul. Hariette, their youngest daughter (who was divorced), was there too with her little boy Philippe. She was tall and very good-looking. Also present were Ida's brothers and their wives. Ida seemed to tower above everybody else as the matriarch of the extended family that now included us too.

---

1.   Romanian for "aunt."

I was able to communicate with them using the English I had learned from Mrs. Murphy, my former English teacher, while Rudi employed the little English he had learned during the courses that the HIAS organization had offered emigrants in Italy.

I was really impressed by Ida's kind offer to call my father. I gave her the number, and soon there was my father Gică's voice at the other end of the line. He was overjoyed when Ida told him in Romanian that we were okay and gave him assurances that she and Sam would be taking good care of us "like parents." Knowing that the eggplant salad[2] is always a hit with Romanians, Ida had included it in the menu. And, indeed, it did give us a taste of home.

Ida was proud of us, and I don't think we disappointed any of those present. Norman was impressed with my decent English and promised to help me land a job. He even offered Rudi, as a present, fifty dollars to use as pocket money. In fact, everybody promised to use whatever resources they had to help both of us find jobs, which we knew was not exactly an easy task. In particular, finding a job in the construction industry for Rudi would be a long shot, both because he lacked American experience and because he was not a Construction Workers' Union member.

As our first evening in the United States came to an end, we retired to bed with feelings of gratitude for everything Ida had done for us. At the same time, the remarks made by Ioana Crătunescu were still ringing in my ears: "In America it is very important for you to be debt free and to have a good credit record with the banks."

* * *

The next morning I set myself the task of calling Edith Răileanu, making arrangements to give her the letter from her friend Irina Luca. In addition, I planned to call George Kandel, who in the meantime changed his name into Kendall, my former virtual brother-in-law, whose phone number I had from my friend Lulu Sarf.

---

2.   A dip similar to the Mediterranean baba ghanoush made of the chopped pulp of a roasted eggplant blended with oil.

When I called Edith Răileanu, after introducing myself, I told her that I had a letter for her from her friend Irina Luca. She was very happy to have news and invited us for lunch the following Sunday. I accepted the invitation, confirming with her that the address written on the envelope was still valid: 110 West Sixty-Ninth Street, Fifth Floor, Apartment A, New York City. Her answer was affirmative, and so as I hung up the phone, I had the feeling I had one less obligation to worry about. (At least that is how I regarded that phone call and upcoming visit to the Răileanus' apartment.)

Then I called George. When I spoke my name, he was really taken aback. "Who's there, Mona from Armașului Lane?" When I said, "Yes, it's me!" he asked where I was calling from. I told him New York and explained that I had obtained his number from Lulu Sarf. After telling him briefly how I had managed to leave Romania and get to Rome en route to Israel—and how I had eventually managed to change gears and come to the States—he asked me right away whether there was anything he could do to help. At that moment, I was reminded that Norman had deposited $500 for us to the HIAS in Rome and that it would be nice to pay him back promptly. So I asked George whether he could lend me that money, and he told me that it was no problem. He offered to come to Ida's house the following day to take us out to dinner, which would give us the opportunity to catch up on all that had happened during the past twenty years. With this phone call, I had started to fulfill Ioana Crătunescu's advice.

For now, my top priority was to find a job and a place to live (although Ida gave us assurances that we were welcome in her house for as long as we wanted to stay).

* * *

So we had the peace of mind to venture out and explore our neighborhood. There were no tall buildings. Most houses were one- or two-family townhouses with brick siding.

Back home, we found Ida already busy calling employment agencies as she tried to find a job for Rudi. I was struck by the fact that every time the call did not go through or she dialed the wrong number, she would call the operator to get a refund. Later on, I saw

19

she did the same thing when using pay phones: after listening to Ida, the operator would promptly return her coin. I never thought that such a thing was possible.

As a newcomer, I was also struck by how Americans would customarily have their dinner in the early evening when everybody returned home from work. Back in the old country, a typical work schedule was from 7:00 a.m. to 3:30 p.m., and we had the main meal of the day in the afternoon, since that was when we got home from work. For a few weeks, until our digestive systems got adjusted to the American way, we were really hungry after each lunch.

In the afternoon, we usually took it easy, and Ida would try her best to give us brief insights into American history and politics. She told us about the Great Depression and what it had meant to most people. I thought that those hard times had really left a mark on her and explained, in part, why she was so careful to get a refund for every phone call that did not reach its target. Then Ida introduced us to the American two-party system, telling us about the Republicans and Democrats. We learned about President Roosevelt's New Deal policy that had been established in the wake of the Great Depression and about the Social Security system that provided a safety net for every working person, including unemployment and retirement benefits. She also described the Medicaid and Medicare systems that provided low-cost medical assistance. Back in 1966 these programs were not yet marred by the financial difficulties of later years, and so Ida had many reasons to be grateful for their existence.

But Ida was still marked by President Kennedy's assassination in November 1963, a true American tragedy, about which we had already heard in Romania. From Ida we learned about the conclusions of the Warren Commission that the assassination was not the result of a plot but the action of a sole individual, Lee Harvey Oswald. Later, in 1985, from the book *Breaking with Moscow* (pages 123–124), by the Russian author Arkady N. Shevchenko, I learned that the Kremlin ridiculed the conclusions of the Warren Commission and that Lyndon B. Johnson's administration absolved the Soviet Union of any role in the assassination. There was additional information about JFK that I found in the book *Killing Kennedy: The End of Camelot* by

TV personality Bill O'Reilly and historian Martin Dugard. The book analyzes Kennedy's multiple problems with the Chicago Mafia, the situation in Fidel Castro's Cuba, and the intervention of America in the Vietnam War. It concludes that Lee Harvey Oswald acted alone and that Jack Ruby, who killed Oswald, also acted alone. But the most interesting part of the story for me is in the afterword (pages 198–199, 287–290, 300), where O'Reilly writes, "In March 1977 a young reporter from Dallas began looking into the Kennedy assassination. He sought an interview with the shadowy Russian college professor who had befriended the Oswalds in Dallas in 1962. The reporter traced George de Mohrenschildt to Palm Beach, Florida, and travelled there to confront him. When he knocked at the door of Mohrenschildt's daughter's home, he heard the shotgun blast that marked the suicide of the Russian, assuring that his relationship with Lee Harvey Oswald would never be fully understood. By the way that reporter's name is Bill O'Reilly," himself the author of the book. (I saw Bill O'Reilly and M. Dugard presenting the book and movie on Fox News, November 30, 2014. I liked the book and the movie.)

* * *

The next morning, on Tuesday, April 29, Norman called to let me know that he had spoken with Dave Bernstein, a CPA, who let him know that one of the companies he was doing accounting for had an opening for an assistant bookkeeper. Norman immediately told Dave to set up an appointment for me with the chief accountant for the following morning. I was a little nervous about my English. So far, most of my practice in the language had been limited to basic conversations. But I was encouraged by the fact that for bookkeeping you had to be good with figures, not with words. In addition, I was confident that my work experience in Romania would help because the job of a "normator" was actually more complex than that of a bookkeeper.

Everybody in the house was very supportive and offered words of encouragement. Even Sam, who was a man of few words, patted me on the shoulder and said, "I am sure you will be up to the mark and get the job." So I kind of considered the job a sure bet and was quite happy that I did not have to go through headhunters and other placement agencies.

* * *

That evening I received the expected visit from George. I was waiting for him, and he was very punctual. When I opened the door, we were seeing each other for the first time since November 26, 1947, twenty years before. I was pleased to find that he had changed very little; he was tall, slim, and smartly dressed. We hugged each other, both feeling emotional about this unexpected reunion.

I introduced George to everybody. I just said he was a "former tenant of ours from Armașului Lane." George promptly gave me an envelope with five one-hundred-dollar bills that I placed in one of our suitcases. Then George drove us to Manhattan's west side on the Henry Hudson Parkway. He got off at the Fifty-Seventh Street exit, and we ended up at a fancy restaurant.

A signature feature of the restaurant was that pipe-smoking patrons stored their pipes in a specially built cassette, retrieving them on their next visit. While I do not remember what we ate for dinner, I do recall doing a lot of catching up. I had many stories that brought George up-to-date on what had occurred during the previous twenty years. I told him what had happened with our house on Armașului Lane, about our family, about how I met Rudi and how we managed to come to America. George, in turn, told us that he was married to an American woman, Linda, and that they had two sons, Colman and Joshua. He invited us to their house to meet his family.

Of course I was impatient to find out about his brother Stephen, my former true love. Finally, George said, "Stephen and Mother are in Toronto, Canada." He went on to tell us that Stephen had been married to a fellow doctor, someone their mother did not like, whom he had subsequently divorced. He remarried an Englishwoman who had a daughter from a previous marriage, and they had their own daughter, Stephanie. George also mentioned how much Stephen had suffered when I was unable to get out of Romania and join him in Italy. George said Stephen's move to Canada had been for financial reasons. And finally George added, "Moving to Canada was very painful for Stephen as, in his mind, it meant a final and painful separation from you." I made no comment. I was at peace with the thought that we had both gone through a divorce and were now happily remarried.

Then the conversation moved on to other subjects. Among other things, I asked George how much Americans knew about what life was like under the communists. His answer was something that stuck in my mind: "With the exception of a handful of intellectuals, Americans cannot relate to stories about communism, and therefore, those stories are of little or no interest to them. My advice to you," George continued, "is to forget about the past. If you get that job tomorrow—or any other job, for that matter—you better avoid that subject when you are at work. It does not appeal to people over here. They cannot bear to listen to what you had been through. I am telling you this from personal experience."

George's advice to Rudi was to improve his English as soon as possible. George recommended the Berlitz School of Languages, a national chain with offices around the country and overseas. Berlitz had an office in downtown Manhattan.

After George drove us home, I thanked him again for the money he had loaned us. Before he left, he said, "See you soon!" I was not sure whether he meant that literally or whether it was just an American way of saying, "Good-bye."

After that day we did have frequent phone conversations as George followed up, with interest, to see how we were doing. I did not call his mother, Rosalie, though I intended to get in touch with her in due time.

* * *

Back home, Ida and Sam were waiting for us, impatient to find out how the evening had gone. Rudi took the envelope that George had given us and handed it to Ida, saying, "This is a payback for our debt to you." Of course Ida and Sam were really impressed. This was especially true for Ida, who felt vindicated because it was she who had mobilized the entire family to support her effort to get us a US sponsorship. She had given everyone assurances that it would be a worthwhile effort as we were expected to do well in America. Ida picked the phone and called Norman to let him know the big news—that we had already paid back our $500 debt.

The next day, Ida, Rudi, and I took the subway to Manhattan for the job interview Norman had arranged for me. The trip with the subway was quite an experience for me as I had never before seen such a diversity of people of all races, sizes, and hairstyles. We got off at Thirty-Fourth Street, Penn Station. Steinberg and Kass, the company where I was going to have the job interview, was located on the fifth floor of the office building at Two Pennsylvania Plaza. The lobby directory showed the company listed with the initials SK, which happened to be my initials. I thought that was a good omen. Ida told the receptionist that Claire from the Accounting Department was expecting us. Soon Claire showed up, invited Rudi and Ida to sit down, and showed me to her office. Next to hers were two other offices with the titles "Steinberg" and "Kass"—hence the initials SK. I concluded those must be the owners of the company. (From what Norman had told me, I learned it was a garment whole-sale company.) Claire had a brief chat with me. Without getting too many details about my education and prior American experience, she offered me the job on a two-week probationary basis starting the very next morning, May 1. Later I realized that she might have had a vested interest in doing a favor for Dave Bernstein; he was working closely with her, basically auditing the company's records and mak-ing sure that there were no problems prior to the annual filing of IRS tax returns.

Claire showed me to my future work area and introduced me to one of my future coworkers, Mary, who smiled and welcomed me on board.

On my way out, I broke the news to Rudi and Ida that I had been hired. Understandably, they were very happy for me.

Back on Thirty-Fourth Street, we agreed that we were all hun-gry, then crossed the street to a place called Horn & Hardart to have a bite. I ordered a ham sandwich and almost went into shock when I saw the sandwich was almost two inches thick. I wondered what kind of a mouth you would need to take a bite from that monster sandwich. Back in Europe they would give you just one slice of ham in a sandwich. But I was kind of getting used to the idea that everything was big in America—the tall buildings, the bridges, the cars, the servings in restaurants, and accordingly, the size of most people I saw in the streets and the subway.

When we got home, another pleasant surprise was in store for us. Henry told Rudi that he had a connection at the Wyckoff Hospital in Brooklyn who wanted to see Rudi for a possible position as assistant electrician. The problem was that the following morning both of us needed transportation. Again, our family members came to the rescue. Sam offered to drive Rudi to Brooklyn while Carl, Ida's son-in-law who worked in the Manhattan garment district, offered to drive me to my new job. (For a while, I commuted to work daily in Carl's Buick until I was comfortable enough to use the subway system.)

Arriving at Two Pennsylvania Plaza, I took the elevator to the fifth floor and went straight to my office, where Mary showed me what she wanted me to do, which was mostly filing and sorting checks and mailing. Mary also handed me two books in which I was supposed to enter the checks, without any further explanation. At some point, Claire showed up with a pile of checks and, without any explanation, put them on my desk. Perhaps she assumed that Mary had told me what to do with them, but I hadn't been told a word. I thought Claire might be doing that on purpose to give herself an excuse to fire me once the probation time was over. Nonetheless, I opened the books that Mary had given me and figured out what to do. Later, the checks paid to us that I had processed were taken by a messenger to a bank for deposit. After the first scare, I found that what I had to do was kind of repetitive, nothing like what I had been doing as normator.

One day during the probation period, Claire called me to her office and requested me to "bring me the Tobias ten thousand voucher from the file." I had no idea what she wanted, but I retained, phonetically, the sound of her request. All I could decipher were the words "bring me" and "ten thousand." Like a parrot, I repeated to Mary what Claire had asked me without actually knowing what I was saying. To my surprise, Mary calmly went to a file cabinet, opened the drawer for the letter *T*, picked the TOBIAS file, and took out a $10,000 voucher from it. That's how I inferred what Claire wanted, and in the process I learned the words "file" and "voucher." I triumphantly took the voucher to Claire's office and put it on her desk. There was no "thank you" from her, but I thanked God that I had not made a fool of myself in what might have been an embarrassing situation.

That is how I started to build my American experience, with a weekly salary of $68 after taxes and all kinds of withholdings. Despite my meager income, I was able to save some money since we were staying in Ida's house without any expenses. My first priority was to pay back the debt to George as soon as possible.

Rudi was also offered a temp job at the hospital, where he did all kinds of odd jobs—such as fixing a toaster (which he had never done before). But Rudi was always very handy, and he somehow finished all the jobs assigned to him. He gradually earned the trust of his boss, who liked him, and eventually secured a permanent position with a weekly salary of $100 after taxes.

* * *

While we were gradually adjusting to the present, some of the new experiences we faced in the new world seemed laughable to us. For example, we could not understand why Ida was throwing away the tasty skin of the roasted chicken for fear that its fat had too much cholesterol, or when all the members of our new family were taking turns inviting us to their houses for lunch or dinner, or why the food was served on disposable paper plates instead of china plates. Again, that was something new to me.

One day when we were invited to Norman's house, a tall guy began complaining that he could not finish remodeling his main bathroom because the seven-foot bathtub that was to replace the five-foot one (which was too small for him) had not been delivered on time. His problem sounded to me like such a trivial problem: my mind went back to our improvised bathroom in the laundry of our little apartment where we bathed by pouring water over our heads from a pitcher that substituted for a shower.

We constantly measured our present against the past that still haunted us.

But there was no way to forget that past. One evening I found a letter on our bed. I recognized my father's writing and opened the envelope in a hurry. Unfortunately, the letter delivered sad news of the passing of my dear Uncle Nicu, who died of a massive heart attack. (He died while we were in Rome, but my father had not wanted to break the news at the time, knowing that we faced other issues that required our full attention.) I loved Uncle Nicu dearly and was literally heartbroken! My beloved uncle had devoted a lot of time to me during my childhood, and I will always remember him. I reflected on how he had endured numerous vicissitudes—having the communists take away all his properties, land and house, while also depriving him of the right to pursue his profession. God should rest him in peace!

* * *

The Răileanu family expected us for lunch the following Sunday. Edith gave us directions, explaining how to get to their apartment via the subway. She warned us not to expect a fancy building: they lived on the West Side of Manhattan, while the more affluent area was on the East Side. We had no problem finding the Răileanu apartment. When I gave Edith Irina's letter, she welcomed us with open arms, greeting us as messengers from her beloved Romania and beloved friend Irina. Her husband, Visarion, though less exuberant, was equally friendly. Until that day I never suspected the value of that innocent letter.

They served us a lunch with a lot of traditional Romanian dishes, such as eggplant salad with roasted peppers and feta cheese with tomatoes. They also served us a Romanian plum brandy, which is the Romanian version of the Hungarian Slibowitz. Even the plum brandy glasses were traditional, just like the ones in Romania.

After the meal we all sat down in the living room, and the discussion dealt mostly with us and how we had fared so far in the new country. We proudly mentioned that we were both lucky to have found jobs already in our first week in the States. The next step, we explained, would be to find an apartment even though we were currently living with relatives in the Bronx who were ready and willing to host us indefinitely. The Răileanus asked whether we had any preference for a particular part of the city where we wanted to look for an apartment. Of course we had no idea which area would have an apartment that would be within our budget and also within easy commuting distance. Then, without comment, Visarion picked up the phone and began talking in Romanian with a certain Mr. Zissu who lived in the building. (Mr. Iancu Zissu was the lawyer of the former Romanian Jewish Community whose president was Willy Filderman, both mentioned in volume 1.) Visarion confirmed with Mr. Zissu that the fifth-floor one-bedroom apartment would be available after a certain Dr. Cosla moved out. Then Visarion said, "I know you are in good terms with the owner, and I have here with me the daughter of Professor George Vrăbiescu from the Bucharest Law Faculty who recently immigrated to the States. Both she and her husband are currently employed, and they are looking for an apartment."

After Visarion hung up the phone, he told me that Mr. Zissu just confirmed that he had been my father's student and offered to check with the owner. A brief ten minutes later, Mr. Zissu called back to inform Visarion that Mr. Cosla, the previous tenant, was not ready to vacate the apartment but that he had no problem subleasing the furnished apartment to us for one year as long as Mr. Zissu was willing to guarantee for us.

We went to the fifth floor to see the one-bedroom apartment with a fully equipped kitchen and nice bathroom. The rooms were sunny, with windows facing Sixty-Ninth Street. We loved the apartment and decided to sign the subleasing contract on the spot for a monthly rent of $120 and with July 1 occupancy. Due to Visarion's intervention and to the fact that Mr. Zissu was my father's student, he recommended that we get the apartment. That meant we would be worry-free for one full year. This marked for us a step forward in a journey that seemed like it had been mapped out from the moment Irina gave me her letter for Edith in Bucharest. It made me reflect that God had taken good care of us even before we arrived in the USA and that there is more to life than we can comprehend.

A year later, when the lease was up, we called Dr. Cosla, fearing that he might not want to renew the contract. To our satisfaction he said that he no longer needed the apartment and was willing to give it up for good. Then we went back to the owner to sign our own lease contract. It turned out that the previous owner had the apartment under "rent control" status. I don't know why, but for some reason the owner offered us the same terms—although, by law, he was under no obligation to do so once the previous "rent control" tenant had vacated the apartment.

Initially, we thought that we would live in the apartment only until we could afford something bigger or fancier, but as it turned out, we found the location very desirable in every respect. Starting on July 1, 1966, we kept the same apartment. We were close to Central Park and also close to the Seventy-Second Street subway station, very convenient for our daily commute. In addition, soon after we moved to the area, Lincoln Center was built just a few blocks away. We were now within walking distance of the Met Opera, NYC Ballet, and NY Philharmonic, which had a really positive impact. The area we lived in soon became very desirable, and apartments were in great demand. As it turned out, our apartment was a big present that fate offered us back in Bucharest through Irina Luca's letter, hidden in my suitcase and not discovered at the customs, toward our new home in our new country. That's what the letter was about!

* * *

Meanwhile my only grievance was my uneasy relationship with my boss Claire and the fact that I found my job increasingly boring.

One morning as I was crossing a large hallway, heading for my office, Claire saw me and asked me to do some task for her from the other side of the spacious hall—again in her usual abrupt and rude tone. Later on, just before lunchtime, she approached my desk, and I thought she would be giving me some other task; to my surprise, she had only come to apologize for the way she had talked to me that morning. I was stunned, because the way she had spoken with me that morning was no different from the way she had addressed me at other times in the past. But later, in midafternoon, Mr. Steinberg came to my desk and asked, "Did she apologize to you?" Apparently, he had overheard how Claire had talked to me that day and thought it was inappropriate. He wanted the relationships among his employees to be civil and polite. Presumably, he had asked her to apologize to me in order to teach her a lesson.

Unfortunately, she did not learn much from that incident. On the contrary, her attitude became even worse. I got the feeling she was now envious of me, thinking that perhaps I had become the big boss's protégé.

With my coworker Mary, I got along fine. We even saw each other socially from time to time. The first occasion was when we invited her and her fiancé Viny for dinner. We had dressed up and were surprised when they showed up in jeans, T-shirts, and sneakers. Again, we were learning the American way the hard way. After a whole week of dressing up every day to go to the office, Americans apparently preferred to dress casually and relax during the weekend.

Another novel experience for me was watching, in awe, as the window washers cleaned the office windows. I could not believe how they managed to work at those heights with only a safety cord hooked up to their belt. When one of the workers entered into our office through an open window, I asked him how much the window washers were paid for such a dangerous job. I knew my accent betrayed me as a newcomer when the guy told me promptly that "in this country salaries are confidential." I learned my lesson: to this day I have never dared to ask anyone else how much money they were making.

* * *

When the hot days of summer set in, Ida and Sam invited us to spend a weekend with them at their summer house in Monticello, a little town in a hilly area in Upstate New York. It was there at a local movie theater that I saw *Doctor Zhivago*, the movie based on Boris Pasternak's novel that won him the 1989 Nobel Prize for Literature. That was such a revelation for me. I could relate very well to the movie plot. I had not been able to read the book; however, although it had been published in the USA in 1959, it was forbidden in Romania. (In fact, the novel would not be published in the Soviet Union until 1987.) As we got out of the movie theater, both Rudi and I were red-eyed from crying. But we could overhear comments from other spectators to the effect that the movie was interesting but too long. It was one more awakening for us to the fact that people who had never lived in such circumstances (portrayed in the movie) could not relate to those realities.

One time, while we were still living in Ida's house, we were taken to a function where we were joined by a number of other people. One lady at our table was not happy with the food for some reason and called the waiter to return it. The waiter took the plate away, showing no sign that the incident might inconvenience or annoy him in any way. Then when the replacement plate came, the lady again found something wrong and once again returned it. That was too much for me to bear. I stood up from the table and left to vent away my frustration outside. Coming from a part of the world where people were standing in line for hours to procure basic necessities, I just could not get over the fact that these people were so spoiled and that they were getting away with it.

* * *

Our moving day came on Tuesday, July 1, 1966. Both Rudi and I took that day off from work. As he had done so many times since our arrival, Sam again offered to help us out, schlepping us and our two suitcases from Wallace Avenue to our new address at 110 West Sixty-Ninth Street, apartment 5A. Ida gave us a few bed sets and towels, kitchen utensils, pots and pans—in short, the bare necessities to get us started in our new home.

Once installed, we went to a supermarket on nearby Columbus Avenue and bought lots of groceries and other household necessities, including a few more pots, detergents, food for the rest of the week, cigarettes (because we were both smoking at the time), sugar, salt, and pepper. The cost was twenty dollars, one-third of my weekly salary. Not bad, we thought, for a country that, according to the communist propaganda, was rotting from within.

Then we moved our bank account to a bank in our new neighborhood. We were surprised how easy the whole operation was. The transfer went very smoothly. It was a really nice feeling to see ourselves on our feet after such a short time in our new country. And we were especially grateful for the fact that, after settling all our payments and expenses, we could still afford to save some dollars every month.

* * *

The next time George invited us for dinner, he came with his wife, Linda. As soon as we saw each other, we pulled out one of the checks that we had just received, printed with our new address, and made out one to them in the amount of $500 to pay back the debt that we had to George. We felt that we had really made a qualitative leap forward in the process of getting integrated into the American society. During our conversation with Linda, we never touched on our Romanian past, as we recalled George's warning that it was hard for her to relate to his past and we should not mention the subject to her at first. Instead, Linda told us at length about her tennis lessons, about her exercises at the gym, and about their two boys. When we got to the Vietnam War, the top political issue of the day, Linda said she thought the Americans had no business going to that remote country. George, on the contrary, expressed the opinion that President Johnson could no longer afford to leave unchallenged the advance of the communist-supported Vietcong. Again, we were surprised to find out how indifferent some Americans were to the steady communist expansion.

Finally, the time was right for me to call Rosalie, who was, technically, my former mother-in-law, at least on paper. When she heard my voice, she responded with a spontaneous outburst of joy. In no time at all, she briefed me on everything she had gone through since her husband's unexpected and untimely death in Milan. Of course she also talked about Stephen's marriages and how she was getting along with her daughters-in-law. As for my own stories, there was no need to tell her anything: George had already informed her about everything there was to know.

* * *

Meanwhile, my mother wrote, urging me to try contacting Mr. Valahu, who was one of her second husband's lawyers. When we called him, he invited us to meet at his wife's office on Fifth Avenue. His wife, Christine Valmy, was the owner of a well-known cosmetics chain. Mr. Valahu knew nothing about my mother's time in prison, and both he and Christine were horrified to hear what she had gone through. Before we said good-bye, Christine Valmy suggested that we join them at a meeting of the Republican Party that was to be held at a Holiday Inn Hotel. She had reserved a big table for the meeting.

At the same Holiday Inn Hotel, on another occasion, we met many friends from the Romanian diaspora in New York. To my surprise, the manager at the Holiday Inn was my friend Călin Alimăneştianu in whose house I had met Lulu Şarf years before. Călin and his brother Constantin (who now lives in Chicago) had fled from Romania by swimming across the Danube to Yugoslavia. It was a great pleasure to see him again, especially when I realized how handsome he was, even at his more-advanced age. He introduced us to Despina Hodoş and Ştefana Cantacuzino, the two sisters. (These were Ioana Crătunescu's friends, the ones she had phoned from Rome when she recommended us.) While we were there, somebody asked whether we knew Sorin Anagnoste, who lived in Manhattan. Of course I knew him very well and was eager to get in touch with him.

* * *

Time passed quickly, and before we knew it we were experiencing our first Thanksgiving Day in America in the beautiful house of Sandra and Norman, in the midst of the entire family and many invited friends. All traditions connected with this American holiday were new to us. We admired the beautifully roasted and plump turkey filled with stuffing that Sandra proudly presented on a big tray lined with lettuce leaves. We marveled at the big fruit platter covered with jelly and at the cranberry sauce, since we had never before seen or tasted such sweet trimming served with meat. To be honest, I missed the pickles and the sautéed cabbage that were usually served with turkey in Romania, but that didn't stop me from tasting all the foods that were new to me. Though they seemed weird then, over the years I have come to like them.

That year, we spent Christmas Eve in the house of Sorin Anagnoste, whom we rediscovered among the Romanian diaspora. Then on Christmas Day we were invited to the Răileanus'. After dinner we went out for a stroll in downtown Manhattan to see the Christmas decorations by night—first, the big Christmas tree in Rockefeller Center, and then on to Times Square. For us it was an overwhelming experience that gave a feeling of euphoria. I was happy for Rudi, who could at last see, in all its glory, the city that he had dreamt about for years. It really is "a city that never sleeps," and it infused us with optimism.

We owed a lot to the Răileanus, special nice people who reached out to help ensure that our future life would be good. In addition, they took us to a show at Radio City Music Hall for the first time. I shall never forget the moment when the orchestra started to play, and, big surprise, it was Enescu's *Romanian Rhapsody*. It was a magic moment that seemed to be designed especially for us—an unbelievable coincidence that made me cry. I realized I truly felt there was more to it, as if there had been a divine intervention to make me feel at home even though I was far away in strange surroundings.

1967

In January Rudi started his English as a second language (ESL) courses at the Berlitz School of Languages. Norman, who used to work in the garment district and was the same size as Rudi, passed him some ten suits that he had scarcely worn. In the morning Rudi was an electrician, in the afternoon the most elegant student at the Berlitz School.

Finally, the time came for us to think about owning a car. From a dealer in Queens we ended up buying a preowned red Chevrolet Monza. We were very happy, and it was then when I took my driving license.

While we were both working at our current jobs, we were already thinking about the next step. Rudi considered starting his own business as a contract electrician. But we found out that you needed years of experience to get a license. The alternative was to attend school and get the diploma of a licensed electrician. As for me, I was also ready to get away from my boring job and from the impossible Claire.

Thus, I decided to approach Dave Bernstein and ask about the possibility of going to school to become a licensed accountant. He was totally skeptical about that, telling me, "Simone, accounting is a man's job," words which made me think, "There we go again!" In Romania I had been discriminated against for sociopolitical reasons, and in America I was again being discriminated against for being a woman. (In America it was only after World War I that women got their right to vote.) Of course, legally speaking, women had the same rights as men, but in practice it was a highly different story. My remedy remained to pray to find a solution for a professional career.

And the answer came when God was speaking to me through a stranger. This happened toward the end of May 1967 when George and Linda Kendall invited us for dinner in their Queens home. We were fourteen people at the table, and Linda seated me next to an Egyptian lady who had fled Nasser's communist regime. As we did have a lot in common, we had long conversations. At some point she asked me how I liked America and asked what I was doing for a living. I told her that I was working as an assistant bookkeeper and that I would very much prefer to do something else more appropriate to my qualification as a graduate of the Bucharest Law Faculty. Then she asked, "Why don't you do what my daughter did? She is also a law school graduate, and she got a degree as a legal librarian."

The lady volunteered to send me a letter with details about the steps her daughter had taken toward being admitted to Columbia University to study for a master's degree in library science. I knew that fate was answering my prayers. If Linda had seated me next to somebody else, nothing would have happened that evening.

A few days later, I got the promised letter in the mail with a detailed description of how many credits were required to earn a degree, what documents you had to submit to apply, where to apply, and so on.

Finally, after twenty years, my law diploma seemed to be worth something. That turned out to be the only asset that the communists could not take away from me.

I called Despina and Ştefana, Ioana Crătunescu's friends, and told them the news. Immediately they invited us for dinner, together with a friend who just got his master's degree from Columbia. That evening at dinner he drafted my application, explaining my past communist experience, the financial immigrant situation, and my desire to study based on my Romanian law diploma.

As instructed, I submitted the application to Columbia University General Studies. My only worry now was to anticipate the letter telling me whether I would be admitted to a master's degree program.

* * *

After one year on the job, I was entitled to a two-week vacation. From our friend Sorin we found out about the little town of Avalon on the New Jersey shore, nearly a two-and-a-half-hour drive from New York City. We checked into a motel called Desert Sand, which had minisuites, each with a little kitchen area, a table, a small refrigerator, a living room with a TV and a sofa bed, as well as a bedroom with a king-size bed. The motel was across the street from the beach and had two swimming pools.

* * *

Many weeks later, I got an envelope in the mail from the Ford Foundation letting me know that I had qualified for a master's degree program with a $1,000 grant that would be paid in two $500 installments. Some conditions were attached, however, including the requirement that I take a three-month course in English offered by Columbia University; if I passed the English exam and got enrolled in the master's degree, I had to get a minimum score of B in the first semester and, finally, attend courses full-time. I read through the letter over and over again to make sure that I did not overlook anything. Rudi was delighted with the news.

A few days later, I went to the Admission Office in the Butler Library at Columbia University. I showed the Ford letter and my law school diploma to the administrator in admissions, who congratulated me on the Ford scholarship award. I was told that my law diploma was equivalent to a BS, which allowed me to start accumulating credits toward the desired master's degree. I thanked her and explained that, despite the scholarship, I could not afford the tuition cost, especially since I would have to quit my job in order to attend courses full-time. With a smile, the admissions worker declared that I had been lucky to get that scholarship, as it was only awarded to a limited number of students. Then she took a piece of paper and started to jot down some figures. She asked me how much I paid for rent and utilities, my car and commuting expenses, how much money Rudi was making, and so on. Then she drew a line, added all the expenses, subtracted them from our income, and figured out how much I had available for tuition and how much money I needed. Finally she told me that Columbia University could grant me a loan for that amount, payable in affordable installments over a number of years once I landed a job. The only string attached was that I must complete the three-month English course successfully. That course was also offered evenings, three times a week from 6:00 p.m. to 8:30 p.m., and the next session started October 1.

The normalcy and smoothness of the entire process touched a chord in me, and by the time she was done explaining all this, I had tears in my eyes. I compared the way I had been treated by the communists in my own country to how I was now being treated under this blessed democracy.

I started the English classes on October 1. Because they were held in the evenings, I was able to keep my job with Steinberg Kass. I took the course completion test in mid-December, and the instructor informed me that the results would be sent to the Admission Office of the Library Science School in a few days. When I checked with the Admissions Office a few days later, they had received the results, and I had the green light to start the enrollment process. I was in heaven! My lessons with Mrs. Murphy paid off.

* * *

Now the time had come for me to quit my job, giving them the customary two-week advance notice of my resignation. I did not want Claire to be the first to know about it. So I went straight to David Steinberg's office and let him know of my intention to resign effective in two weeks, explaining I had been admitted to Columbia University to work toward a master's degree. David stood up, shook my hand, and wished me luck. Then he asked whether Claire knew about my resignation. After I told him that he was the first to get the news, he called her by phone to come to his office. When Claire saw me in his office, she could not believe her eyes. On the spot, he let her know about my intention to resign. Claire had no reaction. Without addressing a word to me, she just assured Steinberg that she would start looking for a replacement right away. Her dry reaction to the news of my resignation was indicative of the bad chemistry between us. But I had learned that there were some extenuating circumstances, as Mary told me that Claire had some personal problems at home. Nonetheless, I was fed up with her, and I am sure the feeling was mutual.

* * *

When I returned to the Administrative Offices of the School of Library Science, the nice lady gave me some forms to fill out. She informed me that each student was being assigned to an advisor and that I was going to see the dean himself.

Meeting with the dean in his office, we reviewed the courses that were offered. Based on my past experience and my plans for the future, we selected the required number of mandatory courses that would prepare me for the librarian career and a few selective ones for general knowledge. When I asked the dean the relevance of my legal studies, he told me the university offered a number of courses on legal issues, domestic and foreign legislation, and government and international organizations, such as the League of Nations or the United Nations. Before I left, I thanked the dean for his time and wished him "Happy holidays." All the way home, I was on cloud nine.

* * *

Before the end of the year, Norman and Sandra invited us for dinner, and we went with the "affidavit of support" form required to bring Gică to the States for a three-month visit. Though we had filled the form, we could not add our signatures because we were not American citizens. As always, Norman was happy to help us. He signed the forms and then wished us "Happy New Year" with the Romanian "La mulți ani" that he had learned from Ida to surprise us.

CHAPTER 2

January 1968–August 1969

Many people hesitate to leave a secure situation even when the change is likely to be for the better. I was not afraid to make such a change. Case in point, my situation with Claire. I was yearning to regain my dignity and capitalize on my law degree. Earned in Romania, that degree had been useless at the time in that country, but now it promised to regain some value. My aspiration was to get to work in academia or in an international organization where I could make use of my command of four languages—German, French, Romanian, and of course, my constantly improving English.

For me, becoming a student at Columbia University was a daring endeavor. Lacking any experience in the American education system, I was at a disadvantage compared to my colleagues, and I had to redouble my efforts to keep up with them.

Following the dean's advice, for the first semester that started in January, I chose three mandatory courses and one elective. Attendance at each course varied, depending on what other students had selected. This was a contrast to Romania, where all students were supposed to take the same courses.

During one class, a young American woman introduced herself as Carol. She was very nice and talkative and curious to find out as much as possible about me. (My accent gave me away as a foreigner.) She told me that her company paid her entire tuition; she did not have to pay a penny out of her pocket.

As time went on, we began to sit next to each other in many of the courses we had in common. One day she brought up the subject of the Vietnam War and told me she was opposed to it. I did not want to comment. I had avoided the subject of my life under communism because I realized that she and I came from different backgrounds and had different life perspectives.

To me Carol was the quintessential American woman. My feeling about her was reinforced one day in the Butler Library. As I was studying there, looking for answers to typed questions that the professor had given us, all of a sudden Carol showed up. She whispered to me that she would have to do that assignment in a hurry to make it to a women's emancipation meeting. As I had already completed the assignment, I offered to share the answers with her. It was an offer she flatly refused. To my surprise she said, "Oh, Simone, how could I copy your answers? My company is paying me to study, not to steal somebody else's work. But I thank you anyway." I was really impressed. To me, her honest attitude was typical of most Americans.

Soon after that, I had another experience along the same lines. Copying some documentation for an assignment, I thought the copy machine did not return a dime that I was supposed to get in change. I had moved away to my table in the library when a girl patted me on the shoulder and said, "I found this dime in the change compartment of the copy machine. I think it's yours." Yes, it was mine. I took the dime and thanked her. Once again, I was impressed with American honesty.

Another fellow student whom I met and befriended in my acquisitions course was Leonarda Wielavski. She was originally from Poland and told me that her parents back home had an agricultural estate and a horse-raising farm. During the war, German soldiers kidnapped her from the street in her native town and took her to a forced labor camp in Germany. As she was a Catholic, she had managed to survive and later married a psychiatrist who had also survived a labor camp. Together they managed to immigrate to the United States, and like me, they went through all the hardships of starting out in a new country, not least of which was learning the language. In addition, her husband had to pass all the equivalency exams before he could become a practicing psychiatrist in New York.

Leonarda and her husband had a beautiful house in Bedford Hills, a few miles north of New York City. We visited them often and would remain friends for years after our graduation. In fact, we were always invited for the Catholic Easter in their house, and she came to us for the Orthodox Easter. For Passover we were always at Ida's. With Leonarda, also known as Lee, I could finally share memories about life under communism. We often discussed present-day events such as the post-Vietnam atmosphere and the anti-Vietnam movements and the communist expansion, which both of us dreaded.

We praised Truman's policy of *containment*, aimed at halting the expansion of communism by providing military aid to the countries that were trying to preserve their liberty. Then we could not understand why Kennedy started the Vietnam War in the Tonkin Gulf just because a tiny North Vietnamese gunboat menaced a giant US warship. Bill O'Reilly put it right in his book *The O'Reilly Factor* (page 48): "So because of this mouse the elephant would eventually put millions of young men in harm's way on the other side of the world for reasons no one ever explained."

Lee and I also talked about President Johnson's conviction that America had to stand up to the Russian-supported communist expansion in North Vietnam by sending fifty thousand Americans to Vietnam and approving big funds to support military action. However, that triggered the violent antiwar movement that spread throughout the country. We believed that left-wing people fueled a climate of support for the communists in North Vietnam.

All that had happened a short time before Rudi and I arrived in the United States—a country that was getting radicalized before our eyes. We were shocked at the violence of the protests, and also by the sex liberation movement, the increase in drug use, and the rebellion against all conservative and traditional values.

But we loved listening to Elvis Presley being proclaimed the king of rock. And in the 1970s, we watched the *Ed Sullivan Show*, the *Today Show*, the launching of the disco music by the successful *Saturday Night Fever* boomers—those born during or immediately after World War II, who were expressing themselves in powerful ways that contrasted with those born during the financial crisis of 1929–1935. And I was reading the major magazines—*Life*, *Time*, and *Bazaar*.

* * *

Then five important events happened. These were Johnson's withdrawal from the presidential campaign, followed by the presidential debates between the Democrat Hubert Humphrey and the Republican Richard Nixon. Then on April 4, 1968, we were shocked by the TV news reports about the assassination of Dr. Martin Luther King Jr. at age of thirty-nine. It struck the country like a thunderbolt. My fellow student Carol, from Columbia, called me, crying as she asked whether I had heard the news. She was kind of surprised to hear that I knew that he had been awarded the Nobel Peace Prize and had heard about his famous "I have a dream" speech expressing the hope that discrimination will be no more. Shortly after that event, on June 6, Robert "Bobby" Kennedy, attorney general during his brother's administration, was assassinated by Sirhan Sirhan in Los Angeles, California, during his run for the presidency. (He had been a resolute fighter against organized crime.)

Two days later, on June 8, Lee—my Polish fellow student from Columbia—called to let me know that her husband had died of a massive heart attack. Now she was left alone taking care of their three children. We were very saddened by this unexpected tragedy in the Wielavski family.

* * *

Regarding my future career, one day Mihai Handrea called me to say that, if I was interested, he might recommend me for a job that had opened up at the New York Public Library, offering a summer internship position for a student who was fluent in at least one foreign language. Handrea was the one I had met in the house of Despina and Ștefana who had a master's in library science from Columbia and who drafted my application for my own master's degree. (I had often asked for his guidance during my enrollment process.) Now he was working for the New York Public Library, which was how he had heard about the job opening in the Periodicals Section. My first inclination was to turn down the offer, but Mihai explained that it would do me no harm to take a break from school during the summer and resume courses in the autumn. That way, he explained, I would gain some experience while earning money at the same time. In the end I decided to interrupt courses and give it a chance.

Mihai set up an interview for me with Eugenia Patterson, head of the Periodicals Section, a very nice lady. We chatted about my background, my education, and the foreign languages that I was fluent in. She offered me the job, starting as soon as I finished the trimester at Columbia.

That summer internship job turned out to be a godsend, because meanwhile, I had received the good news that my father had been given a passport and an American visa. He planned to come on July 15, allowing me enough time to earn enough at the library to pay for his plane ticket. Without that job, it would have been practically impossible for us to afford his ticket since we had been living on very limited resources while I was a student. (We strictly allocated the money for each expense, and an overspending of even five dollars in one week had to be deducted from the following week's budget.)

At the end of the trimester, I passed all midterm exams with grades that met the requirement to qualify for the next $500 installment of the Ford grant. After the exams I had almost two weeks before the July 1 start of my job. Knowing our meager financial situation, Lee told us that we were welcome to stay in her vacation cottage at Cape Cod. We accepted the offer, and although it was kind of out of season for Cape Cod, we were very lucky and had excellent weather, with many sunny days. We often went to the beach and even got into the ocean a few times.

With our batteries recharged by that unplanned but very pleasant minivacation, I reported for my new job on July 1. There was a bus stop at the corner of the street near our house, and that bus would take me right to the library. Commuting to work by bus instead of by subway allowed me to admire the city sights. I was especially impressed by Times Square with its huge neon signs and big advertising billboards. It was, for me, a spectacular sight.

Eugenia Patterson, my supervisor, was the complete opposite of Claire. Whenever Eugenia gave me a task, she would coach me, providing a lot of detailed instructions about what I had to do. So she gave me confidence. But when I had to answer the phone, it was a different story. I was terrified of the idea that my accent might be too heavy. For me, it was always a challenge—that balancing act between being extra careful about my English and trying not to fake an accent. For the most part, however, I discovered that my English was good enough in a city where one heard all kinds of accents all over the place. Moreover, I even got compliments for my English, with many people telling me they would be happy to know a foreign language as well as I spoke English. That gave me a nice feeling. Because Americans never frowned on me because of my accent, I never felt like a foreigner in this country.

* * *

On July 15 we drove to the airport to welcome my father, Gică. I was overjoyed but also a little apprehensive. He was now seventy-six, and I was afraid that the eleven-hour trip from Bucharest might have been a little too long for him. But he did not look tired at all. It was really emotional for us to finally be able to hug each other again. Both of us had tears in our eyes. He had only good words to say about the flight, the service, and the food served on the plane.

On the way home, the sight of the Manhattan skyline, seen at a distance, made quite an impression on him. Once we got home, his first request was to call his wife Florica in Bucharest and let her know that he had arrived and everything was okay. Then he told us he would like to call Sam and Ida to thank them for everything they had done for us. After we had a little snack and a beer, he slept like a log on our sofa in the living room until the next morning.

In the days that followed, he liked to take walks in Central Park, feeding nuts to the squirrels and bread to pigeons. We would arrive home after he'd had lunch and an afternoon nap, and find him quite happy. The only thing annoying him was the fact that he only spoke French and German but did not understand English. In the evening we had to translate the evening TV news, especially when it was about presidential elections.

On weekends, we gave him tours of the city and the surroundings and took him to visit relatives and friends. One day, we took him to Columbia University to show him around the campus. At the School of Law Library we checked the catalogue of publications under the letter *V*, where we found the name Vrăbiescu. Both George and Nicolae were listed along with their doctor's degree theses written in Paris in 1921. My father's thesis was "Contribution to Critical Studies on the Right to Acquit," and my uncle's was "The Natural Obligations and Moral Duties as Independent Notions."

While my father was still with us, on August 21, Soviet troops—aided by troops of other Warsaw Pact member states—invaded Czechoslovakia to crush the Prague Spring reforms initiated by the communist leader Alexander Dubček. The goal of the reforms was an attempt to partially decentralize the economy and grant more democratic rights to the people, even though the country was to retain the communist system and remain a member of the Warsaw Pact. However, those reforms—especially the decentralization of administrative authority—were not well received by the Soviet leader Brezhnev, who sent thousands of Warsaw Pact troops and tanks to occupy the country. Romania's president Ceaușescu criticized the Soviet invasion, calling it an interference into that country's internal affairs.

My father's visit ended. He returned to Bucharest via Paris, where he stopped over for a few days. It was an emotional opportunity for him to again visit the city he had known during his student years and to see my aunt Tancy and the Missirlius. He had also been invited to visit Lulu Șarf, our former neighbor in Armașului Lane with whom I had a brief teenage fling.

* * *

In September I had to resume my courses at Columbia University that had been interrupted during the summer while I was doing my internship. Then one evening, the phone rang. From the first hello I recognized Lulu's pleasant voice. He had become a prominent civil engineer in Paris specializing in high-rise buildings. Now Lulu had come to New York for a few days to view the construction of the foundation for the World Trade Center twin towers, which was in full swing at the time.

At the end of September, we had another event. Rudi's mother, Sylvia, came to visit us from Israel. In contrast with my father, for whom we had to translate the evening news, Sylvia was not interested in politics. She was happy to cook for us.

To amuse Sylvia, Ida, her first cousin, extended us a permanent invitation to spend weekends with her and Sam in their house. One weekend, Rudi drove Sylvia and Ida to Canada to visit Sylvia's sister, Tony. I remained home, busy with my studies, but also because I was not feeling well.

* * *

In fact, I had been feeling unwell for a while and suspected I was pregnant. I went to see a doctor. After a test that came up negative, he blamed my symptoms on the accumulated stress generated by the multitude of adjustments we had gone through since starting our lives in a dramatically new environment. However, one day when I was studying in the library in the evening before the seven o'clock course, I felt a severe cramp in the abdomen followed by a great weakness. I just managed to get to the bathroom, where I felt I was going to pass out. Luckily, a fellow student saw me and realized I was in distress. She helped me to an adjacent room where I lay down on a couch.

I called home. Fortunately, rush hour was over, and Rudi got there quickly. He then called a doctor, who advised that I go to a hospital emergency room immediately. Then he asked a library clerk to call 911. An ambulance arrived a few minutes later. In the ambulance, barely able to speak, I told Rudi, "Remember Tănţica predicted that after two years in my new environment I'll be between life and death, but I'll survive!" That gave me confidence. She had been always right. I was taken to Saint Luke Hospital at 114th Street, only two blocks away. There I was given a transfusion. That helped me regain my strength somewhat, and I was rolled on a stretcher directly to the OR. On the way, summoning the little strength I could muster, I asked the attendant pushing the stretcher whether I would be able to take my test that was a week away. The attendant, obviously annoyed, reproved me harshly, "Ma'am, you are dying and you are concerned about an exam!" It was apparent that his sole concern was to make sure that I survive, whereas my concern was passing the exam, without which I would lose the $500 award, the rest of the credits, and my future career.

The next day, I woke up in an intensive care unit without knowing what kind of surgery had been performed. But I could see I had bandages on my belly. When I asked whether I could speak with the surgeon who had operated on me, a very young-looking guy came to see me. After he asked how I was doing, I requested to see the doctor. It was then I found out that he, a resident student from Germany, had been the one on call in the emergency room when I was brought in. Due to my critical condition, there was no time to reach one of the doctors who was on call. The resident had to perform emergency surgery immediately. I had had a tubal pregnancy, resulting in the rupture of my fallopian tube, which caused extensive internal bleeding. The young resident said I would be able to go home in a few days. He did a marvelous job.

Rudi, at the hospital, was relieved to be told that I was out of danger. His concern then shifted to the question of how we would pay for the surgery and hospitalization. The hospital social worker put our worries at ease by telling us that, due to our limited financial means, we qualified for Medicaid, meaning that all medical costs would be covered even though we were not yet citizens (as Ida had explained us). To that we said, "May God bless this generous, well-organized country."

As it turned out, I was released from the hospital in time to take my tests, and in spite of my week of absence from school, I passed all of them. Soon after, Sylvia left.

1969

We started the new year with a new Republican president, Richard Nixon. He inherited the war in Vietnam, had to face the nuclear arms race with the Soviet Union, and at home the violent antiwar movements spreading across the country. From my perspective, the pacifist antiwar movements were emboldening the North Vietnamese enemy.

At the end of January I began the final trimester at Columbia. The last mandatory courses that I took were legal studies and international organizations (which dealt mostly with the League of Nations and the United Nations). The course was given by Joseph Groesbeck, deputy director of the United Nations Library. I was especially interested in taking that course, still dreaming that one day I would work at the United Nations. I wanted to see how the organization worked and if anything could be done to save Eastern Europe—including, of course, Romania—from Soviet influence and internal dictatorships.

I also elected to take a course dealing with general types of libraries, for which I had to write a review of a book of my choice. My selection was Marx's *The Capital: Critique of Political Economy.* I selected that book deliberately. I wanted to vent my opinion about the harmful impact of Marx's utopian ideology, which endeavors to totally change the functioning of a normal economical system, based on the relation between production and consumption, into one directed by government, promising heaven on earth for everybody. The Marxist system is against human nature, denying personal initiative and private property ownership. From my own experience I know it does not work, a fact which later, after the collapse of the Soviet Union, will prove to be true.

Just before graduation, I made an appointment to speak with Professor Groesbeck. I had learned that between 1960 and 1963, he was Lev Vladimirov's predecessor as UN Dag Hammarskjold Library director. When the professor received me in his office, I asked him point-blank about my chances of getting a job at the UN Library—particularly in view of my proficiency in English, German, French, and Romanian. He seemed very interested. After asking me a few questions about my background and credentials, he set up an appointment to see me in his UN office. I was overjoyed.

Visiting Professor Groesbeck's office at the UN was emotionally overwhelming. I knew I was setting foot in an iconic building. Mr. Groesbeck gave me some tips regarding the kind of position I should be seeking, one that would offer me the best chance to get hired. He asked his secretary to bring me some job application forms, suggested that I fill them out right then and there, and offered to bring them to the Personnel Department.

One of the first pieces of information I had to provide was in regard to my citizenship. I explained to Mr. Groesbeck that, according to the Romanian laws, I had to give up Romanian citizenship as a precondition for getting a passport and exit visa, that I was in the United States as a green card holder since 1966, and the earliest I could apply for American citizenship was in 1971. Mr. Groesbeck explained to me that all UN employees must be citizens of a certain state and suggested I should resume my job application process once I held my American citizenship. Understandably, I was feeling very disappointed by the time I left his office.

* * *

I used to worry about how I was going to find a convenient job. But to my surprise, already in the month of April, prior to the actual graduation ceremony (scheduled for June), Columbia University organized job fairs when headhunters and interested employers interviewed seniors seeking positions. I got four offers—at the law libraries of Columbia University and New York University (NYU) and also with two reputable New York law firms specializing in international law.

NYU was my first choice. Here I had an interview with Professor Julius Marke, which went well. Although the citizenship issue came up again, it did not seem to matter. I liked his personality and left his office hoping that the university would make me an offer.

Very soon, on April 16, 1969, I received the job-offer letter from NYU as a cataloguer, an entry-level position that paid a little less than similar jobs offered by law firms. Despite the salary difference, I accepted the university's offer because my preference was to stay in an academic environment with a view to possibly continuing my studies. Also, I knew that Rudi intended to go to school to get the license required to open his own business. I was really happy and thought I was very fortunate to land a job even before graduation. It was a delightful change, a complete reversal of my experience in Romania.

* * *

One morning, as I entered the university campus from 116th Street, I saw a long table next to a wall filled with books and brochures displaying, on their covers, portraits of the bearded Marx and Engels, as well as those of Lenin or Stalin—all the communist intellectuals and leaders whom I had dreaded and despised so much in my old country. I just could not believe my eyes. I soon found out that the ad hoc book fair was organized by a new left group called Students for a Democratic Society (SDS). I had already seen, on TV, news reports about the violent confrontation between students and police at the National Democratic Convention in Chicago in 1968 and about the student demonstrations in support of the Black Panthers. Also, American blood was spilled during the Days of Rage of 1969 in an effort to undermine the US war in Vietnam. SDS also tried its hand at organizing the poor in the early 1960s. That this effort was led by Todd Gitlin, now a professor of journalism and sociology at Columbia University, has been explained by Matthew Vadum in his book *Subversion, Inc.* (2011, page 12).

Another time, from the Butler Building where we had the library courses, I saw a big three-story-tall portrait of Ho Chi Minh hanging on the wall of the Philosophy Building. I also viewed the unusually violent protests on campus against the so-called Morningside Heights scandal. (Morningside Heights is the name of an area where the university bought a vacant lot intending to build a gym for the faculty and students. The protesters claimed that the facility was going to be used only by white people, not also by African Americans.)

Also, I heard about the SDS Weather Underground terrorist faction, led by Bill Ayres and his wife, Bernardine Dohrn, who were against the capitalist system. This again I could not comprehend. It was like they wanted to take revenge on a system of government that had been successful.

At school, some faculty members were engaging the students in debates about this Morningside Heights scandal. The debates were very heated, and as far as I was concerned, the succession of events that I had witnessed (the book fair and Ho Chi Minh's portrait) made it clear that it was all the work of communist sympathizers. I did express my views, affirming that I believed the agitation was being caused by communist movements. The teacher's opinion was that I had been brainwashed with preconceived anticommunist ideas. I realized that the teacher sympathized with the campus movement, so I decided to shut up since I needed the credits—an attitude that I was all too familiar with back in Romania.

The agitation continued. Even the dean's speech at the graduation ceremony of June 3, 1969, was interrupted by left-wing hecklers who marched in with their left fists lifted up. After police intervened to remove the protestors, the dean continued his speech as if nothing had happened. I was probably the only one of hundreds of graduates present that day who had witnessed a similar event back at the Bucharest Faculty of Law. It occurred when a group of communist students managed to disrupt the course of Istrate Micescu, a distinguished professor and a celebrated lawyer of the time for being considered against the newly installed communist regime.

Years later, as a librarian at the NYU Law Faculty Library, I came across a congressional document with an analysis of the events of 1968–1969 giving detailed references to the student movements of June 1969 at Columbia University. The document presented, as a conclusion, that most movements were organized by the SDS. My first impulse was to go to Columbia University and show the document to my former professor who had disagreed with me, proving that my perception of events had been correct, based on my personal experience with a communist regime, a perspective which she was lacking.

* * *

On this subject I read and found Stanley Kurtz's book *The Radical-in-Chief Barack Obama and the Untold Story of American Socialism* (pages 31, 39, 60, 131, 197–198) very informative. The author describes how, in the sixties, Michael Harrington became the most influential socialist in America when he was heading the Democratic Socialist Organizing Committee (DSOC). Further, the author points out that in 1969 the Students for a Democratic Society (SDS, the group that had carried out the most violent radical leftist protests in the sixties) and the SDS Weather Underground faction, led by Bill Ayres and his wife, Bernardine Dohrn, were preparing to embark on their infamous terror spree against the capitalist system. After the collapse of the socialist SDS, its members were absorbed in 1970 by the New American Movement (NAM). This, in turn, merged in 1982 with Harrington's DSOC to form the new Harrington-led Democratic Socialists of America (DSA). Most DSAers were committed to electoral politics within the Democratic Party. Harrington's overall strategy was to force a realignment by pulling the Democrats sharply to the left.

Furthermore, also in the sixties, the National Welfare Rights Organization (NWRO) was established by the Marxist theorists Richard Cloward and Frances Fox Piven, who guided it with a strategy derived from communist organizing techniques of the 1930s. NWRO members sought a socialist transformation of the United States. They believed that as welfare recipients shed the notions of self-sufficiency and learned to demand government support as their right, a kind of de facto anticapitalist mentality would take hold. For them, however, transformation depended on stoking their sense of entitlement and rage. Cloward and Piven published their famous "break the bank" strategy in the *The Nation* magazine in 1966, which would have further results (described later).

* * *

With my MLS degree from Columbia and my JD from the Bucharest University—and taking advantage of the job offered to me at the library of the NYU School of Law—I thought it would be a good idea to enroll as a part-time student toward a second master's degree in the legal field at NYU. Being an ambitious person, I was motivated to achieve in America what I had been unable to do in Romania. In addition, I thought my Romanian diploma, my Columbia MLS, and my fluency in foreign languages were not sufficient qualifications to help me advance my career and attain my ultimate goal of getting a job at the UN.

So at the end of June, I took my diplomas to the NYU Admissions Office and applied for enrollment to work toward an LLM degree with a major in international law public.

July 15, just a few short weeks after I submitted my application, I received the following letter from the assistant dean of studies from NYU:

> Dear Mrs. Kleckner,
>
> I am pleased to inform you that you have been admitted to the Graduate Division as a candidate for the degree Master of Law (in International Law) to begin your studies in the fall, 1969 semester…You will be required to complete twenty-four credit hours to qualify for the degree… Classes in the fall will begin on September 11.
>
> Sincerely,
> Bert S. Prunty Jr.

That letter was a landmark moment in my personal life.

* * *

A few days later, on July 20, another landmark event took place, though this was on a national level—namely the successful launching of the first mission of the Apollo 11 spacecraft with two astronauts on board. I was moved to tears when Neil Armstrong walked on the lunar soil and spoke his now immortal words, "One small step for man, one giant step for mankind." I was proud for America.

* * *

My surgery, combined with all of my efforts to pass the finals with good marks (so that I could qualify for scholarship), took a toll on my health. All my joints from the neck to ankles were aching. This might have been a flare-up of arthritis caused by my weakened immune system. Rudi, who meanwhile had left his first job for a better-paying one, had been working off hours with an electrician friend to provide a little supplemental income. He came up with the idea that I should visit a spa so that I would be stronger before starting my new job in September. We did our homework and, after considering several places, decided in favor of going for two weeks to the Badgastein spa in Austria. The spa was highly recommended for treatment of rheumatic diseases and stress relief. The idea appealed to me all the more because Austria was the native country of my dear nanny Haagi, who had told me so many stories about that country and its magnificent mountains.

Since Rudi could not leave his job for two weeks, and we could not have afforded the trip for both, I went to the spa by myself.

Checking in at the posh Wuhrer Hotel, I was impressed by its elegance. After a stroll in the spa, I realized that my hotel was, by far, more elegant than any other. When I went to the restaurant for dinner, a maître d' dressed in tuxedo and black tie greeted me and led me to a small table. A waiter took my order while two girls in navy blue dresses and white starched aprons served me. All the hotel guests around me looked very elegant: gentlemen wore jackets and the ladies were in elegant suits, wearing beautiful jewelry, with impeccably coiffed hair. I looked around, and I picked one face that I liked—someone I decided I wished to know during my stay.

Next morning I had an appointment with the doctor who would prescribe my treatments. In the waiting room there was only one gentleman; he had white hair and a distinguished look. He greeted me. We exchanged a few words in German, introducing ourselves to each other. His name was Rudy Boyko, and as it turned out he was not an Austrian but a Slovak who had been educated in Vienna. After a while, the gentleman invited me to have a predinner drink at the hotel bar, indicating he wanted to introduce me to his wife.

When his wife and I met in the evening at the bar, surprise, she was the one I picked among all other ladies the night before in the dining room! In spite of her gray hair, she had the demeanor of a young person. Her name was Rhoda, and she was an American from Philadelphia who had married Rudy Boyko, a widower who had immigrated to the States because of Hitler.

At some point Rhoda asked me about myself. She was totally surprised to hear that Rudi and I were refugees from Romania, that we had been in America for two years, and that I was currently a student. She could not understand how I could afford the most elegant hotel in the spa. When I told her that we had no savings in the bank, she burst out, "My little girl, take it from me. All Americans spend no more than a quarter of their income on housing, one quarter on food, another quarter on vacations and clothing, and they earmark at least one quarter for savings."

Then she turned around and asked me, "Do you know who are the people around us?"

From her I learned most of them were members of the Rothschild family and frequent guests at that hotel. I was curious to find out which members of that famous family were among the hotel guests. The next day before dinner I again met with my new friends at the bar for a drink. Rhoda told me that she had found out that some members of the French branch of the Rothschilds were among us in the hotel. I was amused, imagining the reaction of comrades Gheorghe, Tănase, or Buzescu from the Romanian Ministry of Transportation were I to tell them what distinguished company I was keeping.

During my entire stay at the spa, I saw Rudy and Rhoda every day. Back in New York, I introduced them to my Rudi. He and I have remained friends with the Boykos for many years.

Two days before I left, the hotel management called to let me know that a Mrs. Vorvoreanu was there to see me. That was my former good friend Aimée, now married to my cousin Ion Vorvoreanu.

It was she who—for no reason I could figure out—had pretended not to see us before her departure from Bucharest. Even though she had rudely ignored us on that occasion, however, I told the manager to let her come to my room. Once there, she embraced me and, with tears in her eyes, implored me to forgive her. To my way of thinking, her attitude in Bucharest had been unwarranted and inexcusable. (At the time, Ion had offered to get us out of Romania with him and her, but I turned down his generous offer because I could not have left the country while my mother was still in prison.)

Initially, I was blunt with Aimée, letting her know that I was not interested in forgiving her and letting her past behavior be forgotten. Eventually, though, I caved in and gave her a chance to give me an explanation. In truth, I was curious to find out what motivated her bizarre attitude, both then and now. She claimed that she had been jealous because she thought that Ion was putting her down every time he praised me for my perseverance in finishing my law studies in Bucharest.

Also, I found out about her more recent life. Though she had lived in London for a while, she did not like the cold and damp weather. She had applied for Ion and her to be hired to work for Radio Free Europe in Munich, Germany. They were hired, but she was the only one to go, while my cousin, her husband, remained in London.

That clicked for me right away. Radio Free Europe was subsidized by the Americans, and all its employees could opt for the American citizenship after a certain number of years of employment. But there was a precondition for that—namely to be able to prove that you had a permanent address in the States. So now that I was a US permanent resident, I could provide the required permanent address and residence for her. By reconciling with me, she would be able to come to New York during her annual vacations and stay with us while, at the same time, our sponsorship could help her obtain the much-desired American citizenship.

After my initial rejection of her plea for forgiveness, my heart gradually softened as I put myself in her shoes. I thought about what it would be like for me to be without Rudi in Munich. At the same time, I thought that forgiving her was a Christian thing to do, to follow Jesus's example, not just the doctrine. On a conciliatory note, I gave her our New York address and phone number and said that we would be in touch.

* * *

Back from Austria, and before starting my new job in New York, I decided to pay a visit to Claire. When she saw me at the door, her eyes opened wide. She asked me to sit down, which never happened before. I told her that I had graduated from Columbia University and had a job at the NYU Law Library. She expressed her disbelief, saying, "You foreigners have an advantage over us because you know foreign languages, have strong wills, and are determined to succeed." She was right. Once I had regained liberty, I chose action.

At that moment, I felt vindicated. She was probably thinking about her sons who, from what Mary had told me, gave her some problems.

While in Austria, I had become a little detached from the issues related to the war in Vietnam, but as soon as I returned I got interested in how Richard Nixon was handling the domestic left-wing agitators of the peace movement. I could sense, and was almost sure, that these agitators were being influenced from outside the USA.

CHAPTER 3

New York University, September 1969–November 30, 1974

I have described how discrimination against me under communism, where I had faced so many social or sentimental problems, had not hardened my resolve to get out of that system, and I congratulate myself for not letting fear of the unknown deter me to leave Romania. Also, I have described how we were helped along by Rudi's family, by some friends, and by fortunate circumstances. Now I felt I had reached a point when I was past the beginnings stage. Conceding this, I was finally going to do a job for which I was qualified at NYU, one of the most prestigious universities in the United States. I had also been admitted to work toward a master's degree in the judicial field. That gave me a feeling that the winds were at my back. What else could I hope for?

Starting my first professional job meant a significant step forward when my work would become my life because I knew that I had to make up for the lost years in the old country. This is why I have to describe how I managed to attain the professional positions that I held and reveal what it took to fulfill my obligations in those jobs.

(I will also include, on these pages, some descriptions of my juridical studies and of the offices where I spent a significant part of my life.) It became clear to me that from now on my ambition was to reach my full potentials in a competitive world, an endeavor that now will become the centerpiece of my story.

At the same time, I will express my views about American administrations since politics had a major impact on my life. Those of us who lived under communists perceive the domestic and foreign policies of the United State from perspectives that are different from those who never had that experience. In other words, dealing with the same realities, points of view will differ. In fact, it is my belief that many in the West are poorly informed about the essence of a social-ist system that often leads toward totalitarian communism. Hence, in the pages ahead I will analyze in a chronological way events that unfolded in the years to come.

* * *

September 1, 1969, marks the beginning of my first professional job at NYU. When I got off the subway, I felt as if I was flying while climbing the stairs to the street and stepping onto the university campus. I was beside myself with joy. Reporting to Professor Marke's office, I found that his secretary, Carol, was already expecting me. Little did I realize, as she led me to his office, that I was about to work for an extraordinarily good man, a guardian angel. He would become the cornerstone upon which I built my professional career, someone who would exercise great influence over my future choices. It was the beginning of a remarkable professional relationship that would serve me well in the future. After welcoming me on board, Julius Marke took me on a library tour during which he introduced me to my future coworkers. From the main hallway, we entered the enormous General Reference room, where the manager was Edward Bender, called Ed. Greeting me with a very friendly smile, Ed held out his hand and said, "Nice meeting you, Simone," to which I replied, "Same here, Ed." (It would not be long before we became good friends.)

Then Professor Marke took me to the Foreign Publications section, headed by Dushan Djanovici, who also welcomed me on board and congratulated Professor Marke for hiring somebody from his part of the world. Dushan was a Serb from Montenegro. I, too, was glad that one of my future coworkers came from Eastern Europe.

Then Professor Marke and I went to the Acquisitions section, where he introduced me to Pauline, the section manager, explaining to me that she was the most senior member of the library staff.

Finally, we ended up at the Cataloguing section on the second floor, where I would actually be going to work. Mary Chapman, a young blond-haired girl with green eyes and freckles, greeted us. She was substituting for her boss, who was on vacation at that time. With that, Julius Marke wished me luck again and left me in Mary's care.

In the Cataloguing department Mary introduced me to my coworkers, Suzan Soll, a friendly American, then to a Polish lady. Finally, there was Sushna, the typist, originally from India, who was wearing a traditional silk sari. Then she showed me around. There were five desks along one wall. The middle of the floor was dominated by a big glass-walled cubicle reserved for the department head. In the central area were file cabinets. She explained that the publications on top of some shelves were new arrivals waiting to be catalogued. In front of each desk was a wheel cart with two shelves of books. Publications, assigned by Mary, were placed on individual carts. I soon realized that everything was organized in such a way that we could work in silence.

My duty was to catalogue an average of ten publications a day. Our daily hours were 8:00 a.m. to 5:00 p.m. with two twenty-minute coffee breaks, one in the morning and the other in the afternoon, and a one-hour lunch break that we could take from 12:00 p.m. to 1:00 p.m. or from 1:00 to 2:00 p.m.

After a couple of weeks, the department boss, Marcellia Simpson, returned from vacation. She had a very fair complexion, although—as I found out from Suzan—her parents were African American and Caucasian. From the first moment I saw her, I was impressed with her appearance, with the way she dressed, and with her gentle manner. After some time, Marcellia, whom we all called

Marcy, invited me to go out to lunch with her, and in the days that followed, we frequently spent our lunchtime together. During those relaxed and friendly conversations, we got to know each other better and better. I liked her very much, and as it turned out, the feeling was mutual.

On the other hand, my relationship with Mary, though very friendly, was mostly professional rather than personal. Her political views were very different from mine, which, many times, annoyed me. She was a very assertive individual who expected everybody to share her opinions, and if you were in disagreement, she would try to impose her views. Professionally, though, she was very good, and I learned a lot from her. In fact, I credit her with giving me much of the knowledge that would become useful for me in the future.

During coffee breaks, I would go with Suzan and Mary to the campus cafeteria, where we usually found Dushan and Ed. On occasion, Julius Marke also joined us. Whenever our conversations shifted to political issues, Mary would usually assert her leftist views. Dushan was the only one who contradicted her. That was to be expected because, besides me, he was the only other one in the group who had firsthand experience with life under the communist system. I was always in agreement with Dushan, and the two of us became very close friends.

* * *

September 8 was the long-anticipated day when I had to register for my international law master's degree (LLM). The duration of studies was flexible; how long it took me to attain my degree would depend on how many courses I could take each semester.

At the registration office I joined a short line of applicants. All were men until a blond young woman suddenly joined the line. I went to her and told her that I was happy to see another woman in that all-male crowd. But I learned she was not an applicant. She was a secretary filling out registration forms for her boss who, she informed me, worked for an oil company called CONOCO. She asked me what I was doing and was very happy to hear that I was working for the NYU Law Library. She figured right away that I could save her a lot of effort searching for the documents that her boss would need for different courses, and she offered to pay me by the Xerox page for my effort. I learned that her name was Amy, and she told me that her boss's name was Van Langley.

I signed up and paid for one of the prerequisite courses, International Law Part 1. (I planned to take part 2 in the spring semester.) To start with, I only took a single course because I was not sure how well I would fare. Amy selected the same course for her boss and suggested that I save a seat for him. Since I was the only woman in the class, he would have no trouble locating me.

On the same day, Rudi went to register for evening courses at Brooklyn Polytechnic University. At the time, he had changed his job from the hospital to the US Gypsum Company located in New Jersey, where he took charge of all their electric installations. From that point on, our daily routines changed. We could no longer count on having dinner together in the evening. And during weekends, we were both busy studying.

On September 11, when the courses started, I was directed to a room where students were seated around a long table. As Amy had suggested, I saved a seat for Van Langley. The room had almost filled to capacity when a very handsome guy came in, looked around, and caught sight of me. He approached me with, "Hi, Simone, nice meeting you, and thanks for saving the seat for me." I told him that I was also glad to meet him. It was the beginning of our friendship that continued to this day.

The last to enter the room was Professor Olmstead, who took his seat at the head of the table. He surveyed the students to get a first impression of those attending his course. When he spotted me, I noticed that his gaze lingered a little longer. He was probably not used to seeing women around that table.

Professor Olmstead asked everybody what they were doing for a living and what had determined their decisions to enroll for an LLM degree. When my turn came, I told him that I was a graduate of the law school of the Bucharest University and that, in the States, I also had an MLS from Columbia University. I further explained that I had been unable to practice law back in Romania because I was discriminated against by the communist regime. I also explained that, in the United States, due to the differences in the juridical systems, I was unable to capitalize on that qualification. So my intention now was to finish up unfinished business.

The professor did not comment on my story but told me that, next time, I should sit next to him in the chair on his right. He probably had a hard time understanding my English due to my accent. After that first day, there were hardly any classes during which he did not ask me questions or ask me to comment about the contents of landmark judicial decisions cited in the class's mandatory readings.

I was very pleased that Professor Olmstead's introductory course covered an overview of international law and international organizations. It gave me the opportunity to learn something new about the United Nations, where I still dreamed of working someday.

Looking up the documentation from the professor's weekly list was enough to keep me busy during my lunch hour. I made copies of all materials both for me and for Van. Dushan, on occasion, helped me get some of the cases I needed. Besides, I wanted for myself to read the text of the Atlantic Charter and of the secret Ribbentrop-Molotov Pact of August 23, 1939, both of which affected the destiny of Eastern Europe.

Whenever I needed it, I got some help from Van, who patiently explained things that I was reading, when I had trouble understanding a specific case. Van had gone to school in Buenos Aires, where the atmosphere was quasi-European, and his first wife was French, which made him more receptive than others to European affairs. Through him I also met Patricia Dowling, beginning with her a friendship that has continued to this day.

Looking back, I consider myself very lucky because each of my colleagues at NYU helped me, one way or another, in my work as a librarian or as a student. I had a lot to learn and was given a wealth of advice and encouragement from my boss Marcy whenever we went out for lunch together. Ed Bender was also a very nice, friendly, and calm individual.

As I have mentioned, I also have fond memories of Julius Marke, the director of the library. I learned he was a highly respected personality in the world of legal librarians, and a frequent contributor of articles and essays to professional publications.

*   *   *

Besides taking international studies, I was also eager to learn as much as possible about the fundamental documents of the United States. I was especially fascinated with the Declaration of Independence of 1776, which proclaimed the fundamental concept that "all men are created equal, that they are endowed by their Creator with certain unalienable individual Rights: Life, Liberty and the pursuit of Happiness," which do not come from the government, but from the Creator. A noble thought!

Likewise, I was fascinated by the Constitution, which stated the principle of the separation of powers in the state—legislative, executive, and judiciary—as a way to limit the power of each branch of government. I remembered that the 1923 Romanian Constitution clearly expressed the same principle of separation of powers. Of course I could not help drawing a parallel between these noble concepts and what was going on now in Romania where the executive was the only sovereign authority, controlling the other two powers.

At the same time, given my family's history, I also had an interest in how the idea of property was dealt with in the US Constitution. I found out that the Fifth Amendment requires that the power of "eminent domain" must be coupled with "just compensation" for those whose property is taken. Again, my experience in the old country after 1945 was so dramatically different. The first communist move was to confiscate and nationalize all properties with no compensation whatsoever, resulting in the destruction of civil society and turning citizens into government slaves.

*   *   *

Regarding the war in Vietnam, when I made my daily visit to the NYU cafeteria, I overheard students at nearby tables engaging in heated, often violent antiwar rhetoric. I think most promoters of the pacifist and leftist movements of the time had no experience with foreign occupation through communist expansion all over the world. I think their profound dissatisfaction was not so much with the evils of the war but a result of their worry-free lives. For example, John Lennon of the Beatles, like most musicians of the time, was very vocal in his protest of the Vietnam War. Many of his songs reflected his political activism, indirectly supporting the Black Panthers and the SDS—both organizations that were very active at Columbia University.

I must confess that before I had arrived in this country, I naively thought the United States was immune to communism because it was so fundamentally opposed to everything that communism stood for. But after the opening of the Soviet Archives in 1992, I bought the translation that was done by Timothy D. Sergey, which was the basis of the comprehensive book *The Secret World of American Communism* (Yale University Press, New Haven, 1995) by H. Klehr, J. E. Haynes, and F. I. Firsov. There I read that the Communist Party (CPUSA) was disciplined and cohesive. It was a centralized Marxist-Leninist vanguard organization, assisting the Soviet intelligence in the 1930s, aligning its loyalty to the Soviets. CPUSA was never outlawed, which meant it was able to set up the United States Peace Council (USPC), accepted by many congressional members. I could not detect anyone who took an official position against the crimes of communism in general.

* * *

Moreover, observing the movements confronting Nixon's policy in foreign affairs, I could not understand why that president was accused of not being dedicated to peace, even though he was already withdrawing US military forces from Vietnam. It looked to me as if the peace movement was against America rather than opposing the communists in North Vietnam. To say the least, I was upset to see that the topic of the war had created a domestic conflict between liberals and conservatives. Naturally, it was our ardent wish that some of the people of this noble country would be able to see reality and hold on to the prestige it deserves.

* * *

Being very busy with work and studies, Rudi and I pretty much limited our social life to phone calls, with the exception of our visits with the Răileanu family and Irina Spătaru, who lived in the same building. A few times, we visited Van Langley in his Connecticut home. We also tried hard to find time to attend the meetings of the Iuliu Maniu[3] Foundation, dedicated to providing material help to Romanian refugees and keeping alive the flame of freedom and democracy in Romania.

My father's and mother's letters did not relay much news about Romania. But from our friend Aimée, with whom I'd had a reconciliation of sorts in Austria, came frequent letters with hints that she would very much like to visit New York.

1970

Rudi and I resumed our studies immediately after New Year. I took International Law Part 2, also with Professor Olmstead. As in the previous semester, I sat to the professor's right, with Van seated next to me. I found part 2 more interesting since it clarified for me the structure of the United Nations, its charter, both the political and administrative duties of the secretary-general, and the mission of its three thousand employees.

* * *

After successfully completing the course, I had a pretty busy summer ahead of me. Among other things, I had to decide whether to invite Aimée to New York. I thought that, after all, it was against my nature to bear grudges, especially considering our friendship had been forged a long time ago and had lasted many years before the incident that occurred at her departure. Therefore, in June 1970 Aimée visited and stayed with us in New York. As with all other guests, she slept on our sofa bed in the living room. Though our time with her was limited, we took every opportunity to show her around.

---

3.   A respected Romanian politician who served as prime minister of Romania for three terms during 1928–1933.

She proved to be a very enthusiastic tourist, eager to see everything and liking everything she saw. Aimée was very impressed that our stores were open late and on weekends, which did not happen in Germany. (She told us that most stores there even closed for two or three hours during lunchtime.) She walked to New York's major department stores, where she was capable of spending hours on end. She bought everything in duplicate, one for her and one for me. I always reimbursed her for the expense, but trusted her taste, and to this day I still find some of those items in my closet.

Aimée was a heavy smoker and coffee drinker. She would easily finish one pack a day of Players unfiltered cigarettes. When she had been alone in Munich, her diet had consisted primarily of chocolate and coffee. Even though she was a very good cook, her meals were mainly for her guests. Back home Aimée informed us that she had applied for the American citizenship based on her length of service with Radio Free Europe and now having an address in the United States.

* * *

Good news came in the form of a letter from the NYU secretariat saying that I had been promoted to a higher-paying position as associate curator with no tenure.[4] The letter also mentioned that in order to qualify for tenure, I had to teach a course and write articles to appear in certain publications. Though that opened up an unexpected new perspective, it also meant I had to do additional work. From that point on, without exception, I received a salary increase on each of my anniversaries.

* * *

For summer vacation, Rudi and I planned to go to the Badgastein spa together, on to Munich, then fly home from London after visit-

---

4.   *Tenure* is a form of continuous appointment within academic institutions; librarians with *tenure* are considered faculty members, not professional administrative staff, and are eligible to academic positions.

ing Ioana Herescu and my cousin Ion Vorvoreanu, Aimée's ex-husband. As planned, we flew to Vienna, from there taking a train to Badgastein. We checked in at the same Wührer Parkhotel, where we were happy to reconnect with Rhoda and Rudy Boyko, with whom we had planned, in advance, to meet. As in the previous year, we found out that we were again surrounded by different members of the Rothschild families.

In Munich we stayed in Aimée's apartment in the Schwabing district. Following our arrival, she invited a few colleagues from Radio Free Europe to meet us. On that occasion we met Noel Bernard, the director of the RFE Romanian Section, whose voice we knew. Back in Romania, we had listened to his remarkable news analyses and political commentaries about communist Romania and a variety of other topics. Noel Bernard was an extremely witty, gifted, and courageous journalist with a pleasant and friendly personality. He was committed to promoting the principles of freedom and denouncing the evils of the communist system, a position that made him a pariah in the eyes of the Romanian leader Nicolae Ceauşescu.

From Munich we flew to London where we had an emotional reunion with my cousins Ioana Herescu and Ion Vorvoreanu. Being with them brought back fond memories from Craiova and our youth. In addition, I was happy to see that Ioana remained the same beautiful and distinguished woman I remembered from our last get-together in Paris in 1966. I never brought up the subject of her past health problems.

* * *

Back home in New York, I enrolled for my third course at NYU on European regional organizations, not knowing that this course would give me the opportunity to publish in a professional periodical for the first time. The course dealt with the European Community of Coal and Steel, with the Rome Treaty of 1957, becoming the European Economic Community, known also as the Common Market. (Subsequently, after the 1967 Brussels Treaty, it became a supranational organization with a commission, council, parliament, and court.)

With the knowledge acquired in the course, I realized that European publications in the library were not properly classified, and brought this to Marcy's and Julius's attention. The next day, Marcy told me that I would be solely in charge of a project to reclassify all the publications in the CEE section. With that assignment, I had the satisfaction of being able to apply my course knowledge directly to my job. Moreover, I was now totally on my own, with no obligation to get Mary involved in any way.

* * *

Big surprise! In a letter from Mancy, I learned that she had applied for a passport with an exit visa to Paris to visit her sister Tancy, whom she had not seen since 1942. When I spoke with Tancy on the phone, she told me that her husband, Nicolae Penescu, had worked hard lobbying the French authorities to intervene for Mancy's visit to Paris. I was very happy for my mother.

1971

Immediately after the New Year I started to work on my reclassification project, which I finished in a few months, being what the Americans call a "workaholic." The feeling of accomplishing a goal gives me a lot of satisfaction, and I spare no effort to reach that goal. I think I am fortunate to bring this inborn quality to a competitive environment. In addition, the tenure situation with the conditions required to attain it stuck to my mind. So I wrote an article on my EEC reclassification project, and with Julius's help, it was published in the *Law Library Journal* (volume 68 of 1973, pages 18–26). After the article was published, he told me that the classification scheme that I suggested was already being applied by other law libraries. This was a real reward, and I was more than happy.

* * *

Meanwhile, I was attending my fourth course on commercial law and regional organizations held by Professor Garretson. One of the course requirement was to write an essay. He was interested in knowing more about a commercial communist topic. I chose the 1949 Council for Mutual Economic Assistance, also known as CMEA or COMECOM, an equivalent of the 1947 American Marshall Plan for rebuilding West European economies in post-WWII. Too bad I did not know then what I found out later, reading David Funderburk's *Pinstripes and Reds* (page 47). He wrote that the Soviets required COMECOM members to share any technology they were able to get (illegally) from the West with the other member states. Back then, that was one of the main reasons why COMECOM existed.

A landmark day! February 9, 1971, marked the end of the fifth year of our permanent residency in the States. Having met that requirement, Rudi and I filed our application for American citizenship.

Another special day in February was when all of a sudden I heard my mother's voice on the phone from Paris. Quite a surprise! When Tancy and Nicolas got on the phone, I thanked Nicolas for his lobbying with the French president Giscard d'Estaing, who in turn succeeded in obtaining my mother's visa from the communist officials. Encouraged by her successful trip, Mancy had told us that she would visit us in the following spring.

* * *

In May, at home in the evening, we witnessed on TV new demonstrations that were organized by the peace movement. As I had mentioned, the guerilla strategy in Vietnam turned into street demonstrations marked by rage and violence of students in the United States. Nearly ten thousand people were arrested, in spite of the United States' efforts to shape the withdrawal from Vietnam. It was a national trauma.

About that time, Nixon declared that the United States would not remain indifferent if the Soviets were to attack China, considering China's independence to be indispensable to global equilibrium. I wondered how Nixon would approach the tension between Russia and China, taking into consideration Truman's containment foreign policy, which would not allow contact with the enemy.

* * *

At NYU, there was sudden unrest incited by the unions that wanted to infiltrate the academic world. To me it made no sense to unionize because none of us had any grievances, and there were no interests to defend on our behalf. We all got our salary increases on our anniversaries. Julius made no secret of the fact that he was unhappy at the prospect of union interference in the library administration. At the same time all this was going on, Rudi landed a new and better-paid job with Union Carbide, another positive step forward for us.

Unexpectedly, we got some news that my dear cousin Ioana Herescu had a relapse of the cancer that had been diagnosed in 1966, and Mother managed to come to visit us (although it happened before I had finished my course). Luckily, Mancy was fluent in English, which meant she was able to have a degree of independence even when we were not home. She could watch TV and take long strolls around Manhattan. We derived a lot of satisfaction from the fact that she finally got the taste of a normal life in a free society. One of her favorite walks was to the Metropolitan Museum of Art on Fifth Avenue. She made repeated visits to this museum, and also to the Frick Collection, which reminded her of the Marincu Palace back in Calafat, so intimately connected with the dearest memories of her youth.

But she was torn by conflicting temptations, either to join her sister in Paris or remain with us in the States. In any event she decided that going back to Romania, where she had gone through so much suffering, was out of question. She constantly sought advice on that subject, but we avoided influencing her for fear that if she became unhappy with the decision, she would blame it on us. We just told her that she could count on our support either way.

Once Rudi and I finished with our finals, we started to take Mancy on trips outside the city. We visited Niagara Falls, a sight that none of us had seen before. We also went to Washington, DC, to see former friends from the old country, to my friend Lee's Cape Cod house, and to the home of other mutual friends in Upstate New York. Those were always emotional situations as Mother was reuniting with people she had not seen in so many years.

All of a sudden, a dramatic turn of events occurred. Mancy, totally unexpectedly, got a job offer. One evening at dinnertime she told us that during her visits to the Metropolitan Museum, she had befriended an American lady, Gertrude Fournet, to whom she confided the dilemma about whether to settle in New York City or in Paris. In either case, Mancy told Gertrude she dreaded the prospect of being a burden on us or her sister, but she was aware that, at the age of sixty-eight, her options to live an independent life were quite limited. Hearing my mother's story, Gertrude came up with the idea that my mother might be a perfect fit with a friend of hers, a certain Mrs. Meissner, who lived in Manhattan a few blocks from us. Gertrude told my mother that Mrs. Meissner had fallen and broken her arm and that her son had offered to pay for a live-in companion. "The only issue," Gertrude said, "was that this Mrs. Meissner was originally from Vienna and would prefer her companion to be somebody fluent in German."

That was right up my mother's alley. So the very next day she went to meet Mrs. Meissner. They liked each other, and Mancy also liked Mrs. Meissner's apartment, which afforded a nice view of the Hudson River. Mother was offered, and accepted, a job that would require her to live there six days and nights a week.

Coincidentally, exactly when Mother got that job, we received the postcard that set the day of August 16, 1971, for Rudi and I to take our oaths to become American citizens. After the naturalization ceremony, we felt as if we had won a million bucks. We celebrated the event with Mancy and a few friends. Now that I was American citizen, I could apply for my mother's permanent residency, which, together with the job offer, kind of sealed her decision to remain with us.

Since she was determined to avoid, at all cost, being a burden to us, she asked us to help find her a place to live while she was not with Mrs. Meissner. Rudi found a studio next to our home, and we acted as guarantors when Mancy filled out the lease contract. Now that my mother had a permanent domicile and a job, on October 13, 1971, we filed her application for permanent residency.

Moreover, when A. Valahu, Alecu Radian's good friend and former lawyer in Romania, found out that Mancy was in New York and had decided to stay with us, he came to visit and then invited us to his house. He was married to Cristine Valmy, who owned a prosperous cosmetics franchise in New York. One weekend we visited them in New Jersey, where they were living, to celebrate Mancy's presence among us. Cristine Valmy offered to pay Mother's rent for the first year. After dinner, Cristine took her on a shopping spree and bought her a lot of clothes. We were all very moved by her kindness.

* * *

Back to the work toward my master's degree, I enlisted for the international commercial arbitration course taught by Professor Martin Domke, America's best-known expert in the field. At the outset, Professor Domke suggested that all immigrant students write an essay about arbitration procedures in their countries of origin, promising that he would recommend the best of them for publication in the prestigious *New York University Journal of International Law and Politics*. I accepted the challenge right away, partly because publishing in our journal carried a lot of prestige and partly because any publication would bring me a little closer to qualifying for tenure.

It took a lot of digging to get the necessary documentation, but I managed to write a pretty comprehensive analysis of Romanian foreign trade arbitration, of which, I am sure, many lawyers in the West were uninformed. But writing the essay was a breeze compared to the stress I experienced while waiting for the professor to decide which essays were worth publishing. His verdict would mean a lot in determining whether I would have a future.

Eventually, Professor Domke informed us that he had selected three essays for publication, and one of them was mine. I was really on cloud nine. My essay, entitled "Foreign Trade Arbitration in Romania," was published in the *NYU Journal of International Law and Politics* (volume 5, issue 2, 1972, pages 233–249). All my colleagues congratulated me. My boss Marcy was particularly appreciative that somebody like me who had been in the States for a relatively short period of time had managed to get a paper published in the university journal. Professor Domke even sent a copy of my essay to Grigore Geamănu, a faculty member he had met at Bucharest University. It was not until March 1973 that Professor Geamănu acknowledged receipt of my essay, and he did so while in Paris, probably because he did not want the Romanian authorities to find out that he had any contacts with people in the West. (Just a reminder: Professor G. Geamănu is the former secretary of state who tried unsuccessfully to get me an exit visa from Romania back in 1949 when I attempted to join my first husband in Italy.) I now had the satisfaction of knowing he had read my essay: he had acknowledged it in a letter that Professor Domke shared with me. In the letter Professor Geamănu wrote, among other things, "I am very happy for Simone's successes in the United States, but I am not surprised. Her achievements remind me of the prestigious career of her father, the former professor of our university. Please convey to her my best wishes for a happy personal life and many successes in her profession. It is a shame that we lost a person of her potential."

I felt good about this letter not because of his congratulations but because in the end, he realized that I had succeeded in leaving the country without his help.

*　*　*

1972

When I received sad news from my dear cousin Ioana Herescu in London that she was losing her battle with cancer, I was more than upset. She had been like my sister, and I loved her very much. It was unfortunate that, right now when we had the prospect of seeing each other more often, I was about to lose her. A letter from Ion Vorvoreanu—my cousin in London—informed me that Ioana died in her sleep on January 12, 1972.

E. Lozovan, a friend and journalist who had worked for the BBC, wrote about Ioana: "She was the very image of her father and the last descendent of a well-known family from Craiova. With her death a branch descending from Elena, Prince Matei Basarab's wife, and her brother Udrişte Năsturel will vanish forever. Today, those who never experienced Ioana's charm and dignity should recognize her heroism. At BBC for eighteen years she defended the cause of Romania's liberty with an unshakeable devotion."

I had the sad task of informing my mother about the passing of my cousin, her niece.

* * *

A ray of light unexpectedly entered the darkness of my sadness when, going to work one morning, Julius Marke's secretary, Carol, called me to her boss's office. This was unusual, and I didn't know what to expect. Professor Marke invited me to take a seat, and after making a few positive remarks about my performance in school and in the department—as well as my work on the reclassification project and the publication of my essays—he told me that all my accomplishments had been noticed and highly appreciated.

"You are an asset to us," he said, and then added, "I spoke with the dean of Studies, and management has agreed to fully subsidize your remaining spring courses."

That was such unexpected good news that I impulsively hugged him before I left his office. Returning upstairs, I found Marcy waiting eagerly to find out what Julius had said to me. When I told her, she was really happy for me and congratulated me with a big hug.

* * *

The course that I took in January 1972, on international provocations and regional organization issues, was given by Professor Andreas Lowenfeld. I was on very good terms with him because he often asked me to find documentation he was looking for. Also, as he was married to a Cuban refugee, I think he had a special understanding of my plight under the communists. One of the topics that his course dealt with was the Cuban Missile Crisis of October 1961 when students had to distinguish between two terms—"blockade" during war or "quarantine" regarding the status of the Russian ships in Cuba. From a political viewpoint, on this topic there are divided opinions about what defused the crisis, JFK's firm position or Nikita Khrushchev's decision to withdraw the missiles only when the United States and the Soviet Union agreed to negotiate. At that time, the American envoy to the negotiations in Turkey was Robert Kennedy, the president's brother.

* * *

Back to my question about Nixon's policy regarding the China-Russia issue. It started with a rapprochement with China: indeed, in February 1972, his visit to Beijing was announced. To this day I remember seeing Mrs. Nixon on TV wearing a red overcoat as she stepped off the plane. Shortly thereafter, in May 1972, a visit to Moscow took place. After these two visits I understood that Nixon's administration changed foreign policy by using a different approach from his predecessors'. He launched his controversial foreign policy concept called "détente" with "linkage." He would take advantage of the existing tension between China and Russia to try to withdraw US troops from South Vietnam, also to block Chinese and Russian expansionism in Vietnam by closing after thirteen years of war that had been started by Kennedy.

During the 1972 Moscow visit, due to the concept of *détente*, the SALT Treaty had been amended regarding the limitation of anti-ballistic and strategic weapons. Then based on *linkage*, an agreement had been signed granting the "most favored nation" (MFN) status to the Soviet Union in return for a settlement of the wartime Lend-Lease debt. And, concomitantly, Senator Henry Jackson devised then a means of publicly pressuring the Soviet Union by introducing an amendment, known as the Jackson-Vanick Amendment. The amendment forced communist states to keep a flow of Jewish emigration from those countries. As a result Nixon had swept to a midterm landslide victory by the end of 1972. By then the Watergate affair had already began, lasting until 1974.

* * *

The spring that followed proved to be hectic. Rudi found out that the courses he had taken at Brooklyn Polytechnic University were enough to qualify him for the licensed electrician test. He passed that test, and soon after he surprised me with the news that he had found and rented a street-level commercial space in Mount Vernon, a town in Westchester County, a few miles north of Manhattan, where he intended to start his own business. Soon Kleckner Electric Inc. began doing electrical contracting business all over Westchester County, and after a few years it also started to do business in Manhattan.

Aimée returned for a visit to the United States while Mancy was already with us. Aimée had met my mother back in Bucharest, and now she addressed her as Tante Mancy. And my father, Gică, called to let us know that he had obtained an exit visa that would allow him to visit us again in June. So there was never a dull moment.

After I passed the final test for Professor Loweenfeld's course and Aimee had left, Gică arrived. The funny thing was that Gică's visit made it possible, for the first time in my life, to have both parents around the same table. They got along just fine. My mother played the role of "local" because she was fluent in English, and she felt she was in a position to give Dad tourist advice, providing recommendations about the must-see sights in New York City. She also suggested that the four of us make a trip to Niagara Falls, which my dad had not yet seen. Rudi thought my mother's suggestion would also offer us a good opportunity to make a side trip to Toronto to see my former mother-in-law, Rosalie—thus keeping his promise he had made to me before we got married. I was glad that he had not forgotten a closure meeting with my first husband, Stephen, whom the communist authorities had not allowed me to join in Italy.

I called Rosalie to let her know that we were coming to see her. Her reaction was an explosion of joy. She told me that she could not wait to see my father and me again, and she was eager to meet my mother and my new husband. She added that she would also let Stephen know about our visit. Of course I was emotional at the prospect of that meeting, but I was happy that I had managed to get through the Iron Curtain and do something that the communists had not allowed me to do.

The four of us set out on our trip in our new Oldsmobile car. We stopped for one night in Monticello to see Ida and Sam, and the following morning we continued to Niagara Falls. After staying two nights there, we headed for Toronto.

Rosalie looked very much as I remembered her. She hugged me as if I were her daughter and was very happy to see my father. She gave Rudi an inquisitive look, as if to assess whether he was the right choice for me. From the expression on her face, I think Rudi got her approval. With my mother, Rosalie was a little reserved. That probably reflected her old resentment that during all the years that Rosalie had known me, she knew my mother was missing in action. That was something that she could never comprehend.

All of a sudden, the doorbell rang. Rosalie rushed to open the door. I instinctively followed her. There was Stephen framed by the doorway. He looked at me the same way he had when I first saw him in our house on Armaşului Lane back on February 10, 1947. He gave me a hug without saying a word, and we all returned to the living room, where he greeted my mom and dad and shook hands with Rudi.

Rosalie had prepared lunch for us, and as soon as Stephen arrived, she invited all of us to sit down around the dining room table. Once we were seated, however, there was an uneasy silence. After so many years of believing that such a reunion would be totally unimaginable, I think we were all overwhelmed by the whole event and felt it was kind of surreal. The exception was my mother, who was totally unaware of the situation as she had been in prison during the whole saga of my proxy marriage with Stephen, followed by my three desperate and unsuccessful attempts to join him in Italy.

Eventually, Stephen broke the silence by starting a conversation with my father to catch up with what had happened in Armaşului Lane after their departure. After lunch Rudi addressed me with, "Maybe you and Stephen have a few words to say to each other. Why don't you go to the other room to have some privacy?"

We both headed to Rosalie's bedroom, where Stephen caught me by my shoulders and told me, "I just want to tell you how painful it was for me to leave Europe without you because it felt like giving up all hope of eventually getting you out of Romania…But after my father's death, our financial situation worsened, and we were forced to immigrate to Canada. I loved you more than words can say. At least I hope you are happy with Rudi."

I told him that I too had been heartbroken when I finally gave up all hope of joining him in Italy. But I added that fate had compensated me with Rudi, who was a very good husband.

I asked Stephen why he had not brought along his wife, Pamela, to meet me. He said he wanted to savor, alone, a moment that he knew would never again repeat itself. He took my head in his hands and planted a long good-bye kiss on my forehead. Then he took my hand, and we both returned to the living room. We went straight to Rudi, and he said, "Here she is, all yours, and thanks for your gesture in agreeing to this visit."

Rosalie had tears in her eyes. My father did not say a word; he was probably thinking about the day Stephen came to our Genune estate to propose, just days before he left for Italy. Now my father probably regretted his insistence that Stephen and I postpone the wedding until after I graduated from law school. But how could he have known, at the time, that the Iron Curtain dividing Eastern Europe would keep Stephen and I separated for good!

Witnessing all this, my mother kept asking Rudi whether I was suffering from some illness. She could not understand what I had needed to discuss in private with Stephen, who was a physician. When I heard about my mother's concern, all my emotions melted away, and I burst out laughing. That puzzled my mother even more.

So that was the end of my saga with Stephen, which had started in 1947. After a quarter century, I satisfied my desire to see him, and I also had the feeling we had finally overcome communism at last. Looking back now, my conclusion is that if I had succeeded in leaving Romania in 1948–49, I would not have come to know the full extent of the destructive essence of communism. (I also would not have had the drive to write this memoir, whose main purpose is to show how the benefits of a democratic capitalist system contrast with socialism in general and its communist version in particular.)

From Toronto we returned to New York via Ottawa, the Canadian capital, where the imposing parliament building made quite an impression on us. We all liked that city a lot, but my parents were surprised at the more European atmosphere that seemed to prevail in Canada.

* * *

Shortly after my father's departure to Bucharest, I signed up for the course on legal aspects of international treaties taught by Professor Garretson. One assignment was to put myself in the position of a legal counsel in the US Department of State and analyze an imaginary trade treaty between USA and Romania. I searched Romania's legislature on the matter and indicated what the article of the treaty should include. It was well received by Professor Garretson.

In his turn, Rudi was satisfied that his business was taking off. He was getting more and more contracts. He has an independent and entrepreneurial nature, so that business fit him like a glove.

We spent Thanksgiving, Christmas, and New Year's Day with my mother. On New Year's Eve we were together with Romanian friends at a black-tie party in Mohong Upstate New York. My mother looked beautiful in her long gown. It was hard to believe that thirteen years had passed since her release from a prison term that had also been thirteen years. What a difference her education has made!

1973

The year started with the news that in January the SUA-North Vietnam Peace Treaty was signed in Paris. Following this I was happy to see on TV the prisoners of war, after suffering in the hands of the communists, coming home.

However, at NYU's cafeteria the "peacekeeping movement" atmosphere was still ongoing. I could not understand why I did not hear anything positive about the POW withdrawal process or protests against North Vietnam. I recalled that back in 1969, during my years at Columbia University, I had seen the huge Ho Chi Minh portrait hanging from the wall of a campus building, which clearly indicated to me that SDS students movement could not have been spontaneous but supported and advised by outside forces. Further, in 2013 I read an article by the prominent American journalist Arnaud de Borchgrave saying that the World Peace Council (WPC), founded in Helsinki in 1950, was in fact the brainchild of the Soviet KGB and was entirely under their control. The WPC platform was to promote worldwide peace in opposition to the warmongers in the United States. According to Borchgrave, the Kremlin also ordered the American Communist Party to set up, in 1979, the United States Peace Council (USPC). As many as seventy-seven members of Congress voted in favor of the creation of USPC to promote worldwide peace movements against the war.

And on the same topic, Arkady N. Shevchenko, in *Breaking with Moscow* (page 216), underlines that in a meeting, "Andropov, with unusual bluntness, had remarked 'We'll win the Vietnam War not in Paris but in the streets of America.'" Indeed I witnessed on TV the multitude of young people against the policy of their country, unwilling to fight against the expansion of communism.

When the war was over between the North and the South, it ended in defeat. The South did not get the promised defense spending from Congress when the North violated the treaty and invaded it.

* * *

I needed to take one more mandatory course to qualify for the LLM degree. I signed up for the course on international trade transactions that was also taught by Professor Lowenfeld. As they had in 1965, the Soviets initiated economic reforms that relaxed, to some degree, the centralized planned economy by introducing (though timidly) some free-market elements. Mr. Lowenfeld wanted to challenge his students to come up with ideas about ways to develop East-West trade agreements. As someone who came from an Eastern Bloc country, I was the logical one to get that assignment. As it happened, between February 23 and 24, Harvard Law School organized a symposium on that particular subject. Rudi and I decided to drive to Boston, Massachusetts, to attend that conference. There were many speakers from the United States Departments of State and Trade and from the Export and Import Bank (EXIMBANK). Also represented were executives of several major corporations.

At the conference, Romania's ambassador to the United States was one of the speakers. I was surprised to see how many American lawyers were in attendance seeking to get information on the international trade area. There was an atmosphere of optimism in the hall as many corporations were eager to increase trade relations with the communist bloc. Although they were eager to start trading with the East, they did not know that all organizations were state-owned, the economy was state-controlled, and the prices were fixed also by the state. I found it almost impossible to infuse the same positive optimism into my essay, entitled "East-West Foreign Trade: Subject *en Vogue*." Here I explained that due to fundamental differences between the two systems, developing broad multinational trade relations appeared to be doomed. I believed a hybrid system was not viable and that the only way to develop trade relations with communist countries had to be based on bilateral, mostly barter trade agreements that would take into account the legislature of each country.

I handed in the essay ahead of time because Rudi and I had been invited to a wedding that occurred on April 21. The bride and groom were Patricia and my colleague Van Langley. Van insisted that we stay overnight with them at their home, and we accepted. The wedding was really nice, and the bride and groom made a delightful couple. As they came out of the church after the religious service, we observed the tradition of this country by showering them with rice for good luck.

* * *

My graduation ceremony took place in June. I was so proud to put on my dark blue robe and black cap with a tassel. I had many pictures taken with fellow students and professors. Shortly after, I received in the mail a letter of congratulations from the dean of the NYU Law School that read in part:

> Dear Mrs. Kleckner,
>
> This is a note of congratulation on your having successfully completed the requirements for your degree at New York University. You have many reasons to be proud of your achievement. We have confidence that you will build on the foundation that you have established here and will attain the useful and honorable place in society

for which your studies have prepared you. I send
you my best wishes.

Sincerely,
James M. Hester

With graduation came another salary increase that was announced to me in an official letter. Again and again, I could not help contrasting my experience in this country with what I had experienced under the communists.

* * *

During the summer, Rudi and I again went to the Badgastein spa in Austria. We timed our visit to meet with the Boyko family. From Badgastein we took the train to Munich to visit Aimée. On that occasion we met again with Noël Bernard and other friends from Radio Free Europe.

Back in New York, we went to Monticello, New York, for a few days to visit Ida and Sam. During that time, the hippie festival was going on in Woodstock, which was relatively close to where we were staying. The Woodstock Festival was an icon of the hippie counterculture that involved lots of sex, drugs, and rock 'n' roll. Initially, the hippies had neither defined their ideological or political goals. Nevertheless, the movement was gradually infiltrated by external communist militants who led many hippies to join the anti-Vietnam war and antibusiness protests that were aimed at the destruction of this country from within.

* * *

With three diplomas under my belt, I thought the time had come for me to leave my current job and find one where I could capitalize on my qualifications. Meanwhile, I thought I could use the extra free time to publish something. I thought it would be a good idea to translate the Romanian Penal Code into English, both as homage to my father and with a view to consolidating my qualifications toward a tenured job within the university.

I had to get in touch with Professor Gerhard Müller, the head of the Criminal Justice Department, and seek his approval for the publication of the English version of the Romanian Penal Code in the Foreign Penal Code Series published by his department. Since Professor Müller did not know me, I thought my best chance would be to approach Professor Julius Marke and see whether he would be willing to act as my reference to Professor Müller. I explained my intentions to Professor Marke, telling him why I was motivated to translate the Romanian Penal Code into English. He warned me that translating any penal code was a tedious and difficult job—to which I replied that I had never shied away from challenging tasks. In addition, at the time I had the luxury of having more free time at my disposal to devote to the project. Julius promised to see what he could do, and indeed, after a couple of days, he called to let me know that Professor Müller was waiting for me in his second-floor office.

As I had done with Professor Marke a few days before, I briefed Professor Müller on my intentions and motivations. He gave me the green light pending his review and approval of a sample translation.

Arming myself with an English juridical dictionary and a Romanian-English dictionary, I translated several articles that I gave Professor Müller to review. After a few days he let me know he was satisfied with my job and encouraged me to keep up the good work. I finished the translation in October 1974 and also wrote an introduction. The translation was approved for publication, and the book appeared under my name and the following title: *The Penal Code of the Socialist Republic of Romania* (New York, Rothman, 1976, page 143 , American Series of Penal Codes, No. 20).

* * *

There was a pleasant surprise that fall: Lulu and his new wife, Georgiana, came to New York. As a civil engineer specializing in high-rise buildings, Lulu was interested in seeing the Twin Towers at the World Trade Center, which had been completed at the end of 1973. He wanted to see how the builders had solved the multiple challenges they faced during construction and finishing stages. We saw each other a few times during their stay in New York. It was then Georgiana told me how she succeeded to leave Romania, to meet Lulu, who was divorced and married her. Before they left, they extended an invitation for us to visit them in Paris.

The second surprise came when Mrs. Meissner, the elderly lady my mother worked for, died at the beginning of December. Now, suddenly, my mother had lots of time at her disposal, so she bought tickets for a two-week trip to California.

We too made a trip, going to the Bahamas to see the lot we had inherited from my cousin Ioana Herescu on the island of Exuma. The lot was part of a land development deal that the BBC had arranged for its employees back when the Bahamas were part of the British Commonwealth. (Ioana had bought it while she was working for the BBC.) We stayed at the Peace and Plenty Hotel, where Ioana herself had stayed many times before she got sick. The ocean water was very clear, an intense blue color like I had never seen before. The beach was wide and deserted, with off-white fine sand. It was a beautiful and peaceful image that I shall never forget.

Soon Aimée returned to New York on one of her repeated visits and stayed with us. No sooner did she leave than Rudi's mother, Silvia, returned for a visit, and she too stayed with us.

* * *

Meanwhile, I was still on the lookout for a better job. Nothing came up during the fall and winter of 1973, but then a number of possibilities suddenly arose. One came from our friend Virgil Stăicoiu (a former lawyer to Alecu Radian in Romania), who was working for the Library of Congress in Washington, DC, and about to retire. He told me he had mentioned me to his boss as a possible replacement and said his boss was waiting for me to schedule an interview. We ruled out that possibility of leaving New York because of Rudi's business and because of my mother.

Then I found out there was an opening at the Law Library at Columbia University, following the departure of Mr. Varady, a former attorney of Hungarian origin who was an international law librarian. Almost at the same time, Professor Julius Marke called me into his office to offer me the position held by Dushan Djanovici, who had indicated his intention to prospect other career venues. I thanked Julius and told him I was flattered by his confidence. I answered that I would consider that possibility if and when Dushan actually left.

One morning a short time after that discussion with Julius, the two of us happened to enter the Faculty of Law at the same time. We greeted each other, and while heading to his office, Julius turned around as if he had suddenly remembered something. "Wait a while!" he said. "I meant to mention something that might interest you. I heard that Ms. Virginia Walker from the UN Library is retiring as of January 1975, and they are currently recruiting for a replacement. I would hate losing you, but if you wish, I can mention your name to Mr. Seymour James, who is the head of the General Reference Department and is in charge of recruiting somebody to fill her position."

The prospect of working for the UN seemed surreal, yet it was a dream that might possibly come true, especially since Professor Julius Marke's recommendation would carry a lot of weight. (Not for the first time, I felt like he was my guardian angel.) He also informed me, however, that the offer for Dushan's position was still on the table. When I thanked him for thinking of me for those positions, he replied, "You do not have to thank me because you deserve it." I was happy to be appreciated by him.

With that parting, he headed to his office, and I disappeared among the host of students who were coming to attend their morning classes. At the time, I wondered how he got the idea of mentioning that UN job for me. Maybe Marcellia had told him that my ultimate dream was to work for the UN.

I was so excited about the prospect of working at the UNO that I felt like sharing my excitement with somebody. Reminding Marcellia that we had not gone out for lunch in a while, I asked whether this was a good day for the two of us to get together. She agreed. I could not wait to break the news to her. When I related to her Julius's suggestion about an opening at the UN Library, her face lit up as if she'd had a sudden revelation. She told me she suspected that Dushan had already applied for it. Well, that was not good news, because Dushan was a friend, and I had no appetite for competing with him, especially since he was such a strong candidate for that position. But in any case, I reminded myself, there was a consolation prize, because if Dushan took that job, I had already been offered to fill his vacated position.

The next day, Marcellia's phone rang. After hanging up, she waved me into her office. She told me Julius was on the phone and he wanted me to come to his office. When I got there, he seemed to be in kind of a hurry and told me dryly that he had spoken with Seymour James, who had agreed to meet me. After that, Julius just gave me Seymour James's phone number and told me, "Go talk to him and let me know what happens."

I called Seymour James, who told me to send him a résumé and the names of three people as references. I approached two of my NYU professors, Andreas F. Lowenfeld and Martin Domke, who in fact had promised me that they were ready to give references for me whenever I needed them. For the third reference I provided the name of Professor Julius Marke, chief librarian and law professor at NYU. I put together a cover letter, attached my résumé and the contact information of my three references, and on April 30, 1974, mailed all documents to Mr. Seymour James.

After a week or so, I got a phone call from Mr. James's secretary, Cecilia Tenorio, setting up an appointment with her boss. She informed me that Mr. James wanted to meet and introduce me to the library director, Mrs. Natalia Tyulina. That is how I found out that Professor Groesbeck had been replaced by this Russian woman. (In fact until 1990, most library directors were Russians. They were Lev Vladimirov, 1964–1970; Natalia Tyulina, 1970–1978; Vladimir Orlov, 1979–1985; and Lengvard Khitrov, 1985–1989.) During my years in Romania I had developed a kind of phobia for the Russians, and I began to think I could not get rid of them, even in New York City.

On the day of the appointment, Mr. James received me in his office at the ground floor of the UN General Reference section. He was from Jamaica, where he had received a British education before 1973, when Jamaica was granted independence from the United Kingdom. After a brief chat, he took me to the second-floor office of Natalia Tyulina. She invited us to take a seat and asked me a lot of questions, speaking grammatically correct English with a heavy Russian accent. She looked and behaved like a lady, which made me believe that she might have been of white Russian descent.

At the end of the interview, she told me it would be a while before I heard from them because, ultimately, the decision would be made by the Personnel Department based on her recommendations.

On June 13, 1974, I received a letter from Mr. James with instruction to fill in an attached yellow form with my personal data and return it to him. About one more month passed before Julius called me to his office and, with a broad smile, showed me a letter he had received from Mr. James that said, among other things, "This is just a note to thank you for your assistance in locating suitable candidates for the post of legal librarian at the DHL.[5] As you know we have selected Mrs. Kleckner, who we feel has excellent qualifications, expertise, and the personality to meet our needs. Thanks again. Sincerely, SWJ."

Taking it for granted that my job at the United Nations was a sure bet, Julius asked me to hand in my resignation so he could start the process of recruiting somebody for the position that I was leaving. Since it was Julius's understanding that my job at the UN would start January 1, I wrote my resignation effective November 29, figuring that I deserved a one-month vacation after all the stress I had gone through.

At NYU, which is a private academic institution, the administrative procedures were simple and expeditious, while at UNO, an international organization with three thousand employees, the administrative wheels moved very slowly. Their policies regarding recruiting, promotions, and salaries were rigid and complex, and most hiring decisions were subject to the ultimate approval of the secretary-general.

* * *

At the same time, Rudi and I were glued to the TV watching the final stages of the Watergate crisis. Because Nixon did hide the truth,

---

5.   Dag Hammarskjöld Library.

he faced near certain impeachment, decided to resign on August 8, 1974, and the next day left the White House. Nixon was an able anticommunist-foreign-policy president, and his first term was a triumph, after he succeeded to withdraw American forces from the thirteen-year-long war in Vietnam. I found out that Bill O'Reilly, a media personality, in his book *A Bold Fresh Piece of Humanity* (pages 201–202), referred to Nixon as follows: "Richard Nixon might have been a liar and a crook, but at least he had a clue about the real world and how it works." Indeed, Nixon after Watergate, during his fifteen-year quest for redemption while writing many books, succeeded in working directly with some of the successive presidents, giving them advice on foreign policy matters (as I will further describe).

I saw on camera when his successor, President Gerald Ford, signed the pardon proclamation for Richard Nixon and, in addition, introduced an amnesty for Vietnam War draft dodgers to defuse the tense political climate that was detrimental to America.

* * *

On August 15, I took my entire one-month vacation. We had planned to take Silvia to Montreal to visit her sister, Tony. Just before we left, I received Dean McKay's letter in the mail. He wished me luck and congratulated me for my new job at the UN Dag Hammarskjöld Library. He added that they would miss my high professional qualities, but they were happy to see me advance on a much more important career path.

It would have been a six-hour drive to Montreal, but on the way we stopped for a few days in Monticello to visit Ida and Sam, who were planning to move to Florida a short time later. Ida joined us on our trip to Canada. Both Rudi and I were very happy to help them take this vacation, and I was really relaxed, knowing that I had my dream job under my belt.

* * *

When we returned home, I thought I would find an official appointment letter from the UN confirming the job, but it did not come. I knew procedures at the UN were slow, so I did not panic—at least not yet. Meanwhile, Silvia returned to Israel, and for the first time in months our lives returned to some semblance of normalcy with no guests, no courses to attend, and no translation to do. At the same time, Rudi was happy with the way his business was going. So we now had more time for ourselves and used much of it to socialize with relatives and friends.

With my resignation handed in and no word from the UN, I thought it was time to call Mr. James and ask him the status of my hiring procedure and inquire what I should expect next. He was polite, but there was a trace of boredom in his voice. He explained that I would have to be patient as it took time to screen all the candidates who had applied for the same position. I told him that if I had known they were not ready to make me an offer, I would not have resigned from my job at NYU. When he heard that, he got a little irritated and said that I should have waited for an official offer before I resigned. After ignoring so many potential job possibilities, I was now in a situation where everything was up in the air.

It was around November 1 when Julius caught sight of me in the cafeteria and took me aside to let me know that he had finally received a reference form from the UN and had given them a prompt reply. He said that Carol, his secretary, could give me copies of that form and of the note that had come from the UN. I felt like a huge burden had been lifted off my chest. The note from the UN said, among other things, "Mrs. Simone Marie Kleckner is being seriously considered for appointment as librarian with the United Nations Secretariat. Before making a final decision, we should like to supplement our knowledge of her suitability and background with a candid appraisal from those who have known her or have worked closely with her in the past."

In addition to the copy of Julius's reference, Carol gave me copies of the letters of reference from professors Andreas F. Lowenfeld and Marin Domke. They were all excellent. I could not have asked for more flattering remarks. At that point, regardless of whether I actually got the job at the UN or not, the words of praise made me feel really good. In addition, another piece of good news came from Professor Martin Domke; he sent me a letter dated November

4, 1974, saying, "You will be interested to know that your arbitration article has been mentioned in an article by Jay A. Burgos, 'The Socialist Republic of Romania.' It is chapter 12 of a new book, *East-West, Business Transactions.* With Best Regards, Sincerely Yours, MD."

At the end of November, my NYU colleagues organized a goodbye party on the occasion of my departure for the UNO. Present at the party were all my colleagues, most professors who had taught the courses I took for my LLM degree, and also Professor G. Müller from the Department of Criminal Justice, for whom I had done the translation of the penal code. They all had nice words to say about me. Then it was my turn to say something. I mentioned that after coming to the United States, I had reoriented my career, building on the foundation of the law degree earned in my old country. I thanked my colleagues, giving special mention for the help received from Marcellia Simpson and for her friendship. As a former student, I also thanked the professors Domke, Lowenfeld, and Garretson, who had honored me with their presence. I had special words of thanks for Julius Marke, and I acknowledged the help of the dean of Studies for the financial support the university had granted me in finishing my studies.

When my last day at NYU finally came, my heart was torn. I was leaving a job where I had made many friends who had given me a lot of support—and, most of all, a job that had facilitated my getting an LLM degree. Now I was stepping into the unknown. But I was finally within reach of a goal that I had pursued ever since I arrived in the States. Finally, my hard work and perseverance had paid off.

* * *

With the approach of the holidays, we planned a vacation to Montego Bay, Jamaica, though I continued to be worried because I had not received an official job offer. Using the excuse of wishing "Happy holidays" to Mr. James at the UNO, I called him one more time, hoping to test the waters and find out where we were with my job. He too seemed worried and kind of surprised about the delay. As soon as I heard that note of uncertainty in his voice, I knew that, in all probability, it would ruin my vacation.

* * *

We celebrated the New Year with champagne and felt the joy all around us. But of course I worried every time I thought about what would be in store for me once I returned to New York. My friend from Washington, DC, informed me that the job there had been filled. The job at Columbia University was taken by Blanka Kudej, an attorney from Czechoslovakia who had an MLS degree, and Dushan Djanovici was still in his job at NYU. Even my position of cataloguer had been filled. Therefore, my future was up in the air. I was skeptical about what 1975 held in store for me.

* * *

When I returned to New York, there was still no letter of appointment. Now I was clueless about where I stood with the application at the UN. Understandably, I was under a lot of stress. I even avoided answering the phone or seeing people for fear someone might ask me questions about my new job.

At that point, I got wondering about the cause of the delay. After a few days, the uncertainty became unbearable. I decided to take a chance and call Mr. James once again. He advised me to be patient because he knew for a fact that my file was still under active consideration.

On top of everything, my father was due to come soon for another visit. Like me, he was really excited at the prospect of my working at the UN, and I dreaded delivering bad news. Yet I could not bring myself to start looking for another job while there still was hope of getting an official positive answer.

The whole situation brought back memories of my old country when I used to fear that the communists had found out some facts that had been omitted from my personal file.

But I had no choice. I would have to wait some more.

* * *

CHAPTER 4

United Nations, January 1975-April 1979

On January 24, Mr. James finally called me with the news that he expected me to report to work on January 27, when he would be waiting for me in his office. As soon as I hung up, I called Julius to give him the good news. He was happy to hear it and wished me good luck. Then I called Marcellia; she too was kind of relieved for me, especially since Dushan's position was no longer available, as he decided to stay on in his current job.

On January 27 I reported to Mr. James's office. After the initial exchange of pleasantries, he informed me that the official job offer letter was in the works and that I should receive it shortly. Then he took me on a tour, introducing me to the library director, Mrs. Tyulina, and to my coworkers in the Dag Hammarskjold Library (named in honor of the former UN secretary-general who had died in Congo in a plane accident). Mrs. Tyulina was very friendly and had a satisfied look, as if I was the person she had recommended, and her selection of me had been taken into consideration over what delayed my nomination. She wished me good luck.

The tour gave me an idea about the library organization. In the huge General Reference Department, I was introduced to my future colleagues, Mike Galatola from the United States, Regine from France, and Olia Wang from China. Only Olia offered me help in case I needed it. We then moved on to the Bibliography Section, headed by Britt Kjolstadt from Sweden. Next, Mr. James took me to the Statistics and Geographic sections, and to the Procurement Section, headed by Mrs. Nebehay from Austria. We finished up with visits to the Cataloguing Section and finally the Interlibrary Loan Section, headed by Karina Einola, from Finland, a very nice person whom I later befriended, together with Olia and Britt.

Around 11:00 a.m., Mr. James invited me to have a cup of coffee at the secretariat cafeteria. There we had a casual conversation focused mostly on my impressions of my recent trip to Jamaica. After that, I was received by the library deputy director, Mr. Joseph Fuchs, who seemed to be sincerely pleased that I had been selected for the job. Following that, I met with the head of the UN Department of References, Ivan Schwartz, originally from Chile, and his assistant, Amin Abdel Samad, from the Sudan.

The professionals from the second-floor Reference were located in the Woodrow Wilson Library, named in honor of the American president. Ivan told me that their section held the original books and documents of the League of Nations, 1920–1945.

Finally, I went down to the first and second floors of the basement, where I toured the Periodicals Section, which held no less than four hundred thousand volumes in five languages, and the Archives of the UN Documentation, where documents were stored on microfiche.

By the conclusion of all those visits, it was nearly 2:00 p.m. Mr. James invited me to lunch in the cafeteria. During lunch, there was no business conversation. Only when we got back to his office did he begin to explain what was expected of me. Among other things, he mentioned that Natalia Tyulina, the director, was very particular about getting weekly statistics regarding tasks that had been accomplished; she would check up to verify them. I told him I was not surprised, being familiar with the preference for statistics and planning in the communist system. Mr. James also mentioned that Mr. Louis Garcia would be my assistant, helping sort out the documents received in the domestic mail.

Another subject was the selection of new books for the legal as well as the general library. By the time Mr. James concluded my job description, it was 5:00 p.m., time to leave for the day. On my way home, I tried to recap and digest the mass of information that I had just received. From what I had seen, I estimated that the DHL must have had between fifty and sixty employees.

In my mailbox back home, I found the official letter from the Recruiting Service of the UN Personnel Bureau. From the letter, dated January 27, 1975, I learned that in fact they were offering me the job on a three-month probation basis that they hoped to convert to a two-year fixed-term appointment. The letter gave me a sense that I was finally on solid ground with the job (even though I had only a three-month probation period, rather than six). However, I was happy that I would not be disappointing my father.

Next day, as planned, Mr. James took me to the Office of Legal Affairs (OLA) located on the thirty-fourth floor. To get there, we took one of the six fast elevators that were used by all UN employees (including the secretary-general). We stopped first at the legal library, where I was shown to my desk and where Mr. James introduced me to Mr. Louis Garcia, a Cuban American. He immediately said he was happy that I finally showed up because it was time for him to take his break. Mr. James was visibly irate that Mr. Garcia put his coffee break ahead of his job duties, and he told Mr. Garcia that Mrs. Kleckner would be busy, and he should rely on his colleague to substitute for him, not on Mrs. Kleckner.

Realizing that I was surprised about Mr. Garcia's attitude, Mr. James explained to me that Mr. Garcia had been accustomed to the more relaxed management style of Mrs. Virginia Walker, his previous boss, who had retired. Mr. James asked me to let him know should I have any problem with Mr. Garcia's attitude in the future.

Next we arrived at the office of Mr. Erik Suy, the general counsel of the UN, whose position was the equivalent of undersecretary-general. His secretary, Mary-Lou, a Filipino, announced us and invited us into his office. Mr. Suy, a Belgian, stood up, shook my hand, wished me a warm "Welcome on board," and invited us to be seated. Mr. Suy asked me, among other things, a lot of questions, such as what country I was from, when I had come to the United States, what jobs I had held before, and why I had decided to apply for that job at the UN. At this point, Mr. James interjected to say that I qualified as the best candidate for the job because of my education, my fluency in four languages, and my past experience. Mr. Suy replied that he was glad that Mrs. Kleckner had finally been hired, putting the stress on "finally," as if he was aware that the hiring process had taken a long time. Mr. James agreed and expressed his hope that the Office of Legal Affairs would be happy with the DHL's selection. With that, Mr. Suy suggested that Mr. James introduce me to all division heads.

Our next stop was the office of the assistant general counsel, Mr. John Scott, who was from South Africa. He appeared to me in somewhat of a hurry, and after a polite "Welcome," he gave a brief presentation of departmental functions, though I got the impression he was actually talking to Mr. James rather than both of us. In the end, he suggested that we visit the three divisions under his management—the Treaties Section, the Secretariat of the Administrative Tribunal, and the UN Commission on International Trade Law (UNCITRAL). The last of these, he said, was set up to promote international private trade.

After lunch Mr. James took me to other departments, the General Legal and the Codification Divisions, headed by a Russian. But in the Codification Division in fact we talked to Ms. Jacqueline Dauchy, a French woman, who said she was glad to meet me because I also would be working with her. She explained that her division assisted the International Law Commission in codifying international law and assisted the Sixth Legal Committee of the General Assembly with annual or ad hoc publications requested by the General Assembly as well as the bibliographies for these publications. Mrs. Dauchy, in turn, introduced me to her assistant, Maria Peterman, a naturalized American from Switzerland, whom she described as "my right hand." In total, the Office of Legal Affairs had between eighty and ninety employees.

After two full days of introductory rounds to so many departments, divisions, and subdivisions, I certainly got the impression that the organization was true to its name, as the United Nations obviously employed people from every corner of the world.

At five o'clock, Louis Garcia was ready to leave for the day, and I told him that I would hang around a little longer. Alone in the office, I was finally able to relax. I looked through the huge wall-sized windows that faced the East River. I could view the bridge that we had crossed back in 1966 on our way from the airport. With hard work and perseverance, I had succeeded in reaching my goal, but now I had to show I was up to the task of proving myself in the most legendary international organization.

Free to view the library more closely, I appreciated that it was large and airy with light natural-wood furniture and thick beige carpeting. There was a long counter where the daily books and documents were delivered by internal mail a few times a day. Between my desk and Louis Garcia's desk was a double bookshelf separating us from three large round tables for readers.

A number of impressions accumulated during my first two days on the job. One thing that really intrigued me was the nervy way Louis Garcia had complained about delaying his twenty-minute coffee break because there was nobody to substitute for him in his absence. Trying to put myself in his shoes, I realized I would have never dared to put my personal interests ahead of my job duties, especially in the presence of Mr. James (who was escorting his new boss—me!). I had been told by Mr. James that the legal officers appreciated Mr. Garcia's interim services after Mrs. Walker's departure, while he had been getting information from the Main Reference Desk when he did not know how to handle questions by himself. Then I suspected both that I might have problems with his attitude and that getting help from the Main Reference Desk had to be avoided. Why? In view of the delay in my hiring process and the short probation period, my instinct told me that my performance on the job would be closely monitored, and I assumed other people probably had their eye on my position in case I slipped up or bothered other colleagues for help.

In any case, starting this new job was unlike any other experience I'd had previously, either in my old country or in the States. Despite the diplomas I had earned, at the beginning of any new job, I thought that I would need some direction or guidance from others. But this was not forthcoming, I found. I was on my own, and I had the feeling that I could not count very much on the help of my assistant.

Two things gave me confidence. For one, I had my notes from my courses at Columbia and NYU, and I knew they would turn out to be a goldmine of information. In addition, I could count on the help of my former colleagues, especially Dushan from NYU and Blanka Kudej from Columbia; each was only a phone call away if I needed to pick their brains to avoid bothering my inside coworkers from the Main Reference desk.

When I went down to the cafeteria for dinner, I found it almost full. Taking my seat at one of the tables, I was soon joined by a young Filipino girl who first asked permission to sit at my table. She told me she had caught a glimpse of me when Mr. James was giving me the tour of the Legal Office and figured that I must be the person replacing Mrs. Walker. She said she frequently had to get books and documents from Mr. Garcia, who was always very helpful. Then she added that Mr. Garcia had been hoping to move into Mrs. Walker's position after she retired. I asked her why he did not get it. She explained that Garcia was a general service employee, and he could not move up unless he was a professional employee with the required degree. I was glad that, totally by accident, I now had an explanation for his attitude, seeing that it was probably motivated by resentment.

Going upstairs, I called Rudi to ask if he could come pick me up in front of the building in an hour. While waiting for him, I shuffled through a pile of paper containing question-and-answer statistics, the index cards of legal publications. Before taking the elevator down, I looked one more time through the windows facing Manhattan. As night fell, it was fascinating to see the lights of the skyline. My thoughts went back to our estate mansion Genune, at the cities of Craiova and Bucharest, places that contrasted strikingly with the new reality that I had reached with a lot of hard work, many emotions, and tough decision-making. Those thoughts uplifted me with feelings of self-assurance and satisfaction.

When I got to the street, Rudi was already waiting for me. I got into the car feeling a little tired but in good spirits. I told Rudi that I might have to spend many evenings at the office. That did not surprise him at all because both of us knew what it took to build a new life, and neither of us was sparing in our efforts to succeed.

Next morning at the office, after reading the newspapers, which was a must, the phone started to ring, and people stopped by with questions and requests. I started to fill up statistical sheets with the names and phone numbers of those making requests. For the most part, answering the requests required varying degrees of research that I was able to do myself. For those that stumped me, I called Dushan, who either gave me the answer on the spot or called me back after doing some research himself. A few times, when the issue pertained to US legislation, I called Ed Bender. As soon as I knew the answers, I could report to the people who had made the requests. I was relieved that I could do my job without any assistance from my colleagues downstairs, who might demonstrate that I was not fit for the job.

I have described in some detail the organization of the Dag Hammarskjöld Library (DHL) and the UN Legal Office because those were the places where I was going to spend a good part of my working life. Likewise, in describing my first couple of days of employment at the UN, I wish to portray the inevitable stress generated by the many questions or other aspects of the job. There was much information I had to absorb, plus the host of adjustments that any new job requires. During my first year on the job, there were many days similar to the first ones.

In the days to come, I continued to have an unpleasant relationship with Mr. Garcia. He frequently took days off, and in general, his work ethic left a lot to be desired. One day when he was again missing, Mr. James called me and asked me if I knew of any reason for Mr. Garcia's absenteeism. I did not want to tell him what I had found out in the cafeteria, because I was sure that he and Mrs. Tyulina knew about that. In addition, I had no intention of beginning to complain, especially during my probation period. I was aware I had to be very careful about the image I projected.

The three probation months proved to be difficult for me, because of the stressful situation with Garcia. But exactly on the date when my probation was over, I received a letter letting me know that the initial three-month period was to be prolonged for a year and nine months to January 25, 1977. My position was the same as when I was hired—that is, professional P-3, level 1. I found out from statistical data received in 1974 that out of the total 3,093 employees, only 216 women were P-3 professionals and 41 were P-5 professionals. I was proud to be among the minority of women professionals, but I knew I had a long road ahead if I was going to advance even further up the hierarchy. In any case, financially I had made quite a leap.

Among my responsibilities was maintaining our legal collections, ensure they were up to date—mostly in English and occasionally in French for the legal and main library. For that, I had to know the scope of the UNO Charter, the structure of UNO bodies, the General Assembly agenda, and of course, the major political issues of the time. Downstairs, other collections included materials in English, Spanish, Arabic, Chinese, and Russian.

Also, I had to compile the bibliographies requested by Ms. Dauchy from the Codification Division. The bibliographical work was in addition to monitoring attendance, doing performance valuation, keeping time sheets and statistics, getting required materials on loan, and other administrative duties in the DHL.

Moreover, sometimes the general counsel requested legal sources for a specific subject. The first time I got word that he wanted to see me, I had no idea why. But I soon found out that such visits were routine. He would start with polite small talk, then let me know about his intention of writing an article, an essay, or a book, and wanted me to provide documentation for the subject that he was dealing with. I gave his request utmost attention and top priority. Of course, Mr. Suy never forgot to thank me for a job well done.

To do all that, I often worked long hours, and on countless occasions I also had to come in on weekends. I have to mention here that professional employees were not entitled to overtime compensation. But I had to do what I had to do in order to keep everybody happy to build my reputation. "Everybody" meant James for administration, Codification Division for bibliographies, Legal Counsel for research, and the daily users (many from the UN Missions) whose questions had to take priority.

Meanwhile, I learned that Louis Garcia had managed to get a transfer to the Law of the Sea Unit in the Secretariat. I have to admit that I did not regret his departure. He was replaced by Darell Stewart, an African American, who by contrast was very polite and cooperative. The only problem with Darell was that he was frequently late and often came in looking tired. Every time this happened, he invoked just the kind of excuses that Louis had used. I could have written a book about those myriad excuses.

Friends from that time are Ingrid, the wife of Gerold Hermann, from UNCITRAL, who was hired about the same time as I. I met Ingrid in the Legal Library. I immediately caught her attention because she was beautiful and came almost every day to sit at one of the tables and write letters. One day we introduced ourselves to each other. She and her husband were newcomers to New York from Germany, and at the time they were looking for an apartment. Subsequently, Ingrid and I frequently went out for lunch or a cup of coffee, and after she and her husband settled in their New York apartment, we visited each other often. We remain friends to this day and continue to see each other every time we had an opportunity, either in Austria (where Ingrid and her husband now live) or in Florida, where they have an apartment like ours.

During my twelve years at the UNO, I made many friends in the Legal Office and also in the DH Library. Among the frequent visitors at the library was the Russian Igor Fominov, who loved to read the most conservative American publications. He was always smiling and in good spirits. He spoke English without any detectable accent, and I often overheard him speaking with people in perfect French, German, Italian, or Spanish. I was in awe of what a good education the KGB was giving their people "for export."

I enjoyed working in this multinational environment. The library readers were delegates of member states of UN Missions. There were also members of intergovernmental organizations, press correspondents, and other librarians or researchers working on different projects regarding the organization.

When I started at the library, there were still a handful of the old-timers who had been working there since the beginnings of the organization. They were infrequent visitors to the library as they knew the UN Charter by heart and had no need for documentation in their research. One of them was Brian Urquhart, from Britain, who was undersecretary-general for Special Political Affairs. By contrast, the younger employees spent long hours in the library for having to do a lot of research for their various projects.

Occasionally, I went with my friends to the Delegates Lounge to have our coffee. A huge tapestry hung on the wall of the lounge. It had been designed by the Romanian artist Ion Nicodim and donated by Romania. That lounge was the place where representatives of different missions got together to discuss pressing issues. I heard that it was easier for them to strike a deal there than in the Security Council. Every time I went to the Delegates Lounge, I would invariably see Ivan and Amin, from the UN References desk at the second floor, seated at the table. Though unaware of it at the time, the two of them would turn out to play a role in my future career.

During the fall session of the General Assembly, world-famous jurists came to the Legal Library. It was a pleasure for me to have the opportunity to meet and speak with them. I felt it was necessary to keep myself abreast with what was going on in the General Assembly or in the Security Council. To do so, I was religiously reading UN documents and the daily press, as well as periodicals with articles written by some of those famous jurists.

Another aspect was that all employees with American citizenship (as in my case) were invited by the American Mission to the Christmas party. When I started at the UN, the American ambassador there was Daniel Patrick Moynihan, a Democrat and academic. I never met him because he left this position in 1976, but I heard that he had the reputation of being a staunch anticommunist, and he considered the UNO to be a hindrance rather than an aid in America's foreign relations. (Following Moynihan, Andrew Young was appointed by President Jimmy Carter as US ambassador to the UN. In August 1979 he had to resign because he engaged in direct conversations at the UN with the Palestine Liberation Organization (the PLO), which was not recognized by the American government.)

The one ambassador who stands out most in my memory was Jean Kirkpatrick. In December, when I was invited to the American Mission for Christmas, she hosted the party. I met her at the entrance greeting guests, shaking hands, and exchanging a few words with each of them. When I overheard her chatting in impeccable French with the French delegates, I was very impressed. I complimented her on her French. She smiled and just mentioned that her family owned a villa on the French Atlantic coast, where she spent some time every year.

Jean Kirkpatrick was the first woman to serve in that post, appointed by Ronald Reagan, who advocated US support of anti-communist governments around the world and was a great admirer of Pope John Paul II, whom she considered a courageous man for supporting anticommunist movements in Eastern Europe. Later, I found out that besides being a graduate of prestigious American universities (including Columbia), she had studied at the University of Paris. From some of her articles and essays that I read years later, I learned that she was disillusioned with the way things were at the General Assembly and the Security Council.

Jean Kirkpatrick resigned in 1985. Her replacement was General Vernon Walters, also a highly qualified man. He had been made a general during President Truman's time; later, during Nixon's administration, he was in the CIA.

Romania was very active at the UN, and I met some of the representatives. Their offices were located on the thirty-fifth floor, where the important Department of Political and Social Affairs was located. The leadership of that department was traditionally given to the Russians. At the time I started at the UN, the head of the department was Arcady N. Shevchenko. I never met him, but I caught a glimpse of him once in the elevator.

Among the Romanians, I remember Messrs. Micu, Iftenie Pop, and Traian Chebeleu. I also met Ion Voicu from the Romanian Ministry of Foreign Affairs who came several years in a row to attend the General Assembly sessions. Once Mr. Voicu gave me one of his articles with a note of appreciation that said, "I thank you for the competent help you always gave me at the UN Library." The article was entitled "The Liquidation of Underdevelopment and the New International Economic Order," which cast blame on the division of the world into rich and poor countries and the exploitation of poor countries by the colonial powers.

* * *

When I joined the UNO in 1975, the main concern of the organization was to push for decolonization and self-determination of states. I liked the idea of self-determination but disliked the hasty way decolonization was done. Therefore, it might be useful to give some details as to how the rapid changes came about.

After World War I, President Woodrow Wilson was the first who put forward this idea of each nation's self-determination and creating the League of Nations with a view to ensuring a collective security that would prevent future conflicts. President Wilson's ideas were adopted by President Franklin Delano Roosevelt, another progressive president with anticolonialist ideas. Roosevelt did not appreciate Churchill's ideas that the British empire must be preserved, bringing European civilization and culture to its colonies.

In short, President Roosevelt adopted Woodrow Wilson's ideas and established the United Nations as a replacement for the League of Nations (deemed ineffective because it lacked an enforcement procedure). While the General Assembly was the main deliberative organ of the UN, the Security Council had decision-making power, and five member states had veto power. On Roosevelt's initiative, a decolonization committee was established with a mission to promote, support, and approve the independence of the former colonies. As a result, the United States was in favor of decolonization for free democratic states, whereas the Soviet Union and China were pursuing to implement their Marxist ideology. Under these circumstances, it is no wonder that the first general secretary of the United Nations, Trygve Lie from Norway, once stated that this was the most impossible job in the world, as it was up to him to reconcile diametrically opposed views.

Thus, the new independent states could choose between a free-market system that would have offered them a chance to build a flourishing economy or a rigid, centralized system that always led to stagnant economies and poverty. The problem was that the socialist-communist ideology was then *en vogue*, and therefore, instead of building on the positive contributions of the previous colonizers in education, the judicial system, and medical care, most newly independent states replaced colonial power with the Soviet model.

In my opinion, while the old colonial powers had undoubtedly exploited their colonies, they nevertheless did leave behind some European civilization. Kissinger writes in his book *World Order* (2014, pages 173–174) that "European states built colonies and justified their action by their higher levels of civilizing mission…including democracy. They ensured that after a long period of time the colonized people would demand and achieve self-determination…Also [the European states], abolished slavery in its empires and slave-trading ships on the high-seas.…[Colonization] proved to be one of the shaping factors of the modern world."

In other words, the old colonial powers were taking, but they were also giving, while the Russians did nothing more than taking all they could from those countries' resources. I know that very well from my personal experience when the Soviets robbed us of our resources. Therefore, I was in favor of self-determination, and I hoped that the process of decolonization would develop gradually so that the independent countries would have time to choose and build their own, unique democratic institutions and economic structures when they were mature enough to do so.

In reality, the opposite happened. A hasty decolonization process allowed Moscow to fill in the vacuum left behind by the old colonial powers. Actually, the Russians and the Chinese were competing to impose their hegemony over the resources of those new states. Moscow assumed the role of supporter of the "wars of national liberation" in the former colonies. Marxist groups infiltrated those countries, spreading terror among the population and helping to install totalitarian Soviet puppet regimes all over. The Soviets found in the newly decolonized countries a fertile ground for imposing hegemony the way they had done in Eastern Europe in late '40s, in Korea in the '50s, and in Vietnam in the '60s.

As I have mentioned, the decolonization process was happening very rapidly. When I started my job at the UN in 1975, there were 144 member states of the UNO, and within ten years that number had reached 180. Many of the newly independent states were plagued by corruption and poverty. In spite of their rich natural resources, most of those countries, in what was called the "third world," were struggling with extreme poverty.

This was why, in June 1975, Secretary- General Kurt Waldheim addressed the situation, mentioning that a group of experts recommended cooperation between rich and poor countries, as well as the appointment of a UN director for international economic development to help the poor countries. I wondered how a UN director could deal with the entire economic world. In part, I thought that the situation was created as the result of rapid decolonization and the repudiation of market economies.

The American ambassador to the UN, Daniel Patrick Moynihan, made a number of proposals, including the allotment of $10 billion to the International Monetary Fund and the establishment of a reserve of thirty million tons of wheat and rice as aid to the underdeveloped countries.

* * *

During my twelve years' work at the UN, I followed the course of many conflicts. I will give details so that readers have an idea how the United States, the founder of the United Nations, gradually lost the authority that it had within the organization. This occurred at its inception, largely as the result of increasing Soviet and Chinese influence, together with the decolonization process.

To support this contention, I need only mention that Russia interfered in Angola with the popular movement MPLA, in Algeria through the Palisario Front, and in Somalia through the Revolutionary Party. In Ethiopia the communist movement took over after ousting Emperor Haile Selassie. In 1980, there were alarming signs about the economic and social situations in Libya or Sudan. The fight in South Africa was over the segregation between the whites and Africans, the social structure called "apartheid." Namibia had its SWAPO leadership while Rhodesia (renamed Zimbabwe) had its guerilla movement.

In Southeast Asia, Cambodia fell under the brutal communist regime of the Khmer Rouge leader Pol Pot, who was supported by the People's Republic of China. A UN resolution regarding the withdrawal of the Vietnamese troops from Cambodia, with a view to organizing free democratic elections, was condemned by the Russians as "interference in the country's internal affairs." In spite of the fact that the UN Commission for Human Rights had reported that the Pol Pot regime was practicing genocide against its own population, the General Assembly admitted Cambodia as a UN member state under its new Democratic Kampuchea name.

Most of the new states appearing on the world map as a result of rapid decolonization were gravely affected by poverty, malnutrition, deadly epidemics, high infantile mortality, and other plagues. While many UN resolutions tried to address those problems, the efforts remained ineffective.

During this time, besides decolonization results, other crises of a different nature cropped up around the world. The war in Cyprus resulted in that island being divided between the Turkish and Greek republics. In the Middle East, following the two Israeli-Arab wars of 1967 and 1973, the UN interceded twice—first, with the United Nations Emergency Force (UNEF I) sent to the region to end to the Suez crisis, and a second time, when the United Nations Emergency Force (UNEF II) had to supervise the cease fire between Israel and Egypt. There was also a United Nations Disengagement Observer Force, or UNDOF, that was sent to supervise the Israeli and Syrian forces in the Golan Heights, and the United Nations Interim Force in Lebanon, or UNIFIL, which helped Lebanon restore its authority in the area. (Of course the Israeli-Palestinian conflict continues to this day: the General Assembly granted the PLO observer status, although the United States considered the PLO a terrorist organization and has no relations with it. As I have earlier mentioned, it was the direct talks that the US ambassador Andrew Young had at the UN with the PLO that resulted in his resignation.) In 1975, North Vietnam applied for membership, a move that was opposed by the United States on grounds that the Security Council had previously turned down South Korea's membership application. (Nevertheless, in 1977 North Vietnam had managed to become a member of UNO.) Addressing the Korean problem in 1975, the General Assembly requested the withdrawal of US troops from the region because the Soviets accused the Americans of aggression. (In fact, the division between North and South Korea was triggered by President Truman's fight to contain Soviet expansionism. Today the Republic of South Korea is a democratic state with a flourishing market economy while the People's Democratic Republic of Korea remains a communist state with a bankrupt centralized economy.)

Following the rapid decolonization and the various conflicts that resulted in an increased number of member states, the General Assembly became a populist forum. Newly admitted states, together with the nonaligned states of the third world, tilted the balance of votes against the United States. As I previously noted, this is how the United States, the founder of the United Nations, gradually lost the authority that it had in the first ten years of the organization's existence.

* * *

President Gerald Ford's foreign policy followed the concept of détente. He participated in the Conference of Security and Cooperation in Europe (CSCE) in July 1975 and signed the August Helsinki Accords with the Soviets. The Accords included also statements regarding the observance of fundamental human rights in accordance with the United Nation Charter, the Declaration of Human Rights and Property Rights. On the whole, for the United States, the Accords just meant to minimize the tension between the two countries. But the fact that the Accords included statements regarding the observance of fundamental human rights signed as such by the Soviets, this was very important for East European countries, having a huge, crucial impact for their future. Little by little Soviet totalitarianism had to give in to those rights, and in the end they contributed to the collapse of the Soviet Union and the end of the Cold War. They heralded the beginning of the end of the Soviet empire.

Regarding the existing social issues in the United State, they concerned and saddened me—particularly problems related to the use of drugs, free sex, which produced many fatherless children, and the beginning of political correctness, by not mentioning facts as they were. Some of these trends had already started in the 1960s when we arrived, but they kept worsening.

*　*　*

At home, there was never a dull moment as our apartment became a revolving door with visitors coming and going. My mother found a better apartment close to us and moved out from her studio apartment. At the same time, Rudi's mother, Silvia, wrote to us that she was not feeling well and that she had a hard time finding somebody to help her. Rudi suggested that she move to New York. In anticipation of that possibility, we decided to keep the studio apartment that Mancy had vacated, furnishing it and supplying the kitchen with all the appliances and utensils needed for everyday use. Silvia liked to cook, in contrast to my own mother who would go to a restaurant for lunch and have dinner with us, just so she would not have to cook.

Meanwhile, my father's passport application had again been approved for travel to the United States. Aimée let us know that she, too, was planning to visit us again. Since her visit overlapped with my father's, she slept in the studio that we had prepared for Silvia.

Regarding Mancy's job, after Mrs. Meissner's death, her son gave my mother excellent references, which was the encouragement she needed to begin looking for another job. Through a placement agency, she found employment as general housekeeper for a widower colonel named Arneman, who had a big house in the town of Albertson on Long Island. (For cooking, cleaning, and other chores around the house, the colonel also employed an African American who lived on the premises.)

110

One day as we were driving Mother to Albertson, Mancy unexpectedly said she would like to know where she would be buried. She had heard on radio station WQXR about an all-denomination cemetery in Woodbridge, New Jersey. We were taken aback by her preoccupation with her final resting place. Being totally absorbed by our daily life in the United States, Rudi and I had no time to think about life in the hereafter. But my mother followed up and took care of all arrangements by calling Woodbridge Cemetery. Her only concern was that she would live long enough to see that a final resting place was prepared for her in a mausoleum.

* * *

During this time, Rudi and I met two people at the sports club in the adjacent UN buildings with whom we would eventually become very close friends. In the ladies' sauna I met Pamela Richards. Pam was an Italian American working for a major advertising agency. Rudi, meanwhile, befriended a guy whom he met in the gentlemen's sauna. His name was Chester Frank, better known as Chet, a real estate agent with an elegant office in one of the Rockefeller Center buildings. We often invited Pam and Chet to our apartment for dinner, together with our other American friends—Van, Pat, Ingrid, and Gerold.

We also socialized with a sizable group of Romanian friends and relatives. As my job became less stressful, our social life became more intense. On the whole, those were happy times for us. Only one event cast a pall. Our hearts were filled with grief at the sudden death of Hariette, Ida's youngest daughter.

At the end of July, Aimée and Mancy went with us to the airport to welcome Gică back to New York. He was in great spirits but a little worried about Florica. She had not been feeling well and was unable to join him as had been initially planned. To help us catch up with what was going on in Romania, he told us about an absurd government decree forbidding visitors from abroad to stay with their relatives. He also warned us that the Securitate, Romania's secret police, had increased its spying on individuals and that most phone conversations were intercepted. He warned us that we needed to be extra careful with our phone conversations when we called him in

Romania because the slightest compromising statement could jeopardize his chances of visiting us in the future as well as our chances of getting an entrance visa to Romania.

Gică and Aimée kept each other company on their sightseeing tours in the city while Rudi and I were at work. On weekends, we went together to visit friends and relatives. Sometimes we drove to Avalon, on the Jersey Shore, where we would stay a few nights. We all enjoyed those trips very much.

After Aimée's departure, we all made a trip to Chicago to visit Constantin Alimăneștianu, the youngest of the Alimăneștianu brothers, friends of mine whom I had met back in Romania. We were really impressed with the John Hancock skyscraper, the tallest in the city at the time, where Constantin took us for lunch. It was a pleasure to catch up with things after so many years.

When we left Chicago, we headed south to Ellwood City in Pennsylvania, where we visited Princess Ileana of Romania,[6] who was then the mother superior of the Orthodox Transfiguration Monastery under the name of Mother Alexandra.

My father, Gică, left for Romania, stopping over a few days in Paris to visit friends and, of course, my aunt Tancy, who had married Nicolae Penescu. As my father was leaving, we promised to come to Bucharest the following year to see him and Florica.

Just two short weeks later, we were at the airport again, this time to pick up Silvia. She came with lots of luggage and all the necessary papers required to let her settle in the States. She looked a little weak, and after we had a snack, we took her straight to her studio apartment. She liked it there, especially when she saw that the studio had a fully equipped kitchen and the fridge was full. She was content with

---

6.   Princess Ileana of Romania (January 5, 1909–January 21, 1991) was the youngest daughter of King Ferdinand I of Romania and his consort Queen Marie of Romania. She was a great-granddaughter of Queen Victoria and of Czar Alexander II. After marriage to Archduke Anton of Austria, Prince of Tuscany, she was known as Her Imperial and Royal Highness Ileana, Archduchess of Austria, Princess Imperial of Austria, Princess Royal of Hungary and Bohemia, Princess of Tuscany, Princess of Romania, Princess of Hohenzollern.

her decision to move to the States. Her only concern was that she did not speak English, and as she put it, she would feel like a bird in a cage in New York.

Gradually, though, she made a lot of progress in the adjustment process. She would walk to visit us and also take short walks in the neighborhood. In a word, she was okay.

1976

A very important event in 1976 was the publication by NYU Criminal Law Department of the English translation of the *Penal Code of the Socialist Republic of Romania* by the Rothman Publishing House of South Hackensack, New Jersey. I dedicated it "to my father, George G. Vrăbiescu, former professor of criminal law and procedure, former counsel to the legislative council."

At the end of September, I received my annual evaluation report, which followed a standard format used by the UNO for all employees. The report, signed by my boss Seymour James and by the library director Natalia Tyulina, evaluated my performance in a range of more than ten categories. In each category were boxes that could be checked for "met expectations," "often surpassed expectations," and "outstanding performance." I was happy with Seymour's very positive evaluations and was rewarded for my hard work because I had been unsparing with my time and in my efforts to perform all the tasks at hand. I often had to put in overtime, sometimes working until late in the evening in order to meet deadlines related to the daily demands or to the compilation of bibliographies. I worked as hard and fast as I could, because my career meant a lot to me: my life and self-esteem depended on it. I was aware that, through intense activity, I regained the liberty I had lost in the communist system. I also felt I deserved a pat on the back for the tactful way I had conducted my relationship with Louis Garcia, avoiding any tension or conflict.

* * *

There was one aspect of my professional life that I still had to discuss with Seymour James—namely that I had joined a number of professional associations, and on occasion I needed to take time off to attend luncheon meetings or workshops. The professional associations I was affiliated with were the American Society of International Law (ASIL), the American Association of Law Libraries (AALL), the Association of Law Libraries of Upstate New York (ALLUNY), the American Foreign Law Association (AFLA), and the Association of Former International Civil Servants (FAFICS). Of course Mr. James had no objection to my occasionally taking time off to attend various functions of those organizations, and he made it clear that this would not affect my vacation time (which I considered very generous). At the UNO I had six weeks of vacation time, compared to the four weeks I had been given at NYU.

* * *

That year there were two important elections: the US presidential elections, with debates between President Ford and Carter, and at the UNO, Secretary-General Kurt Waldheim's four-year contract would expire and a new leader would have to be elected.

In September 1976, Anatoli Gromyko, the longtime Russian foreign minister, came to New York to attend that year's General Assembly session. I think his incentive for attending was not to find out the latest in the decolonization process, in which the Russians had a vested interest, but rather to find out who would probably be his counterpart in the new US administration.

* * *

At home, Silvia was not herself; she seemed depressed and would not leave the house unless we were taking her somewhere in the car. Because of that situation, we did not make any major vacation plans for that summer.

Once, just Rudi and I went to the Jersey Shore for a few days. Later on, we received an invitation from Rhoda and Rudy Boyko, the friends that we met in Badgastein, Austria, to visit them at their nice summerhouse in the countryside, where they had an indoor heated pool. When we were invited there during the winter, it was quite an experience for us to be able to swim while, outside, a few deer, attracted by the light shining through the windows, peered in at us. I shall never forget that fairy-tale image, seeing a herd of deer among snow-covered trees.

Another time, when our friend Ingrid's parents came to visit from Germany, we took them on a trip to the West Point Military Academy, founded in 1778. Among the famous graduates of that prestigious academy were two American presidents, Ulysses S. Grant and D. Eisenhower, as well as Generals Douglas MacArthur, George S. Patton, and Omar Bradley. In 1976, the year we visited, women were admitted to the academy for the first time.

America celebrated her two hundredth birthday on July 4, 1976, when a series of events were scheduled. One was a regatta of tall-mastered sailing ships from all over the world sailing down the Hudson River, witnessed by thousands of New Yorkers gathered along Manhattan's West Side Highway (which was closed to traffic for the occasion). Among other famous ships I saw at that parade were the royal yacht *Britannia*, the Italian training ship *Amerigo Vespucci*, and the elegant tall ship *Mircea* (the former Romanian royal yacht that had been turned into a training ship).

In early fall we were invited to the wedding of Nicky Alimăneştianu, the older son of our friend Nana. On that occasion I again saw Călin Alimăneştianu and Mica Ertegün née Banu, and her Turkish husband, Ahmed, the owner of the Atlantic Record House. (Among famous artists who recorded for the Atlantic label were Ray Charles and the Rolling Stones.)

Aimée came in October, about the same time my mother, Mancy, received a letter informing her when she was scheduled to be sworn in as a naturalized American. She was seventy-three at the time. We celebrated the event and were very happy for her. It was quite an emotional moment for her and for all of us, as she had come such a long way from being a detainee in communist prisons and labor camps, where she spent thirteen years of her life, to becoming a citizen of a free country.

* * *

Before her departure, Aimée found out by calling a friend in Munich that Preda Bunescu, the deputy director of Radio Free Europe, had been found dead in his apartment. It was a suspicious death that many attributed to Ceaușescu's secret police. In fact, witnesses said that shortly before Bunescu was found dead, a mysterious person rang the bell of his apartment but left a moment after the door was opened. That led many to speculate that Bunescu might have been sprayed with some lethal gas that caused cardiac arrest. Understandably, Aimée, who worked for Radio Free Europe, now feared for her own life.

1977

This was a good year for me. My contract at the United Nations was extended twice, first from January to February 15 with the same salary, then from February 15 to October 31 with a significant salary increase. Starting November 1, I was offered a permanent position with another significant salary increase. My hard work worked.

* * *

The first major event of the year was the swearing-in ceremony of the new president, Jimmy Carter, who pledged to be a defender of human rights all around the world and to work for the elimination of nuclear arms. Of course, my first thought was the hope he could do something to promote freedom and defend human rights in the East European countries too.

Another event that we watched on TV was the interview of former president Richard Nixon by British journalist David Frost, an interview that would make David Frost quite famous. In the course of the interview, Nixon admitted that not telling the truth had demeaned the office of the presidency, but he still implied that he had committed no crime.

Although Nixon had a foreign-policy vision, he did not have the talent to explain his efforts when faced with the convulsions in the big American cities and universities caused by the antiwar or peace movement. I always had the feeling that they were instigated from abroad after my experience at Columbia University in the '60s.

Therefore, I was not surprised when I read in the *New York Times* in the late 1977 that the CIA, which was following the United Nations Cuban Mission in New York, discovered that a Cuban group had been influencing American youth: the Underground Weatherman were aided by members of the Cuban intelligence agencies, while SDS was influenced by North Vietnam to choose youngsters willing to battle with the police.

This brings to my mind the many in Hollywood who joined the movement, the most notorious of them was Jane Fonda, a political activist, a Vietcong enthusiast, and partner of her antiwar husband, Tom Hayden, whose beliefs became SDS's founding document. (Later, when I heard that Fonda was to play Nancy Reagan's role in a movie, I was speechless with indignation. Luckily that did not happen.)

* * *

At the UNO, after his reelection, Kurt Waldheim made a trip to Moscow in September 1977. The official dinner in his honor was hosted by Foreign Minister Andrei Gromyko because Brezhnev was sick. The dinner took place in a prerevolutionary brick mansion in downtown Moscow where—according to Arkady Shevchenko's book *Breaking with Moscow* (page 301)—they feasted on caviar, smoked sturgeon, beef, and Moldavian champagne in a high-ceiling room with brilliant antique tapestries. Of course, the source of most food was the Danube Delta and the former Romanian province of Bessarabia, seized by the Russians after WWII. The bulk of Bessarabia became the Soviet Republic of Moldavia while the southern part, extending to the Danube Delta, was also seized by the Soviets and presented as a gift to Ukraine, together with other parts of northern Romania. Under the 2014–2015 conflict in the region, this became a dangerous situation for the 1991 independent Republic of Moldova. Russian expansionism never comes to an end since it is in the country's genes.

* * *

As part of my morning routine, I would always listen to the news before going to work. On March 5, 1977, I heard about a devastating earthquake in Romania: scores of apartment buildings in Bucharest collapsed, and hundreds died. My first thought was to check whether my loved ones were okay. I tried to reach my father but could not because all phone lines were busy. As we were desperately trying to get through, Norman, Rudi's cousin, called and asked whether we had any news from Romania. We told him that we were totally in the dark. He then offered to try himself and asked me to give him my father's phone number. Shortly thereafter, as we were making unsuccessful attempts ourselves, Norman called with the news that my father was alive. We asked him how he had managed to get through and how he could communicate with my father, who did not speak English. He laughed and told us that he managed to reach an operator and told her that he had a severe heart condition, that his father was in Romania, and that the anxiety might give him a heart attack. Apparently, the operator believed his story and helped him get through. He said to my father, "Norman, Norman," when he heard him say, "Da, da"—that is, "Yes, yes."

Now that we knew he was alive, a huge burden was lifted off my heart. Later on, when we could finally reach my father, we learned that both the house where he lived and our old villa in Armașului Lane were unaffected by the earthquake but that a lot of downtown buildings had collapsed. In one of them, my friend Tănțica died. I was deeply saddened by the death of my childhood friend who had psychic powers and who had endured so much suffering at the hands of the Securitate after her husband's arrest.

* * *

Meanwhile, Mancy was notified by the Woodbridge Cemetery administration that the building of the new mausoleum where she had bought her interment spot had been completed and that she could come to visit at her convenience. One weekend we drove to the cemetery. The mausoleum was a cross-shaped structure with a replica of Michelangelo's *Pieta* in the middle. A salesperson showed us my mother's niche, right in the center close to the *Pieta*, as was my mother's wish. The salesperson then asked Rudi and me whether we had made any arrangements for our final resting place and delivered a sales speech pointing out that prices would go up soon and that it was always good for the entire family to be together. My mother fully agreed with his point; the bottom line was that we ended up buying a double-casket niche for our own final resting place, an action which we would never have imagined doing that day.

* * *

I had promised my father that I was going to visit him. When James told Director Tyulina that I was going to Bucharest, she asked me to check the UN Document Section at the Romanian Academy Library and gave me a letter of accreditation addressed to the director of that library. At the end of July, I boarded a TORAM airplane (from the Romanian airline service) for a direct flight from New York to Bucharest. Rudi could not leave because of Silvia's illness. Of course, I had mixed emotions at the prospect of reconnecting with my roots and revisiting places where I had spent my childhood and youth, but where, at the same time, I had endured a lot of suffering.

When I arrived in Bucharest, it seemed as if centuries had passed since I left. I stayed at Hotel Lido in downtown Bucharest, the same place where I used to swim in open-air swimming pool with artificial waves.

I unpacked and went straight to my father's house. All those I had left behind in November 1965 were there to welcome me, and we all had tears in our eyes. The only absence was my dear uncle Nicu, who had died, leaving a deep emptiness in my soul. Also, my father's wife, Florica, was lying in bed and seemed absentminded; she had been diagnosed with Alzheimer's disease. Toward evening, other relatives came to welcome me. I did not invite any friends because there was a government decree requiring all citizens to report any contact with foreign nationals. I thought that my relatives did not have to fear any repercussions as they had a legitimate excuse to see me, but not friends. My father had enough income because we regularly sent dollars to some special state-shops which accepted only hard currency, where my father was able to buy various goods and then resell them. Therefore, he could offer guests coffee, chocolate, and American cigarettes.

Most of our conversations naturally centered on what was going on during those times: shortages of all kinds, including groceries, liquor, or sweets, the constant fear that they lived in, and about Ceauşescu's decree that banned abortions for any woman under forty-five who had fewer than four children. Also, Gică warned me that I had to be very careful about whom I talked to and what I said. After twelve years in the free world, all that advice was again frightening. I completed my duty at the academy library and left Bucharest on September 1, with promises that I would be back again with Rudi as soon as possible.

Once seated on the plane headed to New York, I felt regrets at leaving behind so many of my dear ones, but it was quite a relief to get out of that grim atmosphere. Rudi was waiting for me at JFK airport and drove me home, where my mother was also waiting to welcome me back. They told me Silvia was in the hospital, where Rudi saw her every evening. Even though I was exhausted by jet lag, I accompanied him to the hospital that evening and returned again during the evenings that followed.

In the office, first thing, I reported to Natalia Tyulina about the UN document collection at the Romanian Academy. Then, on September 30, I received another very positive evaluation, this time signed by Mr. James and countersigned by Natalia Tyulina and her American deputy, Joseph Fuchs.

* * *

After three days, we learned that Silvia needed surgery to have her gallbladder removed. Following surgery, it appeared that she felt okay, and we all hoped that she was out of the woods. But after another three days, she had internal bleeding that required another operation. She never recovered fully from the anesthesia, and she refused food in spite of Rudi's insistence. A couple of days later, we received a phone call from the hospital early in the morning informing us she had expired five minutes before. Rudi was deeply hurt. Also, we were unprepared, and totally in the dark about what to do. Norman, again, was a lifesaver. He took care of the necessary formalities while Aunt Ida gave us one of the burial plots in a Long Island cemetery that she had bought for her family from her synagogue. Present at the funerals were all our relatives. Even Rudi's ex-wife Veronica and her brother Costel came to pay their respects.

* * *

After Silvia's passing, Rudi wanted to be close to Ida. He decided to drive to Florida but, not wanting to go alone, invited his former brother-in-law Costel to join him. Meanwhile, Mancy, who was again without a job because the colonel's family moved him to a nursing home, said she would also like to accompany them as she had never seen Florida. The three of them left while I remained to work.

I had daily news from Rudi. He kept me informed about everything he was seeing in Florida and described his visit with Ida and Sam. They visited the Miami South Beach area, the impressive Villa Vizcaya, and the surrounding estate that belonged to businessman James Deering, the mansions on the millionaires' row that belonged to all kinds of larger-than-life celebrities, the Everglades nature reserve, and other attractions.

Back home, Rudi remained in a mood for vacations, and with the approach of the holidays, we decided for Puerto Rico. We could not find any rooms available in the city of San Juan, but our travel agent advised us to go to a certain El Conquistador Hotel and Casino not far from the city. Taking his advice, we reserved a room there. A shuttle minibus was waiting for us at the airport and took us to the hotel in time for dinner. I sent Rudi downstairs to see how people were dressed. Rudi reported back to say I could dress as I pleased because the hotel seemed totally deserted. When we went downstairs, we were surrounded by restaurant staff that had nobody else to wait on. The mystery was only resolved when we learned that, indeed, we were the first guests there because the hotel had been closed for renovations. It was the first day it had reopened. Our food came quickly, and after dinner, we headed to the theater hall to see the variety show. It took place as scheduled, but once again we were the only ones present. It was not until the next day that another couple showed up, and within a few days the hotel was filled to capacity.

1978

Back home, Mancy gave us the news that she had found another job. The headhunter agency holding her résumé had placed her as house companion for a certain Mrs. Florence Graf starting January 23, 1978. My mother had previously met Mrs. Graf, who liked her and probably discovered that my mother had excellent references. Mrs. Graf was the mother of the famous New York furrier Ben-Kahn, who was loaded with money and could afford to offer his mother whatever she wanted. Her apartment was on Sixty-Eighth Street, west of Broadway, just a ten-minute walk from my mother's apartment.

Not only was this a better-paying job, it was also a very pleasant one. My mother's only duties were to discuss current events with Mrs. Graf or accompanying her to restaurants, to theater plays, to museums, and to the opera. Not so bad! She would remain in Mrs. Graf's employ for almost ten pleasant years. During that time, I could say that I was worry-free about my parents. Mancy was self-sufficient financially, was paying her taxes, and was making the mandatory contributions to qualify for a Social Security pension income.

As for my father, we were sending him currency on a regular basis to help him buy what he needed at the special shops. Lenuța, the maid, and her daughter helped him by standing in line for hours to procure daily necessities—but he also needed the money to get medical care for his wife, Florica, whose health was deteriorating.

That spring I was delighted to receive a visit from my dear friend Helga Benesch. Our reunion after so many years gave both of us a lot of joy. We both felt as if we had been separated for a very short time, and it seemed like only yesterday that the two of us had been going every Sunday to the Pitar Moș Church.

* * *

During Helga's visit, in the office Mr. James sent me a copy of a letter dated January 31, 1978, from Mrs. Dauchy about the bibliography of the 1976 *Juridical Yearbook* that I had worked on. In the letter Mrs. Dauchy wrote, among other things, "May I ask you to convey to Simone my appreciation for the excellent work she has done?" It was another instance of my efforts being recognized, which of course gave me a great deal of satisfaction.

An unheard-of event, causing a huge shock within the entire diplomatic community, was the defection to the United States of Arkady Shevchenko, the highest-ranking Russian diplomat at the UNO, the one I saw once in the elevator. He had been advisor to the Soviet foreign minister Andrei Gromyko and in 1973 had been appointed undersecretary- general of the UNO. There was silence in the UN, no comments in the Secretariat. It was only after 1985 that I learned about his reasons for emigrating, from his book *Breaking with Moscow*, which I often cite here. (I think this is among the rare books giving direct insight into the dreaded Kremlin.)

Moreover, also in 1978, another incredible event took place, when Ceaușescu's highest-ranking secret police guy, General Ion Mihai Pacepa, defected to the United States. He later wrote *Red Horizons*, a book detailing the Mafia-type criminal nature of the communist and secret police structures.

For me, who had lived with the mentality of the communist totalitarianism, both these events were extraordinarily impressive.

All through 1978 I noticed a sharp upsurge in the number of Soviet officers at the UNO. I asked several people for an explanation, but nobody could give me an answer, and also, nobody seemed to give a damn. To me that signified either apathy, indolence, ignorance, naïveté—or all of the above. Personally, I could not ignore the fact that the surge of the Soviet personnel could influence all kinds of debates and tilt the balance in favor of Soviet interests. Truth be told, all the Russians were very polite, educated, friendly, and very skilled in winning over the hearts and minds of their colleagues. But most, if not all, were undercover KGB officers spying on the United States.

It was only in 1985 that I discovered an answer to that mystery in *Breaking with Moscow* (page 295), where Arkady Shevchenko wrote, "At Ambassador Malik's request, Waldheim's willingness to help the Soviet Union resulted in a substantially increased number of

Soviet nationals working at the Secretariat. Waldheim had permitted the Soviet Union to fill its quota of more than 250 Secretariat jobs."

Since I have mentioned Kurt Waldheim's name, I need to point out that I met him once personally. One morning I was a little late and waiting for one of the six elevators, none reserved exclusively for VIPs. Five of the six elevators were busy, and at the door of the sixth one stood Secretary-General Kurt Waldheim with a bodyguard. I wanted to wait for the next available elevator, but Mr. Waldheim waved to me to get in. The bodyguard pressed the button for the thirty-eighth floor before Waldheim asked me which floor I needed. When I said the thirty-fourth floor, he said, "Ah, you work in the legal department," which I acknowledged. When I arrived at my floor and I got off, I thanked him for taking me in the elevator with him. In fact, such elevator encounters occurred a number of times, when I met other prominent personalities such as King Juan Carlos of Spain or Margaret Thatcher.

* * *

That summer Rudi and I had plans together to travel to Bucharest, the Hague, and Paris. Again, when Natalia Tyulina found out from Seymour James that I was going to the Hague, she gave me an assignment to review the UN documentation sent to the International Court of Justice. She also gave me a letter of accreditation for that job, as she had done when I went to Bucharest.

We stayed at Hotel Bucharest, in a room overlooking the fashionable Victoria Way. Across the street from the hotel, we saw a number of young individuals—all dressed in light gray suits—who were hanging around looking at shop windows, reading newspapers. You did not have to be a rocket scientist to figure out right away that they were Securitate agents planted there to watch the people going in and out of the hotel.

On that visit we found out from friends and relatives that a substantial number of ethnic Germans had been allowed to immigrate to West Germany. We also found that, after the 1977 earthquake, tyrant Ceaușescu concentrated on perfecting his gargantuan program of urban systematization. In the process, a number of landmark churches were demolished.

The family reunions were emotional, as usual. Only, poor Florica no longer recognized us. My father was trying hard, against all odds, to make our visit as festive as possible. At that time, food shortages had reached extreme levels, and whenever some food was delivered to a store, long lines formed in no time, all hoping that the meager supplies would last for everybody. Luckily, my father still had the help of Lenuţa and her daughter, who were doing most of the time-consuming chores.

We went to visit Leana—our old, faithful housemaid who had been hired by my grandmother before I was born and who stayed with me during my marriage to Dr. Cecil Poppa. As I have previously mentioned, Leana was to us what Mammy was to Scarlet O'Hara's family in *Gone with the Wind*. She had aged, of course, but her mind was still sharp. She greeted me with "How are you, miss? I am glad, my little girl, that you did not forget me!" She was really touched that I had come to visit her. When she kissed me good-bye, she said, "This is certainly the last time we see each other." On this sad note, I left. That was my final separation from Leana, a person whom I had known and appreciated ever since I was born.

That visit brought back painful memories about my friend Tănţica, who had psychic powers and who tragically lost her life during the 1977 earthquake. From Tante Maya, her mother, I heard that in the last few years, she had been teaching English classes to her colleagues; on the blackboard she was using, they found the word "earthquake" in her handwriting. They also found a note in her calligraphic handwriting saying she had a premonition about a big obstacle she would have to overcome before her future life would be better. The "big obstacle" was the earthquake.

On the same note, I have another story that I would like to relate here. One of the people dear to us whom we saw on that visit was Uncle Ionel, the general who contributed to King Michael's coup in August 1944. He came to my father's house to see us. At some point, Uncle Ionel pulled me aside and told me in a whisper that Urania, a distant relative of ours, after consulting a pack of tarot cards, had predicted that he would not die before he had a chance to shake hands with the deposed Romanian King Michael I. Then he told me if that were true and monarchy would be reinstalled, I should return to Romania. Of course the prediction and his conclusion seemed extremely farfetched, almost ludicrous, at the time. However, in 1992, King Michael returned on a visit to Romania and attended the religious service at the Saint George Church in downtown Bucharest. In the church Uncle Ionel came and shook hands with His Majesty King Michael. My uncle died a few months later at the age of almost one hundred. The prediction had come true, but different from my uncle's expectations.

Going to the Black Sea shores with relatives and friends, I traveled with my cousin Matei Mirica, who asked me to intervene through the United Nations to get him and his family out of Romania. I explained that the organization did not interfere in member states' domestic affairs, but I said I would inform Nicolas Penescu and ask if he could do something through the French authorities.

On August 1, we flew to Paris. Waiting for us at the airport were Sandu Missirliu and Tante Cellica. Sandu Misirliu and his elder brother Dinu went out of their way to make our stay in Paris as pleasant as possible. It was most rewarding from a tourist point of view: we saw all the major sights and also made a trip to Versailles. We visited my aunt Tancy and her husband, Nicolas Penescu, who had lobbied with the French president to facilitate my mother's exit visa from Romania to visit them. It was then I told him about my cousin's request.

From Paris we travelled to the Hague by train. We had a stopover in Brussels, which has become an important European city as it hosts both NATO and the main European Union organizations. In Brussels we were really impressed with the Grand Place, the central square, the most important landmark in the city.

In the Hague we went straight to the Peace Palace, which houses the International Court of Justice. I contacted my colleague Ralph Zacklin from the New York Office of Legal Affairs, who was teaching a course within the United Nations Institute for Training and Research (UNITAR). Ralph introduced me to the chief librarian,

Mr. Bernard Noble. I handed him the letter from Natalia Tyulina, and he facilitated the review of the documentation sent from New York. He later wrote to the chief judge of the court the following: "I would like to call on your attention that Mrs. Simone M. Kleckner, the United Nations legal librarian, spent a whole day to check on the documentation needed by the members of this court. Considering the exceptional attention given to this vast collection, I would like to know if you agree that a copy of this letter be forwarded to SMK to thank her." The chief judge made the following handwritten note on Mr. Noble's letter: "I agree. I am grateful for her gesture."

We returned to Paris by train, and after another round of goodbye visits, including visits with Lulu and his wife, Sandu Missirliu drove us to the airport.

* * *

I remember the year 1978 for another unusual event. It was the year with three popes. Pope Paul VI was succeeded at the end of August by Pope John Paul I, who died unexpectedly at the end of September. He, in turn, was followed by the first non-Italian pontiff, John Paul II, born Karol Józef Wojtyła in Poland. When Wojtyła was elected as Pope John Paul II, my colleague and friend Manuel Rama Montaldo, a Catholic from Uruguay, was taken aback by the news. He came to me to get my take on this unprecedented event. I told him I was very happy with the new pope because he had experience, having lived through both Nazism and communism. Hopefully, I said, he would be determined to engage the Catholic Church in the fight against political oppression in general and, in particular, against the communist regimes in Eastern European countries. I think Manuel liked my comments and left with a lighter heart.

While witnessing the changes in the Vatican, we received a phone call from Bucharest with the sad news that my father's wife, Florica, had passed away and that my father took it very hard. I had great appreciations for Florica, who had been always there for me in difficult moments and had provided steady support for my father after our departure. We had a memorial service at our church for her. Then Uncle Sam died of a sudden heart attack. We had special feelings of affection for Oncle Sam too. He was a good man, father, and husband, and he had been very good to us during our tough beginnings in our new country. May God rest their souls in peace and reward them for all the good deeds they did during their lifetimes.

* * *

Toward the end of December, Natalia Tyulina's contract expired. There was a big good-bye party prior to her departure, where many praised her qualities and her leadership. I was personally sorry to see her go back to the USSR, because somehow I felt that she did not fit over there. In addition, I appreciated her management style. She was very friendly, polite, and fair, but at the same time strict in her expectations that people would meet their deadlines.

We decided to spend Christmas and New Year's on the Caribbean island of Barbados, which offered us another exotic experience. This was the first time in our lives that we welcomed Santa Clause in our swimming suits.

1979

When I returned to the office, I heard that another Russian, Vladimir Orlov, had been appointed to replace Natalia Tyulina. His contract was to extend from 1979 to 1985. Marking his appointment, a welcome party was held in his honor, hosted by Deputy Director J. Fuchs.

Changes also took place in the Office of Legal Affairs. At the suggestion of Kurt Waldheim, who was from Austria, the Commission on International Trade Law (UNCITRAL) was moved from the thirty-fourth floor of the UNO headquarters in New York to the Donaupark building in Vienna. I regretted the move because, in the process, our good friends Gerold and his wife, Ingrid Herrmann, were transferred to Vienna. From that point on, we would see each other only occasionally in Vienna or Badgastein and, much later, in Florida.

To get my father out of his apartment, where everything reminded him of his dear Florica, I thought it would be good for him to pay us another visit. So I filled out and mailed another affidavit of support to help him get his passport and American visa.

* * *

During that same period, I received my first invitation to attend the convention of the American Association of Legal Librarians, to be held in San Francisco in June. I took a few vacation days so that Rudi and I could combine the convention with a trip to get to know parts of the beautiful West Coast.

We flew to Reno, Nevada—dubbed "the biggest little city in the world"—which was situated in a desert valley at the foot of the Sierra Nevada. From there we drove to San Francisco, passing through the beautiful ski resort of Lake Tahoe. In San Francisco we stayed at the grand Fairmont Hotel, situated on top of one of the San Francisco hills, where many celebrities had also stayed (as we ascertained from pictures hanging in the lobby and hallways). In 1945, the Fairmont had hosted international statesmen for meetings that culminated in the creation of the United Nations. In fact, the United Nations Charter was drafted in the hotel's Garden Room, and a plaque at the hotel memorializes the event.

There we also met with my friend Blanka from Columbia University and her husband, Svatia. The four of us ate at the restaurant at the top level of the hotel, which offered a breathtaking view of San Francisco and its iconic Golden Gate Bridge over San Francisco Bay. We could see the Alcatraz Island situated about a mile and a half off the coast. The island, now a tourist site, held what was formerly a maximum-security prison where famous detainees such as the gangster Al Capone had been incarcerated.

Blanka and Svatia decided to join us on a trip to Yosemite National Park, which is a protected natural wonder. Just seven miles long and never more than one mile across, it is flanked by walls of near-vertical granite cliffs, streaked by tumbling waterfalls, and topped by pinnacles forming a jagged silhouette against the sky. During the trip, Blanka mentioned to me that she would be interested to get the NYU position that had been vacated by Dushan Djanovici. Then we returned to San Francisco, where I attended the convention. Also attending was Julius Marke, who was glad to see me and introduced me right and left to other participants, either librarians or legal writers. I took the opportunity to say a few words to Julius about Blanka, whom I warmly recommended as an outstanding candidate for Dushan's job. Julius told me there were a few other candidates recommended by different professors, but said he would certainly keep Blanka in mind.

After the convention, Rudi and I took a bus trip down the beautiful Route 1 along the California coast all the way to Los Angeles. Visiting Los Angeles, I remembered that in response to the American-led boycott of the 1980 Summer Olympics in Moscow, fourteen Eastern Bloc countries (with the sole exception of Ceaușescu's Romania) boycotted the games. In Los Angeles we visited Hollywood, Disneyland Park, and Universal Studios. Then we drove to Las Vegas, where we were lodged at the MGM Hotel. From there we made a trip in a small plane, probably an eight-seater or so, to the Grand Canyon. It was a frightening experience as at every turn of the plane we thought we would hit the rocks. When we finally landed on solid ground, all passengers looked pale and scared.

Back from this beautiful trip, a pleasant surprise was waiting for me at the office. I received the fourth evaluation report, which was again very flattering. At the same time, I was notified that I had received another advancement to grade P-3, step III, signed by Seymour James and countersigned by Joseph Fuchs and the new director, Vladimir Orlov.

* * *

I received an unexpected call from William B. Simons, a prominent American jurist, who asked me whether I would like to translate the Romanian Constitution for him; he needed it for a book entitled *Communist Constitutions* that he was working on. I accepted the proposal on the spot, because the text was quite manageable, and I could do the job in a few evenings if I dedicated myself to the work. I was thinking that having translated the *Penal Code*, my name must have come up as someone who could translate Romanian legal language into English.

* * *

An outstanding event was Pope John Paul's visit to the United Nations on October 2, 1979, when he spoke at the thirty-fourth session of the General Assembly. In his address His Holiness underlined that the Vatican would never cease to support peaceful coexistence and collaboration between nations. He also said that it was very important for the organization to respect Christ's message of truth and love, which, for him, were the most important life principles. I was among the Secretariat personnel who had gathered to greet the pope in the beautiful rose garden. There was one moment when I was within a few feet of him, and he blessed me. That made me very happy!

Near the time of the visit of Pope John Paul II, I had another close encounter with a celebrity, another John, of a different kind. Coming out from the UN-DC buildings where the swimming pool is located, I came face-to-face with John Travolta. His face looked so familiar that I said, "Hello," and a few seconds later, when I realized who he was, I said, "I am so glad to see you in real life"—to which he replied, "I am also glad to meet you, have a wonderful evening," planted a kiss on my forehead, and disappeared into the elevator.

At work I had another satisfying moment when Alain Plantey, undersecretary-general of the West European Union, wrote a letter to our legal counsel, Eric Suy, in which he said, among other things, "I hope to see you soon. In the meantime, allow me to tell how much I have appreciated the help given by your librarian, namely Mrs. Kleckner. AP." Indeed, I had spent many hours in the library helping him find the documentation he needed for the subject he was working on, and I was grateful that he was kind enough to acknowledge it and that Mr. Suy gave me a copy of his letter.

As one with an international law degree, I was regularly invited to attend the annual meeting of the International Law Association. In 1979 I went to their meeting and dinner marking the ninetieth anniversary of the association. That was an honor and a privilege for me.

* * *

During this summer my father, Gică, managed to come again on a two-month visit, which again made us very happy. As we greeted him at the airport, we thought he looked a little aged and a little more frail than the last time he had come to New York. He walked with a cane, but was uncomplaining. As on his previous visits, we took him to see friends and relatives, and as in the past, we made one-day trips to Jones Beach on Long Island. We also spent a minivacation in Avalon, New Jersey, where our friend Chet and our friends Jacques Debaucheron and George Sanders joined us. And one weekend, we made a trip to Washington, DC. We visited the usual tourist sites on the Mall, the National Art Galley, and the Space Museum (where Gică was very impressed with the Lunar Module). Staying with us clearly recharged my father's batteries, and by the time he departed for home, his whole demeanor had visibly improved.

* * *

I was stunned, therefore, by the November news that a group of Iranian militants had seized the American Embassy in Tehran and taken American hostages, demanding the return of the shah for trial. The shah, who had been a staunch ally of the United States, was now suffering from terminal cancer. What saddened me even more was that President Carter had caved in to the militants' demands and had forced the shah to move from the United States to Panama, though even that gesture failed to win freedom for the hostages. In my opinion, if Carter had supported the shah's Westernization of Iran with its women liberation, he might have spared us the threat of Iran becoming a nuclear power, a development that started after the 1979 revolution.

What disappointed me further was the Soviet invasion of Afghanistan in December, just after President Carter had signed the SALT II agreement with Brezhnev, but never ratified by the Senate. Furthermore, President Carter broke off diplomatic relations with Taiwan, hoping to improve relations with communist China, and he signed a treaty agreeing to return the Panama Canal Zone to Panama.

At last, Rudi and I were happy that Margaret Thatcher had been elected as the new British prime minister. Her reforms aimed at dismantling the welfare state reshaped almost every aspect of British politics—reviving the economy, reforming outdated institutions, reducing the size of government, and reinvigorating the nation's foreign policy.

Likewise, we were happy when the Republican Ronald Reagan, a former governor of California, announced his candidacy for the presidency of the United States. I was glad that in Reagan's first day as president, the fifty-two American Embassy hostages in Iran were liberated after having been imprisoned a full year during Carter's presidency.

* * *

That year, we spent Thanksgiving with friends, and for Christmas and New Year we went to the Bahamas, where we said good-bye to our fifteenth year in America and greeted the sixteenth. At that time, I had already been with the United Nations for five years. It had not been an easy job, especially at the beginning, but with hard work (sometimes lasting till late evening hours), I managed to build a good reputation for myself and felt many kinds of satisfactions.

Initially I had been hoping that working for that organization, I might find out how it could contribute to improving the situation in Eastern Europe, including my old country. Unfortunately, that turned out to be wishful thinking because the Charter does not allow the interference in any country's internal affairs (which was something I had known from my international law courses). However, even if the Charter had allowed the interference in internal affairs, this would not have helped. The organization, over the years of decolonization, increased the number of member states mostly dominated by populist and prosocialist ideas, where the influence of the USSR and China were predominant. So Ceaușescu's Romania remained the same anticapitalist bastion where human rights were systematically violated and the majority of the population was struggling to survive in an atmosphere of fear and poverty.

* * *

With five years of experience on the United Nations Legal Library job, I was already thinking ahead. I intended to explore ways to emerge from the anonymous mass of legal librarians in the USA and Canada. The idea came to me while attending the Convention of Legal Librarians in San Francisco, and in time I got more and more obsessed with it. I had no idea how I could achieve that goal, but I knew in my heart that where there is a will, there is a way—and it helped to pray, as I always did.

CHAPTER 5

United Nations, 1980–April 1987

Back in the office after our vacation in the Bahamas, one morning, I met Jacqueline Dauchy in the corridor. She noticed my tan and asked where I had been vacationing. That was the start of a conversation, and she invited me to sit down in her office for a chat. Among other things, she told me that the Second World Convention on International Documentation would take place in Brussels, Belgium, in June 1980.

When I heard that, I took the opportunity to suggest that it would be great if the UN could make a presentation at the convention with bibliographic data about the publications of our Legal Office. In support of my idea, I mentioned that such a presentation might turn out to be useful reference for librarians working in legal libraries across the United States and Canada.

Ms. Dauchy found my idea interesting and asked me whether I would consider getting involved in such a project. I said I was more than ready and willing, but that, in view of the volume of work involved, I might need somebody to assist me. Ms. Dauchy advised me to talk with Seymour James about my idea and said that she too would approach him to discuss it. I did not know whether my project would ever materialize, but I thought that such a presentation would help me stand out, as I was hoping, from the multitude of anonymous legal librarians.

I started to work on the project right away, taking advantage of any occasional free time I had. I set for myself a tentative March deadline for completion, knowing that I could be sidetracked by any number of unexpected projects. In addition, I was planning to attend the Convention of the American Association of Legal Librarians (AALL) in April, which was another departure from my normal schedule. In order to avoid potential deadline pressures, I came to the office several weekends to make progress on my presentation. I knew I had to work, more and more.

After a while, Ms. Dauchy informed me that she had mentioned my project to Mr. James, and in fact he liked the idea. Sooner than I expected, Mr. James came to my office to break the news that upper management had approved a new position and I could hire another assistant. Indeed, this was good news!

Toward the end of February, Ingeborg was hired on a probationary basis. She was originally from Germany. I introduced her to people in the Legal Office, and she turned out to be a blessing. Hiring her meant that I could now concentrate on the more complex projects on my plate, as well as on the project for the World Convention on International Documentation, which I entitled "Major Publications of the United Nations Office of Legal Affairs."

Moreover, I decided my presentation could also be published in the *Law Library Journal* of the American Association of Law Librarians (AALL). I asked approval from both Seymour James and the new library director, Mr. Orlov, arguing that it would be useful to United States and Canadian librarians for research. Once I got the approval, I sent Julius the text and asked if he could recommend it to AALL for publication.

* * *

In April I went to Atlanta, Georgia, to attend the seventy-fourth annual AALL Convention. That also marked the seventy-fifth anniversary of the association. As at any such conventions, different speakers—mostly holding leadership positions in their organizations—made presentations in the main auditorium on a number of topics of interest to our profession. There also was a hall at the convention with stands of different publishing houses specializing in legal publications, such as OCEANA, Rothman, Sijthoff & Noordhoff, and many others, where sales representatives were presenting their latest publications and advertising their services. Besides giving me the opportunity to learn from other people's experiences, the convention gave me a chance to reconnect with other fellow legal librarians or former colleagues. There I met Julius Marke, my former boss from NYU, and Francis Gates from Columbia University. (In fact, the convention was presided over by Francis Gates, who was serving as the AALL president.)

At that convention I also reconnected with my dear friend Blanka, who, based on my recommendation, had been hired by Julius to fill the position that became available after Dushan's departure. Now I had the opportunity to thank Julius for hiring her and, at the same time, for recommending my article to the AALL *Law Library Journal.*

I remember with great pleasure that on my return from Atlanta, Seymour James broke the news that I had been designated to go to the Brussels symposium, scheduled to take place in June, helping me to distinguish myself in the world of legal librarians.

* * *

Shortly after my return from Atlanta, we invited Julius and his wife, Silvia, to our apartment for dinner. I had special feelings for Julius. I really owed him a lot, considering that he had helped me in so many ways since 1969, when he hired me as legal librarian at NYU. It was thanks to him that NYU had agreed to waive payment for some of the courses I took to earn my LLM degree. It was also due to his support that I had been able to work by myself on the collection of the European community publications and that I was entrusted with the translation of the Romanian penal code. Last but not least, it had been through him that I found out about the position that opened up at the UN Legal Library.

In short, as I have often said, ever since Julius offered me a position with NYU in 1969, he had acted as my guardian angel. Unquestionably, when I had to choose among New York University, Columbia University, or other two law firms for my first professional position, I definitely picked the right place and boss when I accepted his offer. Fate had been watching and helping me.

The evening that Julius and Silvia came over, we also invited Blanka and her husband, Svatia, as Blanka was now reporting to Julius at the NYU Legal Library.

* * *

Finally, the time came for me to leave for Brussels to make my long-anticipated presentation at the World Convention on International Documentation. In addition to the legal librarians attending the Brussels convention, there were also many leaders of international agencies, including some of the top legal minds and a number of world-renowned personalities. Rubbing shoulders with all those people was a really nice experience for me.

At the end of the convention, I attended the cocktail party hosted by the Belgium foreign minister at the impressive sixteenth-century Egmont Palace, located in the beautiful Petit Salon Square area of Brussels—a site that, today, houses the Belgium Ministry of Foreign Affairs. The cocktail party was an overwhelming display of old-world elegance, and I was thoroughly impressed by it all. Once again, I felt my initiatives and hard work were being abundantly rewarded.

I loved flying because up in the air there were no disruptive phone calls and no deadlines to meet. That is why, alone with my thoughts on the flight back to New York, I had the peace of mind to think about future projects.

During that seven-hour flight, it occurred to me that a reference document that the Dag Hammarskjold Library had prepared back in 1976 needed to be brought up to date. In addition, I thought it should include a host of foreign materials useful for researchers, legal scholars of international law, diplomats from the foreign missions, and even for major law firms specializing in international law. I also thought the revised document had to be restructured, as I had learned during my LLM studies at NYU, in accordance with article 38 of the Statute of the International Court of Justice (or the Permanent Court of International Justice that had existed during the time of the League of Nations). I thought this could be done by organizing the primary sources into (a) treaties and conventions, (b) state practices becoming custom, (c) general principles recognized by civilized states, and (d) judicial and expert decisions.

I was convinced that such a project would be of great use to legal librarians everywhere; while most had expertise in common law, they were less knowledgeable about international law. My plan was to work on that project at my convenience, and only when it was done would I let Mr. James know that I had updated the 1976 document and restructured it into a format that was universally accepted in the legal world.

However, in the office, I had to dedicate most of my time in preparing the bibliography for the *Juridical Yearbook* requested by the Codification Division, through Ms. Dauchy, before I could start to work on my newfound personal project. Meanwhile, some of the regular questions coming my way, which I also had to handle, were very time-consuming.

Despite my preoccupation with this project, I found time to invite my mother, Mancy, to have lunch with me in the Delegates Dining Room. As one who appreciated refined surroundings, she liked the elegant atmosphere in that hall, and she thought I was very lucky to be working in such a fancy environment. It took a long time to reach the point where she could say she was proud of me.

* * *

In 1980 we had presidential elections. We were hopeful that things would take a turn for the better when, on July 17, the Republican Convention nominated Ronald Reagan as their candidate. It was high time for a change, because under President Carter's domestic policies, unemployment and inflation grew to unprecedented levels, interest rates went through the roof, and gas shortages caused people to stand in line for hours at gas stations. All that created a state of general discontent in the country.

Having experienced communism, which brought about nation-wide poverty, I had been interested in the US policy called "war on poverty" adopted by President Carter. I found out that some other American presidents had also declared war on poverty, including President Johnson, who, in 1964, pushed through Congress the Economic Opportunity Act (EOA). This was modeled on FDR's New Deal of the 1930s, which had been followed by Truman's Fair Deal and by Kennedy's New Frontier. Carter's war on poverty is described by Stanley Kurtz in his book *Radical-in-Chief* (pages 161–162). He writes that in the seventies President Carter placed VISTA program (Volunteers in Service of America), an EOA program, a surviving remnant of the original War on Poverty, in the de facto control of die-hard radicals from the sixties, once again making federal government a ready source of bread for leftist political agitation. The capture of VISTA by the left was with the help of the Midwest Academy and the Association of Community Organizations for Reform Now (ACORN), by distributing grants directly to national networks.

I have to emphasize the ACORN since it would have direct implications for the administration of President Obama, by citing the findings of M. Vadum, who devotes his entire research only to ACORN in *Subversion, Inc.* (pages 1, 2, 8, 12, 14, 17, 31, 45, 49, 141–142, 184). The author informs us that ACORN was established in 1970 by Wade Rathke and became the most powerful and dangerous organization in the country, arising from the cluster of violent new left groups. ACORN pushed for more government control, the establishment of a health-care monopoly, and an open-door immigration policy. It opposed capitalist profits and targeted corporations, and it was also involved in election procedures. M. Vadum defines community organizers as professional activists who believe that something is truly wrong with America and that they are the ones to fix it. The guru agitator, who manufactured crises to inflame the community, is identified by Vadum as Saul Alinsky.

Further, the author states, with regard to entitlements in America, that so far they have been controversial. In short, the liberal Democrats believe that government-sponsored entitlement programs can reduce and eliminate poverty. By contrast, the Republicans believe that the government's role is to provide job opportunities for the poor through economic growth and that the policy of entitlements actually perpetuates poverty while encouraging complacency and dependency on government aid. For all the above reasons, in domestic matters, as well as in foreign policy, I am in agreement, based on my experience with the later alternative. Controversy has certainly dogged Carter's presidency.

* * *

When it came time for the presidential election, my mother, Rudi, and I were glued to the TV as we followed, with excitement, the election coverage. We celebrated every time another red state appeared on the map, displaying electoral victories marking another Republican victory. Finally, Ronald Reagan won in forty-four states while Jimmy Carter took only six. That was a clear indication, to us, that the people were ready for a change. Moreover, Ronald Reagan was an anticommunist in the '40s due to his experience as president of the Screen Actors Guild during his battle with their presence in Hollywood.

1981

President Reagan nominated the Fulbright Award winner David B. Funderburk as US ambassador to Romania, who would serve from 1981 to 1985. (I would have later the privilege of meeting both Ambassador David Funderburk and his wife, Betty, in 1990 in New York.) Reagan continued to support the Helsinki Act of 1975, signed by President Ford, and named Max Kapelman, his chief arms control negotiator with the Soviet Union, as his ambassador to the Organization of Cooperation and Security in Europe (OCSE). In his book *Pinstripes and Reds: An American Ambassador Caught Between the State Department and the Romanian Communists, 1981–1985* (pages 158–159), Funderburk wrote that Max Kampelman (his parents had come to the United States from Cernăuți in Romania's Bucovina region) "had shown courage in defending U.S. interests in talks with the Soviets and block allies." In London in December 1982 Max

Kampelman told American ambassadors that "the Soviet Union represents the most serious threat to our society and values in this century." Now I might add, also to the following twenty-first century.

* * *

Also, 1981 brought back political communist horrors. At the beginning of February 1981, my aunt Tancy called from Paris to tell us there had been an attempt on the life of her husband, Nicolae Penescu. The attempted assassination occurred after he attended the post-Helsinki conference in Madrid, where he denounced the deplorable state of human rights in Romania. I later found out details of that attempt on Nicolae Penescu's life in Şerban Orescu's book *Ceauşismul, Romania between 1965–1989* (pages 36–37): "Part of the Securitate contract with terrorist Carlos (also known as the Jackal) was to intimidate three important Romanian dissidents in the West: Paul Goma and Nicolae Penescu in Paris, and Şerban Orescu in Cologne because their protests covered by the international press, were an annoyance to the activity of the Romanian delegation attending the Madrid Conference on European Security." Even in the West, my family continued to be harassed.

Our friend Aimée called us from Munich to tell us that, in February, Noël Bernard had had surgery in New York. She also told us that a terrorist bomb had exploded at the Radio Free Europe headquarters in Munich, which understandably terrified her. Later she called to give us the good news that Noël Bernard was feeling better and had resumed his work at the radio. However, the bad news was that Emil Georgescu, another Radio Free Europe commentator, had been stabbed several times in a parking garage by two French mercenaries. Georgescu escaped with his life either out of sheer luck or because the order was to intimidate him rather than kill him. All these happenings at Radio Free Europe were caused by the Romanian president Ceauşescu's secret police. Its tactics were often used to silence inconvenient opponents against its regime.

And I will never forget when on March 30, in the hallway at the UNO, I ran into my colleague Manuel Rama Montaldo, who asked me, "Did you hear the news? Ronald Reagan was shot! They are now rushing him to the hospital." I was in shock and could not even say a word. I went to my desk and immediately turned on my little portable radio. From news reports I learned that Reagan had been shot in Washington, DC, by David Hinckley, who acted alone. I was extremely impressed and sorry for him and the country. Luckily, the president recovered.

*   *   *

We planned a vacation in France with my colleague and friend from the UN Jacques Deboucheron and his friend George Sanders, together with our friend Chet. As usual, we hooked up with family and friends first and then flew to Cannes on the French Riviera at the seaside. Renting a car, we made frequent day trips through the surrounding countryside. Jacques was a connoisseur of the region and took us to places that were off the well-trodden tourist paths, Eze and Turbie, very picturesque villages where we enjoyed typical French cuisine.

We also made a trip to Monaco, the principality ruled at the time by King Rainier III, best known outside Europe for having married American actress Grace Kelly. We were enchanted by the town of Monte Carlo.

Following my mother's advice, we also visited the town of Menton, dubbed "the pearl of the French Riviera," where she had spent many childhood vacations. Again we followed in my mother's footsteps when we flew to Lausanne and sought out Hotel Cécil, where my grandmother Manini had lived for about eighteen years with her daughters, Mancy and Tancy.

*   *   *

After this beautiful vacation, I returned to the real world, where I set about answering questions regarding the many crises mushrooming in every corner of the world—South Africa and Namibia (formerly Southwest Africa); Algeria and Morocco over Western Sahara; Vietnamese troops supported by the Russians, refusing to withdraw from Cambodia; Afghanistan still occupied by Russian troops; Israel bombing the Iraqi nuclear plant near Baghdad (where, it was believed, the Iraqis were making nuclear weapons intended to destroy Israel); and last but not least, the United Nations Convention on the Law of the Sea, to be held in Geneva, for the signing of this international agreement (one that the United States refused to ratify).

At the beginning of the General Assembly September session, I believe due to the hasty decolonization process, the secretary-general again reminded the assembly that 52 percent of the world population lived in poverty and foreign aid was needed. I was of the opinion that it was a viable market economy, not foreign aid, that would help those countries emerge from poverty.

This UN fall session was more eventful than usual, as that was the year when the secretary-general had to be reelected. Kurt Waldheim offered to serve another term. My only concern with that election was related to the fact that each secretary-general usually appointed his own legal counsel, the highest-ranking legal officer, and chief of the Office of Legal Affairs, where I was working. (In December, after the election, I found out that the Security Council nominated and the General Assembly approved Javier Perez de Cuellar from Peru as the new secretary-general. I heard through the grapevine that he was a modest, civilized, and very cultured man. Now I was really interested in seeing whether Perez de Cuellar would keep Erik Suy as legal counsel.)

Earlier, on September 30, I received my fifth performance evaluation report covering the period from October 1979 to September 1981. This time, too, the report rated my job performance as excellent on many levels.

That autumn we were pleased to be visited by Johann Schobel with Dorle, his wife, who came from Frankfurt-am-Main. We were all very happy to see them, the reason being that he had been faithful as administrator of my mother's Radomir estate and later helped bring in his car the family's jewelry from Romania to my aunt in Paris. My mother took them to the Metropolitan Opera, to museums and concerts, and we showed them around, taking them to Upstate New York, where we admired the spectacular foliage season.

* * *

Again, Julius was the one to give me good news by calling to say that my article on UN publications would be published in the *Law Library Journal.* He told me he had forwarded to me a facsimile of the publication. I expressed my deep gratitude to him for using his prestige and influence to help me. I showed the facsimile to Ms. Dauchy, who was extremely happy to see that the work of the Legal Office was publicized outside the UNO. Then I called Seymour James and invited him for a cup of coffee in the elegant Delegates Hall. After I showed him the facsimile, he, in turn, displayed it with pride to my colleagues from the General Reference Department. I was delighted.

Moreover, I was really surprised when a gentleman from the Japanese Mission came to my desk to let me know that the Tokyo National Library had translated my article into Japanese for one of their publications. Mr. James took a copy of the Japanese text to show other directors. It was nice to know that my work was also being appreciated in the Far East.

* * *

Having to follow daily the newspapers, I read that the Polish leader Jaruzelski had proclaimed a state of emergency in his country, an attempt to counteract the actions of the Solidarity Union that had emerged at the Gdańsk Shipyard under the leadership of Lech Wałęsa, claiming human rights. I did not know, then, that this was the beginning of the end for the communist regimes in Central and Eastern Europe. But I liked what I was reading.

* * *

After the good news regarding Noel Bernard, unexpectedly Aimée called saying that he had died in Munich on December 23. We were very saddened because we greatly appreciated his integrity and intellect. He had tirelessly used all his multiple journalistic talents in the service of truth and had unmasked the lies of communist propaganda in Romania. Our feeling of loss was all the more painful as we suspected that his cancer occurred under very suspicious circumstances. Indeed, later we read an article by reporter Andrei Bădin (published on page 5 of the December 23, 2007, issue of the Romanian *National*

Journal) that the assassination of Noël Bernard through irradiation had been approved by Lieutenant General Pleşiţa of the feared Romanian secret police, the Securitate. Noël was the first victim of a series of similar assassinations, using radiation, ordered by the communist regime of Nicolae Ceauşescu.

Before Christmas there were parties at the UN and at the US Mission. I organized a little buffet party in the Legal Library for Ingeborg, whose contract had expired. She was a really good worker, and though I regretted her departure, I wished her luck in her future endeavors. Anne Salzberg was hired to replace her. She too was very smart, with a pleasant personality.

Rudi and I threw a party for our friends from the UNO and, shortly afterward, celebrated our friend Chet's birthday. After that holiday season, we went with some friends on a short vacation to the Hudson Valley resort of Mohonk.

1982

Unfortunately, the new year started with a phone call from Tancy to let us know that her husband, Nicolae Penescu, had died of a massive heart attack, which almost certainly had a lot to do with the shock caused by the bomb explosion after his statements in Madrid. He was another victim of a series of assassinations ordered by Nicolae Ceauşescu's communist regime. My poor aunt Tancy was a widow for the second time.

Later in spring, my mother fell and broke her arm. That was troublesome because during her recovery, she needed a lot of help. Luckily, we found Lydia Maghici, a French teacher from Romania, whom we hired temporarily. In addition, we cooked for my mother and delivered her food daily, or brought her to our apartment for dinner and then took her home again.

On my birthday on March 7, I was pleased to find on my desk a card from Mr. James that read: "Another birthday rolls around. I hope you will continue to display that youthfulness, vibrancy, and charm which is so much a part of you."

As they say, it is nice to be nice! Another compliment came from Benjamin Ferencz, who offered me a copy of one of his articles with the following dedication: "To Simone-Marie Kleckner, the best librarian and the busiest."

* * *

Now real good luck started to boost my career. During one of our frequent phone conversations, Blanka came up with the idea that the two of us might conduct a seminar on international and foreign law at the next AALL Convention, which would be held in Detroit. I immediately embraced her idea and promised to talk to James about it while she informed Julius of our plan.

Concomitantly, James advised me to send a memo to Mr. Orlof, our director, requesting the change of my employment grade from P-3 to P-4. He thought I deserved it and wanted to see it happen before his retirement. To my surprise, shortly after I sent that memo, I received a note from the Personnel Department informing me that I had, indeed, been promoted to professional grade P-4 with a substantial increase in salary. Before I even had a chance to thank Mr. James, I found on my desk an internal mail envelope with the following note from him: "Simone, for many years, I have recommended scores of staff members for promotion and have seen many of them gain their advancements. However, none of them had given me greater satisfaction and pleasure than your recent promotion to the P-4 level. Your thoroughness, competency, and professionalism are some of the reasons which brought you this deserved recognition. I would like to wish you continued enjoyment and success in your career with the United Nations. With sincere wishes, Seymour."

I called to thank him for his nice words and support, and after lunch we went together to the Delegates Hall. Over a cup of coffee, I told him my intent to update and restructure the United Nations document, which, in fact, I was already working on. In addition, I told him about the idea of conducting a seminar at the upcoming AALL Convention in Detroit. He was all for it, but warned me that I would need to be very well prepared because I would be representing the face of the UN Library.

Being in a good mood, Mr. James decided to tell me (after eight years) what had caused the delay in my hiring process. I was all ears. He told me that both he and Ms. Tyulina had selected me for the job that Virginia Walker vacated, but the Legal Office was behind a candidate who wanted a transfer from Geneva to New York and who had the support of John Scott. I asked what tilted the balance in my favor, to which James replied with a smile, "Your credentials— more precisely, your additional LLM major in international law from one of the most prestigious American universities." Mr. James added that Regine from the General Reference section had also wanted my position, but Tyulina held her ground and stuck to her original selection. He explained that was why Regine had later been appointed to become head of the Cataloguing Department to make up for the fact that she had been bypassed in my favor.

Finally, I saw why John Scott had been somewhat reserved when I was introduced to him back in 1975, and I also understood why—of all the others—only Olia Wang had been kind enough then to offer help anytime I needed it. In any case, I patted myself on the back for being smart enough to avoid, at all costs, asking my colleagues for help, always preferring to request guidance from my former colleagues from NYU, Dushan and Ed Bender. Here at UNO, there was competition.

*　*　*

Shortly before the Detroit Convention, I found out from Blanka that, through Julius's intervention, the convention organizers had included our seminar on the list of optional seminars offered for the participants. I barely had time to prepare my speech before I left to the convention on June 16.

There, with Blanka, we registered and decided which seminars to attend. Then we went to see the room assigned for our presentation that was entitled "Sources of International and Foreign Law" and was scheduled for the following afternoon at 2:00 p.m. We thought that the room, holding about fifty seats, was more than adequate.

The next day, we got there ahead of time. To our surprise, people started to come in shortly before 2:00 p.m., and before we knew it, the room was filled to capacity. With all seats taken, some attendees had to stand. The convention organizers, Tom Reynolds from the University of California at Berkley and Claire Germain from the Duke University in North Carolina, immediately decided to move us to a bigger room. Although the new room was five times larger, it too was immediately filled to capacity, and again there were some who had to stand. It came as a surprise to us—and obviously to the organizers—that the subject of our presentation had generated so much interest.

Tom Reynolds introduced me briefly, mentioning my background, credentials, and education, and then gave me the floor. Although I had little experience speaking in public, I was not nervous because I was well prepared, and I was encouraged by the obvious level of interest in my subject.

Subsequently, Tom introduced Blanka, who spoke about sources of foreign law—a presentation that was also followed with great interest. All of a sudden, everybody considered us experts on those subjects, approaching us with questions during the convention and afterward. As a result, I received many phone calls in the library from people seeking my assistance.

Back in New York, I was happy and proud about what Blanka and I had accomplished. And so was Rudi. Through his antennas, Seymour James already had been informed about how well we had done in Detroit, and he congratulated me as soon as he saw me. Blanka, in turn, wrote me a letter to thank me for my "excellent and professionally prepared presentation at the AALL Convention," concluding with, "I am glad that our hard work and effort have been so highly regarded and appreciated."

Encouraged by our success, Blanka and I decided to try to make a similar presentation at the United Nations. I presented the idea to Seymour, asking whether we could reserve the Auditorium Hall for one afternoon and if he would act as the moderator. My request seemed to take him by surprise, but he was flattered by my suggestion and told me he was all for it. We set a tentative date for autumn because my father was again coming to visit us that summer and had plans to go overseas that year.

* * *

As planned, Gică arrived in July. He was ninety at the time, and though we had ordered a wheelchair to take him from the plane door to the waiting area, he categorically refused and walked on his own. Rudi had great admiration for how gracefully my father bore the burden of all those years and asked him, once, how he felt at his age. Gigă's reply was that he was worried about his advancing age only until he turned eighty, but after that he did not care anymore. He said that as long as he was in good health and felt young inside, age was irrelevant for him, though, unfortunately, he could not prevent what others saw.

Besides the usual rounds of visits to friends and relatives, we took Gică to Avalon, New Jersey, knowing how much he enjoyed going there. Ever since his arrival, we noted that he both looked and felt better. To our regret, before we knew it, we were saying good-bye again.

We drove my father to the airport. While we were in the waiting room, a man in a wheelchair waved us over, and Rudi went to see what he wanted. When he came back, Rudi told my father, "That gentleman asked me whether you are Professor Vrăbiescu. When I confirmed that indeed you are that person, the gentleman said that he was once your student and that he was glad to see you." Gică was pleasantly surprised that somebody could still recognize him after about half a century, and he walked over to shake the hand of his former student and exchange a few words. On that positive note, my father's last visit to New York ended.

* * *

This year's September UN session opened with the new secretary-general Javier Perez de Cuellar making his first speech in front of the General Assembly. He emphasized that he found the world to be in an extremely dangerous situation, and then called on member states to fulfill the organization's mission by preserving peace and security. Although the UN was meant for negotiations, the Security Council could not act in a decisive way, even when resolutions had been unanimously accepted and adding that resolutions had not been respected but, rather, ignored by the powerful members that could afford to impose their own way. The secretary-general also referred to different conflicts in various parts of the world. Indeed, there were many ongoing conflicts. The only one to be resolved was in April 1982, when Argentina occupied the Falkland Islands and Prime Minister Margaret Thatcher immediately dispatched the British Navy. Within two months British sovereignty was reinstated.

*   *   *

The United States now had a powerful president, Ronald Reagan, who believed in America's core values. I appreciated his determination to advocate peace by strength. Reagan reversed Carter's policy by increasing the military budget while installing several Pershing rocket launchers in Europe and calling the Soviets "an evil empire." Those who had suffered under the Soviet yoke, like me, knew they had a staunch supporter in the White House. Reagan was nicknamed "the great communicator" because his speeches galvanized people, giving renewed hope after the post-Vietnam, post-Watergate, and Carter eras, both in the United States and beyond, in the world.

Reagan's anticommunist experience started during his Screen Actors Guild presidency. And Reagan's anticommunist feelings and his relationship to Nixon is described in Bill O'Reilly and Martin Dugard book *Killing Reagan*, (2015, page 81–85), and also in *The Presidents Club* (2012, pages 191, 357–359, 364), by Nancy Gibbs and Michael Duffy. They state that "Richard Nixon and Ronald Reagan defined Republican politics in America from 1966 until Nixon's death in 1994....The dominant topic was U.S. Soviet affairs...[when]...Nixon warned Reagan that no matter how appealing Gorbachev may seem, he was nonetheless a classic Soviet apparatchik...Ronald Reagan thanked him for sound suggestions. [However,] Reagan made his name as an anticommunist crusader, by dismissing Nixon's détente policy as being too accommodating to Moscow."

That brings me to Ronald Reagan's anticommunist foreign affairs. He understood the effect of rapid decolonization; his policies were just the opposite of that promoted by the UN General

Assembly and the Security Council. Dr. Kissinger had explained it best in his book *Diplomacy* (pages 768, 774): "Reagan's political doctrine meant that the United States would help anticommunist counterinsurgencies wrest their respective countries out of the Soviet sphere of influence....In other words, this meant arming the Afghan in their struggle with the Russians, supporting the contras in Nicaragua, and aiding anticommunist forces in Ethiopia and Angola, etc." Personally, I appreciated his approach and hoped he would do something for Eastern Europe. However, Reagan's policies revived peace movements at home that were reminiscent of Nixon's day.

* * *

As Blanka and I had planned, it was time to approach Mr. James with the idea of holding a seminar on international and foreign legal research when he reserved the auditorium for the afternoon of October 27. We agreed that we should call the seminar "Taking the Mystery out of Foreign and International Legal Research" and offer it to legal librarians from the entire New York metropolitan area. As in Detroit, again our presentation drew a full house. "International," "transnational," and "multinational" were terms that many found confusing, and I believe this was one of the reasons why so many people wanted to attend. Present in the auditorium were not only legal librarians but also people from the Secretariat, the Office of Legal Affairs, and various law firms.

Mr. James introduced us and cracked a few jokes, as the Americans always do, to lighten up the atmosphere, then gave us the floor. Again, those present received our presentation with a lot of interest, and people applauded us at the end. After the seminar, Rudi and I took Blanka, her daughter, and Seymour to a restaurant to celebrate.

The following day, I opened an interoffice mail envelope with a copy of a note that the DHL deputy director Joseph Fuchs had received from Edith Ward, officer of the International Analysis Division. She wrote, "Yesterday evening at the UN Auditorium the DHL presented a program entitled 'Taking the Mystery out of Foreign and International Legal Research.' I attended that meeting and found it both informative and enjoyable. Mrs. Simone-Marie Kleckner of the Law Library delivered a fascinating talk. It was well organized, well expressed, and contained invaluable information. I am writing this to request that Mrs. Kleckner's talk be issued as a United Nations' document. The content would be of very great interest to the legal research community as well as to myself. The rapt attention of the audience, consisting mainly of persons who were not members of the Secretariat, indicates to me that such a document would be well received."

It was not the text of my presentation that was issued as a UN document but my last project entitled "International Law and Organizations: A Selective Bibliography 1982" (p. 102, ST/LIB/38).

I was very proud of myself when the library received the *International Journal of Legal Information* (vol. 2, no. 1 & 2, 1983), in which (on page 16) I found an article that called readers' attention to the essay "A Small Jewel published by the United Nations entitled 'International Law and Organizations: A Select Bibliography' (102 p).. This publication prepared by the Dag Hammarskjold Library under AT/LIB/38 in 1982 is a reactualized version of a document requested in 1976 by a mission."

I was gradually building a reputation for myself. As a result, I received a letter dated November 19 from Roy M. Mersky, chief librarian and law professor at New York City Law School, who occupied a position similar to the one that Julius held at NYU. Roy was teaching a course on advanced juridical research, and in his letter he asked whether I would be available on March 1, 1983, to give his students a lecture on the difference between international law and foreign law and a review on UNO documentation. I accepted the invitation, figuring I had plenty of materials and time at my disposal to work on that project—or so I thought at the time.

Wishful thinking! Seymour called me to his office and, with a smile on his face, handed me a piece of paper to read. It was an official request signed by my friend Eduardo Valencia-Ospina from the Codification Division informing the DHL that Director Romanov wanted us to prepare a bibliography on the "Succession of States in Respect of State Property, Archives and Debts in Accordance with Resolution 37/11 of November 1, 1982." I raised my eyes to Seymour, waiting for an explanation. Again smiling, he said he wanted me to work on that project. What could I say after he had been kind enough to moderate my presentation? I had two assistants reporting to me now, so I was in no position to excuse myself from taking on this additional task. The fact that I had committed myself to do the presentation for Roy was none of his concern, and I could not invoke that project as an excuse to decline the task. Therefore, I said, "Okay." Mr. James thanked me, and I turned around and left.

On top of everything, we had vacation plans for Christmas and New Year. As they say, sometimes when it rains, it pours. The only way to get everything done was to put in a lot of overtime and to sacrifice weekends.

In the month of December, Seymour James had to retire, an event that I had dreaded because he had consistently supported me, and I really owed him a lot. As a matter of fact, the whole library regretted his departure, and we all chipped in to organize a nice good-bye party for him. A lot of people came, even from outside the library, to wish him luck. There were speeches by Eugeniusz Wiezner, undersecretary for conference services; Vladimir Orlov, the library director; Joseph Fuchs, the deputy library director; and Ivan Schwartz, who was supposed to assume Seymour's responsibilities, with Amin Abdel Samad to be his deputy.

Upstairs in the library, we had another good-bye party for Darell, who had managed to get a transfer to another department. Before leaving, he gave me a little jewelry box with a gold chain and a little star pendant as a thank-you gift. That really moved me. I was very saddened when I heard, a few years later, that he had died because of his immunodeficiency disease. He was replaced by a young Canadian, Chris Flood.

Before Christmas, I received an article on Namibia that had been written by my friend Ralph Zaklin, with the following dedication: "To Simone, with all my thanks for your unfailing assistance. Ralph, T 29-IX-82." I also received a card from Ambassador A. C. Korona from the Sierra Leone Mission. Along with the season's greetings, he thanked me for my help and support. Another season's greeting card came from my assistant Anne Salzberg, who wrote, "For Simone Kleckner, merry Christmas 1982! With deepest thanks for all the help and friendship you've given me and for all I've learned from you. I know that I'll owe you a good deal of success in the future for having had the good fortune to have worked for you. Much love, Anne." I am always ready and willing to share my knowledge, and it warmed my heart to see that somebody appreciated that.

*   *   *

As planned, Chet, Rudi, and I made a trip to Brazil during the holiday season. We visited Manaus, famed for its rubber tree plantations and an opera house that is an architectural replica of the Palais Garnier Opera in Paris. We also made a boat trip on Rio Negro, whose waters, a chocolate-milk color, flow into the Amazon River. From Manaus we flew to Salvador Bahia, the old capital of Brazil, and then to Rio de Janeiro.

In Rio, from our balcony we had a superb view of the Copacabana beach, which, during the day, was like an ant's nest of people. During the night, the beach was lit up with a multitude of candles and flowers that locals pushed out to sea on small three-foot boats. Walking along Copacabana, we were struck by the opulence of the ocean-front hotels, in sharp contrast to the extreme poverty of the slums (or *favelas*) only a few blocks away. Also, we took the cable car to the top of the famous Sugar Loaf rock, from which we had a breathtaking view.

Another day, we took the tram car to Corcovado Park, where the iconic twenty-five-foot-tall statue of Jesus Christ—called *Christ the Redeemer*—stands with arms outstretched. Unfortunately, crime is rampant in this beautiful city. Every time we went out, the hotel staff cautioned us not to wear jewelry and not to leave any unattended valuables on the beach.

From Rio we flew to São Paulo (this time, without Chet, who remained behind in Rio). There we met with Rudi's cousin Nelu Stras, who gave us a tour of the city in his car. The following day, Nelu drove us to Campos do Jordão, not far from São Paulo.

1983

When I returned to my office, I found that I could rely on both Chris and Anne, who were very knowledgeable and always on time. Taking advantage of their help, I concentrated on the project that Seymour had assigned to me and finished it by the January 30 deadline.

After a few days, I heard that Erik Suy, the general legal counsel, had been appointed general director of the Geneva Bureau of the UNO because the new secretary-general had appointed Carl-August Fleischhauer from Germany to replace him. However, any changes in the Office of Legal Affairs did not affect the Legal Library from an administrative viewpoint, because the DHL was under the Conference Services Department, headed by Eugeniusz Wiezner. But working for the Office of Legal Affairs, this could eventually affect the Legal Library's service, an aspect that concerned me.

The Office of Legal Affairs offered a good-bye party for the general legal counsel's departure. Beforehand, I went to Erik Suy to wish him well, when he thanked me for my efforts to provide him and the office with all material they needed. I was sorry to see him go; moreover, I regretted that his new job did not necessarily require his legal expertise. In my opinion his appointment had to do with his reputation of a conservative legal scholar, very outspoken about his legal opinions, whose ideas were definitely not in line with the views promoted by the Soviets, who wanted to rapidly promote the development of international law. That also partially explains the reason why the General Assembly often approved an ad hoc commission or conference to operate outside of the Sixth Legal Committee or outside the International Legal Commission, whose members were some of the best legal minds and diplomats in the world. However, with the initiative of a number of new member states in the General Assembly from the third world wishing to speed up modern development of international law and the rapid codification of various subjects, new ad hoc committees were set up, as well as the United Nation Institute for Training and Research (UNITAR). In short, the majority of members of both the Legal Committee and the International Legal Commission had conservative views, whereas the new members were in favor of rapid development of international law.

* * *

At the end of January, I handed over to Ivan the bibliography on "Succession of States in respect of State Property, Archives and Debts" that Seymour had assigned to me. Ivan gave it to Mr. Wiezner, who, in turn, gave it to Mr. Romanov, chief of the Codification Division. Eventually, it ended up on the desk of Eduardo Valencia-Ospina, who already knew that I had finished it. Joseph Fuchs then sent me a copy of the letter of thanks that Eduardo had sent to Mr. Orlov. The letter read, among other things, "I wish to express the appreciation of the Secretariat of the United Nations Conference on Succession of States...for the Bibliography prepared by the library, since it concerns three rather specialized aspects of international law, it is comprehensive not only as far as the substance coverage...but also in terms of the various materials listed, the date span, as well as it includes a spread of authors from different legal systems. I have no doubt that the Bibliography will be of great usefulness not only to the participants in the Conference, but to a large audience. Thanks are due to Mrs. S. M. Kleckner of the Legal Library...in completing her task in a highly competent fashion with the relatively short time at her disposal."

Indeed, I had spent many more weekends finishing this bibliography on time and preparing material for the class on international law requested by Roy Mersky.

* * *

Julius Marke, who had brought me luck ever since I met him, called me to let me know that the American Society of International Law (ASIL), together with the NYU Law School and the OCEANA publishing group, would sponsor a seminar on international law as applied to international trade. The seminar was to be held in Washington, DC, on April 12, two days before the seventy-seventh annual meeting of the American Society of International Law. He suggested it would be a very good idea for me to repeat, at that meeting, the presentation I had held in Detroit, which turned out to be very beneficial for librarians and would be equally beneficial for the society members. He further suggested that it would also be very useful to include my bibliography published as UN document ST/LB/38. He said that, with UNO's approval, OCEANA might duplicate the document to be used as handouts for the participants.

When I first thought about the international law project in an airplane, I had no idea that it would turn out to be my way to success. Following the Detroit convention, and the presentation in the UN auditorium, this was the third time I was being asked to talk on that topic. Of course, I accepted Julius's offer on the spot because it offered me yet another opportunity that I had never dreamt would become a reality.

I discussed Julius's invitation with Joseph Fuchs, who offered to bring it up to Orlov and Wiezner and ask them whether they had any objection to my attending the meeting in Washington, DC, and whether OCEANA could make multiple copies of the UN document I needed for my presentation. I prayed for approval!

*   *   *

On March 8, I taught a class at New York Law School at the invitation of Roy Mersky. Afterward, he took me out for lunch with Tom Reynolds, the person who had made the introductory speech at my Detroit presentation and happened to be in town from Berkley, California.

It was a nice feeling to know that people now considered me an expert in that field. In fact, shortly after the class, Roy sent me a letter in which he wrote, among other things, "I hope that you will give me any suggestions you may have about our project for sharing resources in the international and foreign field. I would appreciate hearing your comments. Sincerely, RM." I was flattered by his request, but this time I had to say no, because I had enough on my plate at the UN. Also, I could not allow myself to be pulled in different directions, especially at a time when we had a new legal counsel.

I was delighted when Joseph Fuchs informed me that I had received the green light from Mr. Wiezner to participate in Julius's meeting at the American Society of International Law and to have the requested UN document duplicated by OCEANA. As soon as I had a chance, I went over to Julius's office to hand him the document. That was when he told me he had been appointed president of that ASIL meeting, which was to take place at the Mayflower Hotel in Washington, DC. He also told me that the meeting agenda included an announcement of the presentation that I was to make—again jointly with Blanka.

* * *

On April 2, we celebrated Rudi's birthday. We had a few friends over. As usual my mother was invited. Actually, Mancy was always present when we had guests either from our Romanian or American group of friends because everybody enjoyed her. She knew how to start a conversation that was right for the audience. To our Romanian friends of the younger generation, she would tell stories about her experience in the communist political prisons and about what Romania was like between the two world wars. With our American friends she discussed opera, theater, or city restaurants that she got to know better than any of us, while working for Mrs. Graf.

As usual, in April Aimée came to New York. This time she complained about health and her work as she had not done previously. I felt sorry for her and went with her to the Boston Mayo Clinic, where she had an appointment with an eye specialist. After being spoiled by her parents as a child and as a young woman, she was now faced with problems that she had to address by herself now that she was separated from my cousin Ion. Every time she came to visit us, she said she felt like she was coming home. When I left for Washington, she remained with Rudi and Mancy.

* * *

I checked in at the Mayflower Hotel and met with Blanka.

When Blanka and I got to the OCEANA bookstand, there was our bibliography entitled *International Legal Bibliography*, prepared by Simone-Marie Kleckner of the Dag Hammerskjold Library in cooperation with Blanka Kudej, special collections librarian at the New York University Law School, with a foreword by Julius J. Marke of the New York University Law School, New York, OCEANA Publications. We were delighted!

The first speaker at the meeting was Judge Edward Re, head of the Federal Court of International Trade and a professor of international law. Then it was Julius's turn to speak. As the meeting president, he stressed its importance. Then as a moderator of my presentation, he said the usual introductory words about my background and credentials before giving me the floor. I spoke in front of an audience of lawyers from major law firms, judges, law professors, and some legal librarians, all of whom shared an interest in the topic of my presentation. For me that presentation was easy because it was identical to the ones I had given previously. For Blanka, though, it was slightly more demanding as she had to put together a new bibliography about sources of international trade. Both presentations, however, turned out to be very successful, as all those present considered us experts in those respective fields. I was happy about that, but at the time had no idea then how important my presentation would turn out to be for my future.

During the seminar, I attended other presentations, such as the one on the American military program. In 1983 Reagan had just launched his Strategic Defense Initiative, popularly known as Star Wars. And some in the audience, diplomats from the Soviet Embassy, criticized the program. The more they criticized it, the happier I was. Arkady N. Shevchenko reinforced my view later in *Breaking with Moscow*, where he remarks on page 158: "They [Russians] are concerned about American military programs, particularly the 'Star Wars' initiative. Their greatest fear is that they will be left behind in an uncontrollable competition for more and more technologically sophisticated strategic or space based weaponry…and to adjust to the deployment of American Pershing II and cruise missiles in Western Europe."

After the meeting, Julius sent me a thank-you letter that impressed me so much I was brought to tears. In the letter, he wrote, "Dear Simone, I would like you to know how impressed I was by your presentation. You very effectively brought out the problems involved, and this added considerably to our knowledge of the subject by your wise and sophisticated comments on the materials in the field. I would like you to know that your talk was very well received by the participants in the seminar, and there is no doubt that your presentation contributed significantly to the success of the session. I would also like you to know that the bibliography is a significant source of information and should play an important role in the research activity of international lawyers as well as the development of standards for law library collection development in international law. With very best wishes, I am. Sincerely yours, JM."

I called Julius to thank him for his nice words and congratulate him for organizing that meeting. Julius replied that it was not only he who appreciated my presentation, but Edward Re, chief judge of the US Court of International Trade, also had words of praise for me and expressed his appreciation. Further, when I went on April 22 to the regular luncheons given by the American Association of Foreign Trade, by coincidence, Edward Re and Professor Hazard from Columbia University spoke. From what I recall, both were in disagreement with the "progressive" resolutions of the Law of the Sea and related conventions. Even better, a few days after, I received a letter from Judge Edward Re: "Dear Simone-Marie, It was good having seen you again at the American Foreign Law Association luncheon. As always, it was a great pleasure to have heard Professor Hazard speak. I hope that you too enjoyed his remarks. Pursuant to our conversation, I enclose an article which deals with the work of the court. Cordially, Edward Re, Chief Judge."

I was flattered that such a prestigious judge remembered me from Washington, DC. I read the article about the court and filed it in my little personal archive. In my turn, I wrote him a thank-you letter as follows: "Dear Edward, thank you very much for the reprint of your article and your nice letter. I was privileged to have heard you recently in Washington, as well as in New York, and want to congratulate you on the scholarly and lively way you delivered your lectures and speeches. Certainly, I know now more about the US Court of International Trade and its chief judge. I enjoyed professor Hazardt's remarks, too. If you ever need any information or want to see the UN Collections, please do not hesitate to contact me. Sincerely, SMK, Legal Librarian DHL, UNO."

Again, I could not have foreseen the importance of meeting the chief judge. This had been a God-given encounter with future implications, like Irina Luca's letter to her friend Edith.

* * *

Meanwhile, we celebrated the Orthodox Easter in our house. Then Ida visited us from Florida, and as she had done many times in the past, she told us how proud she was of her instrumental role in bringing us to America.

At the beginning of summer, we made a two-week trip to Canada with our friend Chet. Our first stop was in Quebec City, in the French-speaking eastern part of Canada. Here, Chet—who never drank—had a *sangria* with us, which put him in a really good mood, something we had never seen before. We visited the iconic Château Frontenac. We took a boat cruise on the Saint Laurence River and visited the Saint Anne de Beaupré Cathedral. After Quebec, we returned to the States and made a stopover in Maine, where lobster fishing is the primary industry. Of course, we feasted on lobster. We also visited Mount Desert Island and the Acadia National Park, with its rugged scenery dotted with granite peaks.

From Maine, we crossed to New Hampshire and stopped in the old town of Bath, and then we stopped in Plymouth Rock in the state of Massachusetts, where the *Mayflower* Pilgrims disembarked and founded the Plymouth Colony in 1620.

Our last stop was in the Port of Hyannis, where the Kennedy family compound is located and the site of a John F. Kennedy museum.

* * *

In August, Rudi's brother Aristide and his wife, Coca, came to visit us. They enjoyed New York and visiting friends and his relatives. On the very day that Aristide left, on September 1, 1983, Soviet fighter jets shot down a Boeing 747 airliner from South Korean KAL Airlines in the Sea of Japan. This was a big issue at the UN.

I gave details about this flight 007, en route from Alaska to Seoul with 269 passengers (including sixty-one Americans and the crew) killed in the attack, since UN had a say on the issue. We saw

President Reagan's TV address to the nation in which he called the tragedy "the Korean airline massacre." The Soviet Union initially denied knowledge of the incident, but the next day at the Security Council meeting, Ambassador Jeanne Kirkpatrick played a cassette recorded at Japanese ground sites revealing conversations of the Soviet pilots with their own ground control—proof that the Soviets deliberately shot down the plane. Faced with such solid proof, as usual the Soviets changed their story and claimed that the plane was on a spy mission and the incident had been provoked deliberately by the United States. I saw a picture from the Security Council meeting showing Soviet ambassador Troianovski listening emotionlessly and playing with a pen while Ambassador Kirkpatrick delivered her speech.

At the United Nations, Ronald Reagan's presence was felt as well. Secretary-General Perez de Cuellar was in a very difficult position, finding himself caught between the increased influence of the Soviet ideology and Reagan's intransigence toward the Soviets. Moreover, the United States, the biggest contributor to the UNO budget, threatened to reduce contributions because of the inefficiency of the organization. Also, after the introduction of martial law in Poland in December 1981, Ronald Reagan denied the Soviet airline Aeroflot the right to fly to the United States. As a result of that action, and in view of the Korean airplane incident, Soviet foreign minister Gromyko refused to attend that year's fall session of the General Assembly. But I did attend. For Reagan's address to the General Assembly on September 26, the room was packed full (as opposed to the attendance at Carter's UN speeches).

In accordance with Reagan's doctrine, the United States provided overt and covert aid to anticommunist guerrillas and to resistance movements in an effort to "roll back" Soviet-backed communist governments in Africa, Asia, and Latin America. For example, the United States supported both the Contras movement fighting the Soviet-supported Sandinista rulers in Nicaragua and the rebels fighting the Russians in Afghanistan. At the request of the Caribbean states, the United States invaded Granada, being concerned that the airstrip being built by Cuban workers on that island would allow arms from Cuba to be transferred to Central American insurgents. First, the Security Council and then the General Assembly were quick to pass two resolutions condemning the United States and requesting the immediate withdrawal of US troops from Granada. But Reagan decided that the troops would remain there until December, and after the situation calmed down, the United States left a small contingent of American police to ensure stability.

* * *

I was pleased to help a colleague from the Legal Office, Gabriele De Ceglie, when he asked me to compile a list of documents on different subjects before his transfer to the Food and Agricultural Organization (FAO) in Italy. That was a relatively unimportant event because I was routinely getting such requests, but the letter of thanks that he sent me gave me a feel for what the Legal Office people were thinking about me. In his letter Gabriele wrote, "Dear Simone, thank you very much for the documentation you have sent me, which is really interesting and useful! I think you have done a very wonderful job, and I am not the only one to hold this view; everyone else in the Legal Office has the same opinion. Thank you again. Yours, GDC."

Then, unexpectedly, Anne Salzberg resigned by the end of December. She had been in a car accident, and on doctors' orders she was forced to stop working. Chris was okay professionally but lacked the necessary experience to face the world just by himself. I needed a replacement for Anne.

* * *

In September, Chief Judge Edward Re invited me to a luncheon at the Law School of Saint John's University in Queens, where he was delivering a speech about the Law of the Sea. I decided to go since I was curious to hear his point of view. At that time, it was a hot topic as the Reagan administration and the US Congress did not want to abide by the Law of the Sea Convention (and, as it turned out, never did so).

* * *

That autumn, I had some bad news from Bucharest. Liky called to let me know that my father had a little accident. While he was doing his daily walks in the Bucharest park of Cişmigiu, a rotten branch fell from a tree and hit him, knocking him to the ground. He took a cab home, and as he lived on the third floor of a walk-up building, he barely managed to get to his apartment. Before the accident, he had been going up and down those stairs at least a couple of times daily, but afterward he was practically confined in his apartment, which made him very depressed. Luckily, there was no fracture, but he was in pain because of the swelling and bruises resulting from the fall.

As the four-day Thanksgiving weekend was approaching, I decided to take that whole week off to fly to Bucharest and be with him. I boarded a Romanian TAROM direct flight to Bucharest. Over there, it was brutally cold, not only outside but also everywhere—in the airport, in the taxicab, and in the hotel lobby. Although I was wearing very warm clothes—including a fur coat, fur hat, and boots—I was shivering with cold. I checked into a hotel in the heart of Bucharest that had been built in the midfifties, later purchased and fully renovated by the Howard Johnson chain. Without realizing that the receptionist was dressed in a heavy coat and was wearing a hat, I told her I could not wait to get to my room and take a hot bath to warm myself. She looked at me suspiciously, suspecting that I was kidding, and said, "There is no heat in the building, and we have hot water only in the mornings between 7:00 and 8:00 a.m." Really? I thought she could not be serious, but unfortunately she was. I went up to my room, unpacked a few things, and—still shivering with cold—returned to the lobby, where I called for a cab. A few minutes later I was at my father's house.

Miraculously, it was lukewarm in my father's apartment. We hugged each other, and then I went straight to the terra-cotta stove to turn up the heat. It had a methane gas burner. But I found out gas was rationed too. It was turned on just a few times a day, and even when it was on, the pressure was very low. Luckily, the terra-cotta absorbs a lot of heat and releases it slowly, so the stove remained warm even when the burner was off. I put my back against the stove and managed to warm up a little.

My father looked okay, but kind of frail. As usual, my visit attracted relatives, and those social interactions had a therapeutic effect on him. One can tell that I was my father's daughter because I thrive being with people—and fortunately, so does Rudi.

When I returned to the hotel in the evening, it was already dark. Our nephew Dan insisted on accompanying me because, he said, there were a lot of pickpockets in Bucharest operating under the cover of darkness. That night and every other time I left my father's house, I took along a bottle of hot water wrapped in a towel. Back at the hotel, I slipped it under my bedsheets to warm them up.

The days I spent in Bucharest were a real torture for me as I always suffer from the cold. In the morning when I could finally, briefly, take advantage of the warm water, the bathroom filled with steam because the air in the room was so cold.

From what I observed during my short visit, Lenuţa was taking good care of my father. But the big problem continued to be the procurement of bread that was rationed. Luckily, everybody liked Kent cigarettes. One pack would open many doors and went a long way toward getting what you needed. Even the government-controlled TV shows were rationed. I departed from Bucharest with a heavy heart, knowing I was leaving behind people who had to put up with so much suffering.

* * *

We spent Christmas with our neighbors the Răileanus and other friends. For New Year's, we accepted an invitation from Van Langley and his wife, Patricia, to come to their beautiful house near Wilmington, Delaware. Van insisted that we also bring along my mother, which we did, all three of us staying for a couple of nights.

There were signs that the new year would be a good one. On a political level, we were satisfied with Reagan in the White House and Margaret Thatcher as British prime minister. On a personal level, Rudi was doing better and better with his electric contracting business, and I was satisfied with my professional successes.

1984

As I was always preoccupied with keeping abreast of the latest developments in my field, I ordered a book by Edward McWhinney. Its title, *United Nations Law Making*, sounded interesting to me as I always had questions about the UN codification procedures. As I have mentioned, member states of the General Assembly sometimes circumvented the Sixth Legal Committee serviced by the Codification Division. This book (pages 150–161) confirms that the new third world member states found ways to bypass the Sixth Legal Committee or the International Law Commission because they considered them too conservative for their taste; in exchange, they asked for special or ad hoc committees.

The author also gave examples of issues that were never discussed because there were some who did not want the topics raised. For example, there was a request by third world countries for a study of the "veto practice in the Security Council" related to article 27 of the UN Charter. Another was a request related to article 51 of the Charter regarding "self-defense." It is mentioned that both requests mysteriously died in the Codification Division. To me that seemed very plausible because the heads of the Codification Division were always Russians, and they could control the juridical activity. It was obvious that the Soviet Union was not interested in having its veto right challenged in the Security Council. However, I wondered why the third world members never followed up on that request, especially since they were always very vocal on other political issues.

McWhinney's book also analyzed the situation in the International Law Commission either on its internal organization or on selection of the topics of interest. In view of its organization, the large number of members in 1981, the roll call was abolished, which led to absenteeism, the result being that one could no longer establish who decided what—and when—during consultations, thus a lack of transparency. Regarding the decision-making in the commission, some countries thought it was independent from the General Assembly, others thought the General Assembly was just suggesting topics for the commission's work, and evidently, the Soviet Union insisted that it was the General Assembly that had decision-making power over the commission mandate, thus member states having a say on the topics that should be selected.

Later, Margaret Thatcher pointed to similar aspects in her book *Statecraft, Strategies for a Changing World* (page 256), where she discussed the Convention on the Prevention and Punishment of the Crime of Genocide. (This was the UN's first legal response to the mass murder of Jews by the Third Reich.) When it came to the framing of the document, the Soviets introduced all kinds of amendments that suited them. For example, they ensured that "politically" defined groups did not count. Going by the Soviet definition, *genocide* was the attempted destruction in whole or in part of groups that were identifiable based on nationality, ethnicity, race, or religion that counted. Going by that definition, Stalin, with the blood of twenty million Soviet citizens on his hands, would not be covered by the convention. Nor would Pol Pot's extermination of two million of his fellow countrymen in Cambodia between 1975 and 1979 be covered. In other words, only the German atrocities counted, while those committed by the Soviet Union both at home and abroad were ignored.

My reference to McWhinney's and Margaret Thatcher's books is only meant to illustrate the impact of the Soviet influence on the UNO.

*　*　*

As in previous years, this year, too, during the month of March, Roy Mersky invited me to deliver some lectures on international and foreign law and documentation at the New York City Law School.

Once again, during the month of April, I attended the annual meeting of the American Society of International Law (ASIL) in Washington, DC. That year, Jeane Kirkpatrick spoke at the luncheon sponsored by the American Bar Association. She referred to the differences between Jimmy Carter's and Ronald Reagan's administrations. In her view, the main objective of Reagan's foreign policy was to preserve the security and liberty not only of America but also of all US allies. She mentioned the Soviet domination in Europe, Africa, and the Middle East. Kirkpatrick received a big round of applause, not only for what she said, but also for the vigorous way in which she delivered her messages. Her words expressed what I believed.

Back from Washington, I found an invitation from the dean of the NYU School of Law to attend the banquet celebration of Julius Marke's retirement, to be held in the Vanderbilt Hall of the university on May 10. Julius had told me of his intention to retire, but he expected to continue as professor at the Law School of Saint John's University in Queens, New York. At the retirement party, I had the opportunity to see and talk with many of my former colleagues and professors, and all of them greeted me very warmly.

Soon after Julius's banquet, I was invited to another good-bye party for my colleague Eduardo Valencia-Ospina from the Codification Division. He had been given a position at the International Court of Justice at the Hague.

* * *

After Easter, Julio, my new assistant from Peru, who had replaced Anne, put an envelope on my desk that had been sent to me via US mail. That was unusual, and I opened it immediately, curious about what was inside. There I found an official letter dated May 4, 1984, signed by a certain Nancy Johnson, whose name did not ring a bell. The letter read, "Dear Simone, I have the pleasure of informing you of excellent news. Your excellent *International Legal Bibliography* has been selected as this year's recipient of the Joseph L. Andrews Bibliographical Award. The award was established to honor a significant contribution to legal bibliographical literature. The recipient is selected after a vigorous process of evaluation by the Awards Committee. The award will be presented to you at the closing banquet on Wednesday, July 4, in San Diego. On behalf of the Awards Committee, I would like to offer you my sincere congratulation! Sincerely, Nancy P. Johnson, Chair, Awards Committee."

Thank God I was sitting down, because I was overwhelmed with emotion when I read that letter. I felt like jumping up and down with joy, but I could not do that. Still, I thought I should share the news with somebody in the office. If James had still been working there, I would have called him right away. But he had retired. Then I thought of calling Julius to break the news to him. But when I called, it was only to discover that my award was no surprise because he already knew about it. That I should have expected, because nothing happened in the world of legal libraries without his knowledge or advice. Julius congratulated me, as he had other times, and added that I deserved the honor. Still, I felt like sharing the news with somebody at the office. I thought that Ivan Schwartz might not be interested because he was kind of detached from the legal world. So I bypassed him and carried the letter to Joseph Fuchs, who was really impressed and happy for me. I replied to Nancy Johnson with my thanks, confirming that I would be attending the San Diego convention.

I also received another letter from Kathleen Price, president of the American Association of Legal Librarians (AALL), who congratulated me for the award. Shortly after, I heard from William H. Jepson, executive director of AALL, who sent me an official invitation to attend the San Diego convention, saying that Mr. Anthony Grech, a former member of the Executive Committee, would be handing me the award.

Finally, OCEANA publishers contacted me to confirm the publication of my bibliography and asked my permission to publish it in conjunction with the one on trade law that Blanka had written. I had no problem with that.

Because I intended to spend some time visiting Southern California after the convention and then planned to fly to Bucharest again to visit my father, whose health was slightly deteriorating, I approached Ivan Schwartz to make my vacation plans.

Of course, the award was excellent news in itself, but I was particularly happy that the news about it had also spread within the UNO. Even James had heard the news, and he wrote me a brief congratulatory note: "Simone, your work becoming the Annual Bibliography is an award well deserved, and I am glad and proud of you. Seymour."

Shortly after that, on June 4, another bombshell memo surprised me. It came from Carl-August Fleischhauer, undersecretary-general and legal counsel, who was the new chief of the Office of Legal Affairs. He wrote, "Simone, I am pleased to hear that your

International Legal Bibliography is recognized as having a significant merit and that you will be honored with an award. Your exceptional performance has always been appreciated by us, those in the Legal Office, and the missions. Receiving this award is very welcome and honors also the United Nations Organization, as well as yourself. With sincere appreciation, Carl-August Fleischhauer."

And attached was his note to Mr. E. Wyzner, undersecretary-general for Conference Services, informing him that "Mrs. Kleckner, who works at the Legal Office as librarian, but belongs to your department, has received a prestigious bibliographical award. Her performance is characterized as being excellent and dedicated."

On July 12 I was in San Diego with Rudi. After checking in, we met with the Kudej couple. As during previous conventions, a big hall had been reserved for stands belonging to legal publishers. When we reached the OCEANA stand, we saw a poster with my picture, next to the cover of my book. Phil Cohen, the owner of the OCEANA group, was at the stand and congratulated me. That was nice, but most impressive of all was Rudi, who was beside himself with pride.

At the banquet, all participants were sitting at round tables. I sat at a table with Rudi, the Kudej couple, and with Anthony Grech. After dessert, Mr. Grech, Blanka, and I went to a podium at the front of the hall. Mr. Grech made a few introductory words, introduced me, and handed me the mike. I expressed my sincere thanks, telling the audience, of almost 1,800 people, how proud I was to receive that award and how happy I was to be able to emigrate from an oppressive communist country where all doors had been shut in my face. By contrast, I said, in America all doors had been opened for me, offering me the possibility of growing professionally and reaping the fruits of my labor. Mr. Grech then introduced Blanka and gave her the floor. Blanka said basically the same things with regard to her own past in a communist Slovakia and her new life in the States. These were moments of deep satisfaction that more than made up for the multiple humiliations that I had experienced under the communists.

* * *

After the convention, Chet joined us one evening for dinner. We rented a car and drove north along the Pacific coast to San Clemente. President Nixon had a home in San Clemente known as La Casa Pacifica, the Pacific Home or the Peaceful Home, and also called the Western White House. It was in that home that Nixon had received Russian premier Leonid Brezhnev and Japan's prime minister Elsaku Sato.

Our next stops were in Laguna Beach, in Santa Barbara—also known as the American Riviera—and in the picturesque little Danish town of Solvang. That city is still home to a large Danish community.

Our last stop was Los Angeles, and from there we flew home. After a brief stay in New York, we quickly repacked our baggage and flew to Bucharest.

We found my father a little feeble more than on my last visit. This time, he sat in an armchair most of the time. But of course he was happy to see us. From relatives who visited us we learned that Ceauşescu had extended the forced collectivization of agricultural land to the mountain regions, where vast forest areas had been cut down, something that none of his predecessors dared to do. Nevertheless, Ceauşescu was still appreciated in the West for such gestures as refusing to boycott the LA Olympic Games as the other "brotherly" satellite states of the Eastern European bloc had done.

From Bucharest we flew to Paris, where we saw my aunt Tancy for the first time since the death of her husband. When we told Aimée about our plan to be in Paris for a few days, she drove from Munich to see us. From Paris, Aimée followed us by car to Reims, where we all visited the beautiful cathedral Notre Dame de Reims. After having lunch, we then said good-bye to each other, and Aimée returned to Munich while we continued to Strasbourg on the Rhine and Baden-Baden close to the confluence of the two sources of the Danube. Between Aimée and me, it was a simple good-bye. I had no idea that, that was the last time we would see each other.

Next we passed through Vaduz, the capital of the principality of Lichtenstein. That small country is one of richest in the world. Many businesses give Lichtenstein as their corporate address due to the advantage of low taxes and simple banking regulations.

Our last stop was Vienna. Here we met with Ingrid and with Gerold Herrmann (my colleague from UNCITRAL) before flying to New York, where my mother was impatiently waiting to discuss the latest developments in national politics.

* * *

At the beginning of the UN General Assembly September session, Secretary-General Javier Perez de Cuellar announced in a pessimistic tone that the organization's vision was shadowed by the conflicts in the Security Council. In his view, those conflicts among the big powers made it impossible to achieve and maintain peace.

A new source of interest that had surfaced in 1983 and continued in 1984 was Antarctica; there were plans to convene an international conference on the exploitation of the minerals in that strategic area, similar to the Conference of the Law of the Sea.

As usual, in September I receive my sixth performance evaluation. This time Ivan signed it, together with directors Fuchs and Orlov. The grading was identical to the previous one signed by James.

On September 24, I went to listen to President Reagan's address to the General Assembly, which followed his talks with the Russian foreign minister Andrei Gromyko on reduction of the arms race. Everything seemed to go well with the Soviets. However, it was only a few days later that Andrei Gromyko, speaking at the General Assembly, blamed the United States for the arms race and the stalemate in the arms reduction negotiations! No wonder. Russia always blames somebody, and mostly the USA.

I was looking forward to the presidential elections that were held this year. Ronald Reagan secured a clear landslide victory in both popular and electoral votes, winning forty-nine of the fifty states, the highest total ever recorded. Rudi, Mancy, and I were happy for him and for America. As refugees from a communist country, we had a good perception of the political reality of the time.

Here I will refer to the Captive Nations Week, which began in 1959 under President Dwight D. Eisenhower. (Every successive US president observed it, prior to the administration of President Barack Obama.) It was aimed at raising public awareness of the oppression of nations under the control of communist and other nondemocratic governments.

From David B. Funderburk's book *Pinstripes and Reds: An American Ambassador Caught Between the State Department and the Romanian Communists, 1981–1985*, I knew that on July 16, 1984, at the Captive Nations Week's twenty-fifth anniversary, Reagan addressed those nations lacking liberty. He said he would continue to speak up on behalf of those persecuted and illegally imprisoned. I had great hopes, as well as expectations, that finally Reagan would succeed in helping Eastern Europe.

* * *

While I thought I was entering a period of calm in my life, bad news was just around the corner. First, George Kendall called to let me know that his mother, Rosalie, had died unexpectedly in Toronto of a massive heart attack while her other son Stephen with his wife and daughter Stephanie were vacationing in Florida.

Then on November 27 our neighbor from the sixth floor, Irina Spătaru, called and told us, in a shaky voice, that our friend Aimée had died in Munich. Irina had befriended Aimée during her frequent visits to New York, and some mutual friend from Munich who did not have our phone number called her with the news. I was flabbergasted, because I had talked with Aimée on the phone just a few days before. I asked Irina if she knew any details about the circumstances of her death. She told me that Aimée had gone to a gas station in her neighborhood for a fill-up. Later, the police found her car pulled over onto the sidewalk with Aimée inside, her head resting on the driver's wheel. She was already dead when they found her.

Irina also said that her friend in Munich had told her to contact us and tell us to call the US general consul in Munich because Aimée had taken an American citizenship, and her will indicated that we were her only next of kin. No sooner had I finished speaking with Irina than Mrs. Fegar from the American Consulate in Munich called to ask me when I could come to Munich. I told her I would let her know as soon as I was able to get a plane ticket.

The news of Aimée's sudden and totally unexpected death struck me like a thunderbolt. It deeply affected us as well as all our friends who had met her during her visits.

Rudi bought me a plane ticket to Munich. I called the American Consulate and Radio Free Europe to let them know that I would be in Munich on December 2. In the plane I begin jotting down notes about what I was going to say at the funeral. I was nervous because, while I had no problem speaking in public, I am an emotional person, and I was afraid that I might choke with tears while I delivered the eulogy.

In Munich our friend Ion Ioanid, who also worked at Radio Free Europe and lived in the same building with Aimée, invited me to stay with him and his wife. We went together to Aimée's apartment but could not get in as the authorities had sealed it. The next day at the funeral, between tears, I managed to say the few words that I had prepared. We buried Aimée at the Westfriedhoff Cemetery. From that point on, I remained the only one who, over the years, paid the fee to the cemetery administration for the maintenance of her tomb.

Before I left, I took care of all the formalities with German and American authorities and saw to the execution of her will. It was only then I learned to my surprise that, as of July 1980, she had included me in her will as the only next of kin, a fact that she had never disclosed to me. I received her death certificate from the German authorities in May 1985.

1985

At the beginning of January, J. Fuchs assigned to me the task of writing another bibliography on "Treaties Between States and International Organizations, and Among International Organizations," requested by the Codification Division with an end-of-February deadline. It was less than two months before the deadline, and of course, again, I had to put in a few Saturdays to finish the compilation.

* * *

Regarding our apartment, we had been in it for twenty years. Since we liked it very much, especially because of its wonderful location in the middle of Manhattan, in 1985 we decided to try to buy it. We approached the owner, Mrs. Hart, to let her know of our intention, but she would not sell. We then started to prospect the area but could not find anything that we liked that also fit our budget. Therefore, we decided to stay put in our rental apartment. But since we were going to live there for the foreseeable future, we decided to make a number of improvements. Of course, as tenants we were going to benefit from those improvements, but the main beneficiary was, in fact, the owner, Mrs. Hart. Anyway we submitted in writing, for her approval, what we wanted to do—namely to knock down two doors, upgrade the bathroom and kitchen, remove the ugly wallpaper, repaint, and so on. Mrs. Hart obviously had every reason to agree to our plans since she would end up with a modernized apartment at our expense. We bought the materials, and Rudi put in all the work. He started the project in March and finished it in June.

* * *

Forty days after Aimée's death, as is the custom in the Christian Orthodox Church, we had a requiem mass for her. As our house was a mess during construction, we invited about sixty people to the social room of the church for snacks and drinks in Aimée's memory.

On our twenty-fifth wedding anniversary, April 23, Saint George's Day, Chet invited us to celebrate at Tavern on the Green, a beautiful restaurant and garden on the west side of New York's Central Park. Chet was like family to us. We had gone on many vacations together, and he was present at all our family events and major holidays. We were the ones to celebrate his birthday.

* * *

Meanwhile in the office, there was another change in the DHL management as director Vladimir Orlov departed, only to be replaced with another Russian, Lengvard Khitrov. I was still reporting to James Fuchs, a very rational and polite person with whom I got along very well.

The period that followed had to be, for a change, uncharacteristically tranquil both at home and at work, though I was concerned about my father's health. But the tranquil period did not last. Diana Vincent-Daviss, who took Julius's position at NYU, wrote me a letter inviting me to attend the seventy-eighth AALL Convention that she would be presiding over, to be held in New York between July 7 and July 10. Also enclosed was an invitation to attend a wine-and-cheese reception in honor of Julius Marke, marking one year since his retirement. The reception, offered jointly by the American Bar Association in New York and the AALL, was to take place at NYU on July 9 between 6:00 p.m. and 9:00 p.m.

I had hardly finished reading the invitations before the phone rang, and there was Diana again, letting me know that the AALL Committee on International, Foreign and Comparative Law was planning to organize a seminar on "The Role of the International Court of Justice and Arbitral Tribunals in the Peaceful Settlement of International Disputes" and that my name had come up as a possible speaker. She took it for granted that I would accept and suggested that it would be a good idea if I also prepared a bibliography on the subject. I asked who else was going to speak, and when she mentioned, among others, Robert Rosenstock, legal adviser to the US Mission at the UNO, and Shabtai Rosene, a distinguished author, lawyer, diplomat, and university professor, I accepted on the spot. When would I have again the privilege to speak alongside such distinguished lawyers? I was familiar with this vast subject based on article 33 of the Charter, dealing with peaceful settlement of disputes, namely negotiations, investigations, mediation, reconciliation, and arbitration. I started working on the project right away.

* * *

As it often happens, just as I was now really busy with office work and the new project, I got a phone call from Bucharest informing me that my father was not well and suggesting it would be a good idea for me to go there. Consequently, I informed Ivan and Fuchs that I had to take time off to go to Romania. The plane ticket was for a week's stay in Bucharest.

I arrived there to find that my father was physically weak. He could only move with great difficulty, and his vision was very poor. For that reason he preferred to lie in bed most of the day, but doing so, he missed his daily walks and suffered from lack of social interactions that he was so used to. Luckily, especially during my visit, Liky, my cousins Cristina, Nicuşor and Ioana, Rudi's brother Aristide, his son Dan, his wife Dana, and many others came over to see us, which invigorated him a little.

I had no idea whether I was going to see him again, but I was glad I had been able to make that short visit to Bucharest and be with him at least for a little while.

* * *

Shortly after returning to the office, it was more than urgent to work on the July project. As the time approached for the convention, I found out that my seminar was scheduled for the third day in the afternoon of July 9. The luncheon speakers were Edward Re, chief judge of the Federal Court, and Professor E. Wypyski. Our Committee was with the following speakers: Robert Rosenstock, legal adviser, US Mission to the UNO; Ted Borek, assistant legal adviser, US Department of State, Office of the Legal Adviser; Shabtai Rosenne, distinguished author, advocate, diplomat, professor; Marie-Louise Bernal, Library of Congress Law Library, European Law Division; Simone M. Kleckner, law librarian, United Nations Legal Library; and Helen von Pfeil, chair of AALL Committee on Foreign, Comparative and International Law, law librarian of the Office of the Legal Adviser, US Department of State.

I spoke for half an hour about the legal aspect of peaceful settlement of disputes as well as on the various sources of documentation. After the seminar, I received many compliments from Julius, Judge Re, and Diana, among others, who came to congratulate me.

I was happy, both from the satisfaction of my accomplishment and for having the opportunity to be a speaker in the company of so many distinguished names in the legal world. This was my frame of mind as I attended, with Blanka, the reception to honor Julius. On that occasion, his portrait was unveiled and placed alongside those of other retired professors and deans of the university. The following day, I took Rudi with me to the convention's closing banquet.

After the convention, I received a number of congratulatory notes. One was from J. S. Ellenberger, the librarian of the famous Sherman and Sterling Law Firm, who thanked me on behalf of the Law Library of Greater New York (LLAGNY). Another was from Maureen Ratinski, who wrote, "You represent one of the American success stories, an impressive experience! Bravo!" I appreciated Maureen's words because she was a colleague who worked on the second floor for the UN Documentation Section with Amin. (I had heard she was a very good professional, but I also understood there had been some problems since Ivan took James's place.) Finally, Diana Vincent-Daviss, the convention president, sent me a letter that said, among other things, "Your paper was extremely interesting and informative and was well received by the room-capacity audience. I found I learned a lot from it myself even though I have been working in the area for many years. I hope you will consider publishing your paper in the Law Library Journal or another legal periodical."

On September 11, I attended the luncheon of the American Association of Foreign Law, where the keynote speaker was Andreas Lowenfeld, my former NYU professor and one of those who had written a reference for me when I applied for my UNO job.

* * *

I had become familiar with the taste of many separations—from my governess, my cousin Ioana, my good friend Ioana, my fiancé Stephen, my grandmothers Maman Titi and Manini, and my dear uncle Nicu. Now, in early fall, at home after dinner, I got a phone call from my cousin Cristina to let me know that my father had passed away on the night of October 11. He was ninety-three years old. Because he had been lying in bed for an extended period of time, he got sick with pleurisy and high fever, which were ultimately the cause of death. He did not suffer much, but his physical energy gradually burned out like a candle. When I had left him four months before, I was kind of preparing for his death, but when it really happened, it was very painful. Gică had been the pillar of my life. With Cristina's announcement, all the memories of the life I had spent together with my father came back to me in an avalanche of painful feelings.

Rudi took the phone, gave instructions about the final arrangements, and gave details of our plans to travel to Bucharest. We arrived on October 13, and the religious service took place at the Cenușa Human Crematory of Bucharest, and then my father's remains were transferred to Craiova in the Vrăbiescu family's crypt next to those of Uncle Nae, Maman Titi, his brother Nicu, his wife Florica, Viorica her sister, Valodi Missirliu with his mother, Anetta. My father was the one who had taken care of the final arrangements for all the others, and now it was his turn to take his place among them.

I was overwhelmed with emotion when I went to my father's apartment. There, I was stunned to see Mitică Georgescu, the former administrator of our Genune estate, who had come from the town of Craiova to be close to Master Gică. That brought back memories from the good old days, as Mitică, always loyal and caring, was part of the universe of my childhood and adolescence.

After the funeral, we remained in Romania for another six days, during which I felt an urge to reconnect with my roots. Liky drove us to Craiova and from there to Bârca, where Manini's estate and mansion once were. The state had been turned into a machine and tractor station. It was a sore sight to my eyes, because the beautiful green grass and flowerbeds around the mansion had all been paved over.

From there we drove to the village of Lazu, but could not bring ourselves to go to the place where our Genune mansion once stood. The house had been demolished and the whole place turned into grazing ground. While we were strolling through the village lanes, a few villagers, hearing that I was there, came and showered us with a lot of affection, which really touched my heart. I had known them all since childhood.

We returned to Craiova, where Dr. Parhon had invited us for dinner. We accepted the invitation mostly to shake off the moroseness of what I had seen on our former estates. To my astonishment, I found, cramped into the rooms of Dr. Parhon's apartment, who was obliged to move, Manini's old dining room set that I had sold to them to supplement my mother's income after I left on November 15, 1965.

Now forty-five years after that day when I was dining with Manini and the Russian militaries unexpectedly barged into the dining room and grabbed my arm, I was sitting at the same dining room table, eating from Manini's china, and drinking from her crystal glasses, all well remembered from my childhood. Ironically, I had originally accepted Dr. Parhon's invitation to detach myself from my memories, but now, instead, I found myself plunging deeper into the nostalgia of a haunting past.

From Bucharest we flew to Munich, where we attended a memorial service marking the one-year anniversary of Aimée's death, organized by her colleagues from Radio Free Europe. At that time, I paid the cemetery for a twenty-year lease on her burial plot. We left Munich for New York on October 20.

* * *

October 20 was, in fact, the very day when celebrations were taking place to mark the fortieth anniversary of the creation of the UNO. The United Nations Office for the Coordination of Humanitarian Affairs (OCHA), which was designed to coordinate the UN response to emergencies and natural disasters, revealed that nineteen million people in Africa were starving. In fact the entire African continent was struggling with desperate poverty, complements of the so-called "national liberation movements," which had imposed on them Soviet-style hardships.

On October 24, 1985, General Secretary Javier Perez de Cuellar closed his address to the General Assembly session with a "hope for a better future," declaring 1985 the International Peace Year.

Indeed, there appeared to be some hope on the horizon. I had been astonished to read that for the first time, in December 1984, the USA and the USSR had jointly condemned the hijacking by the Palestinian Liberation Front of the Achille Lauro ocean liner. In fact, during that year there were other encouraging signs in the international arena. There was talk about a possible unification of Cyprus, about an exchange of prisoners between Iran and Iraq, about a deadline to withdraw the Russian troops from Afghanistan, and about the withdrawal of Vietnamese troops from Cambodia. All those positive signs had a lot to do with Mikhail Gorbachev's ascendancy to Soviet leadership. He understood that the USSR had reached an economic impasse and that he had no choice but to withdraw from regional third world conflicts that the Soviets had been fueling before his time. In addition, Gorbachev resumed diplomatic relations with South Korea; reduced Soviet aid to Cuba, Vietnam, and Syria; and reestablished diplomatic relations with Israel. Without a doubt, Ronald Reagan's "peace through strength" doctrine accelerated that process too. Right! I believe that only a strong America is the key to peace.

* * *

An important event of the year for me was the publication of the book *Breaking with Moscow* by Arkady Shevchenko, the highest-ranking Soviet diplomat to the United Nations who, before his defection to the West in 1978, was undersecretary-general for the Department of Social and Political Affairs. I cannot resist giving details from this book which I read immediately and assiduously, because many of my readers probably never had the occasion to know it.

Shevchenko started his memoirs with recollections of being a student at the Moscow Institute of International Relations. "During that time," he wrote, "I believed in the essence of dialectic Marxism and was convinced that the system was a good way to lead a country." He became a Communist Party member in 1958.

Then in New York, Shevchenko realized the difference between what he had been indoctrinated to believe and became aware of the contrast between those teachings and the reality of life in the capitalist world—differences that I had witnessed myself.

He became increasingly disillusioned with the Soviets' policies and described in detail his torment and soul-searching prior to his decision to defect.

In the book, Shevchenko described the personality, tenacity, memory, and vast experience of his mentor Andrei Gromyko, who took part in the Yalta and Potsdam conferences, led the Soviet Delegation to the conference that drew up the United Nations

Charter, and dealt with all American presidents from Franklin Roosevelt to Ronald Reagan. In the Soviet Union, Gromyko served all the leaders of his time, starting with Stalin. "Gromyko," Shevchenko wrote (pages 147–150), "was well informed and had become a Soviet institution—a symbol of the regime's continuity and stability."

Regarding America, on the one hand, Shevchenko wrote (pages 297–299) that the Soviets respected America for its economic might, the capacity for technical innovation, and the productive strength that they wished they could emulate. But, on the other hand, the Soviets thought the absence of a solid, coherent, and consistent policy was America's big flaw. In addition, the Soviets abhorred the American military strength for what it could do to frustrate Soviet expansionism.

Regarding the United Nations, the author appreciated that the organization was a place where representatives of the world could informally discuss a spectrum of serious and interesting problems that led to better understanding and tolerance than could be achieved with public talk. Shevchenko thought that, from the inception of the organization, many different factions used it for shallow or destructive purposes. And further he believed (page 222) that the Security Council was, more often than not, paralyzed by disagreement among its permanent members. And yet, all this granted, he recalled there had been circumstances where the UN proved to be irreplaceable in deterring potential explosions. In most respects, the Soviet Union disdained the UN, but that did not stop them from using the organization to shelter KGB spies and to vent Soviet propaganda. Compounding the UN's weakness was the fact that the United States and other major Western nations had lost confidence in it.

Also, Shevchenko described the UN secretary-generals (pages 293–294). Dag Hammarskjold, he said, was adventuresome and flamboyant. He noted that Trygve Lie declared that without the cooperation of all five members of the Security Council, the UN and the secretary-general were impotent and unable to take decisive action. As for U Thant, Svhevchenko described him as a man who spent most of his time twiddling his thumbs. Shevchenko noted that Kurt Waldheim had tried to retain the favor of all states, while Perez de Cuellar, a Peruvian, had given more responsibility to his deputies, especially to Briant Urquhart, who dealt with the Middle East problems. Furthermore, Arkady wrote about the Secretariat (pages 220–221). As defined by the UN Charter and in the staff regulations, the duties and obligations of members of the Secretariat are supposed to be "not national but exclusively international." Theoretically, all members should live up to the oath or declaration swearing that they will only act in the interest of the United Nations. But in taking the organization's oath, any Soviet national had to commit perjury, because, before an individual's candidature was submitted to the Secretariat's Office of Personnel Services, that individual undertook an obligation to do his or her best in the interests of the Soviet Union and to use his or her prospective job to achieve this purpose. The Soviet Mission, Shevchenko concluded, maintains full control over the daily work of Soviet nationals in the Secretariat.

His long years of exposure to Western life convinced Shevchenko that the Soviets were "taking the wrong path," both economically and politically. In 1975, he briefly considered resigning his position with the UN but instead decided to defect, which he finally did in 1978. It was very interesting to read how he made up his mind to defect, how he was in touch with the CIA through messages left in the books in the General Library, and how fearful he was—until he finally got US asylum—about what might happen to him if the KGB found out about his CIA contacts.

Finally, I found Shevchenko's book fascinating because it gave the reader rare glimpses into the inner workings of the feared Kremlin that brought about such dramatic changes in the lives of those who were under the Soviet yoke in Eastern Europe. The contents of that book have relevance today for the present generations. It would make very useful reading since Russian political thinking never changes. Watch Putin's foreign policy in Ukraine and the Middle East. In 2015 Russia is once again becoming a problem.

* * *

Toward the end of this year, I received several invitations to give lectures at several institutions of higher education. For example, on

November 21, I gave a lecture on international law and UN documentation at the invitation of Professor King, director of Legal Studies at New York's Baruch College. Some other similar invitations came my way.

* * *

For Thanksgiving, when we were done with the apartment renovations, we had a few friends over for a traditional turkey dinner and lots of UN friends. The apartment had been painted white, with a big mirror wall in the living room and new, abundant lighting that Rudi had installed. Upon entering, all our guests remarked how big the apartment looked compared to what they recalled from previous visits.

On December 16, I was again invited to the Christmas party at the US Mission. That year's party was hosted for the last time by Jeane Kirkpatrick, who had resigned and was to be replaced by Vernon Walters. The next day, I went to the Christmas party at the Office of Legal Affairs, where John Scott was particularly nice to me. He had no idea, of course, that by then I had found out he was the main reason why I had endured such a stressful period in January 1975, when I feared that I might not get the UN job after all and losing all other options.

1986

All through the '80s my professional stature had been climbing steadily due to my publications, speeches, and lectures, and I had managed to stand out among my peers. Unfortunately, there was no room to advance any further at the UN because the organization required one to have more seniority before being considered for a higher position. Within fifteen months, willy-nilly, I had to retire because the mandatory retirement age at the UN was sixty. This put me in a stalemate. Elsewhere in the United States the normal but not mandatory retirement age was sixty-five. There were rumors that the General Assembly might discuss raising the mandatory retirement age to sixty-two, but those turned out to be just rumors.

Already, in the autumn of 1984, I had started to think about retirement, but the busy times at work as well as the deaths of Aimée and of my father had prevented me from worrying too much about it. Now, however, the prospect of retirement life frightened me, not for financial reasons, but because I felt I could not live without sharing a structured life with active people. Many people, I know, look forward to retirement as a time when they will finally be free to pursue their interests, to travel, or read—in a word, to be masters over their own time—but that was not my case. I reflected that I had been in the States for twenty short years, during which time I had earned two master's degrees and accumulated a lot of experience, and I needed more time to reap the fruits of those efforts. I was fully aware that finding a job at age fifty-nine was a very long shot, but felt it was worth trying anyway. I decided to start spreading the word that I was on the market looking for employment. Haagi's words still sounded clearly in my ears: "You will always find a way through prayer." And that was exactly what I did while going on with my life.

At the library, it was always the same old routine; but at the beginning of April, I was awakened from this apathy by a phone call from Deputy Director Joseph Fuchs, who asked whether I could spare some minutes. He invited me to come down to his office to talk about something, but since he did not mention a topic, I had no idea what he wanted to discuss with me. When I got to his office, he told me Ivan Schwartz had given notice of his retirement and that he wanted me to take his position as head of the Reference and Bibliography Section, which was the position that Seymour James had held. Mr. Fuchs thought that I had both the professional experience and the seniority at the UN to qualify for that position.

Some pieces of information about frictions at the Documentation Section had reached my ears, and I was aware that Ivan had recommended Amin Abdel Samad to replace him after his retirement. I had not paid much attention to all those rumors because I was far removed from that area. In any case, Mr. Fuchs's offer took me by surprise, and I asked him whether he was aware I would reach the retirement age in March 1987, and told him I already had firm vacation plans for the summer. He told me he was aware of my upcoming retirement age. However, he was counting on the fact that, in view of the organization's financial problems (caused by cutbacks in funding from the Reagan administration), the trend was to promote people from within rather than hire from the outside. As to the vacation issue, he said he had no problem substituting for me while I was away. He seemed genuinely interested in hiring me for that position. To further convince me, he added that in the process my salary grade would go up from a P-4 to a P-5 level. That would translate to an increase of my final average earnings, which would be a factor in calculating my pension income. Finally, he added that he would like me to work in Ivan's office on the second floor, close to his own office, and not downstairs where Seymour's office had been.

I told him I was going to think about his offer and get back to him soon. As I returned to my office and looked around, I thought that, in retrospect, and with the sole exception of the first year, I had spent many happy years there. My work had also been very rewarding on many professional levels. The idea of leaving that place for a purely administrative position, with scores of employees reporting to me, was not very appealing.

Feeling torn by the difficult decision I had to make, I called my Finnish friend and colleague Karina Einola and asked whether she would like to have a cup of coffee with me during the afternoon break; there was something I wanted to discuss with her. She said yes.

When we met in the Delegates Lounge, I told her about Mr. Fuchs's offer and asked her to give me some background information about what was going on in the area. She told me that Amin was the crux of the problem. He was smart but a nonperformer, and Ivan, who was his friend, always covered up for him and gave him favorable evaluations. Fuchs disagreed with those evaluations, which had been the source of friction between Ivan and Fuchs. As a result, Ivan, who was buddy-buddy with Amin, decided to retire, but Amin was still expecting to get Ivan's position. Now it made sense to me why, for many years, I had often observed Ivan and Amin together in the cafeteria.

Later on, I planned to find out all details about Ivan's retirement. But for now, I was aware of how I would be trapped in a spiderweb if I accepted Fuchs's offer. That evening I went to the gym pool to do my laps, and while I was swimming, it occurred to me that it would not be a bad idea after all to accept the new position. Anyway, I had been intending to look for another job outside the UNO, and being aware of the difficulties of finding a job at my age, I thought it might help if my résumé showed more extensive administrative experience. That convinced me. By the time I left the gym, I had made up my mind to accept, which was a crucial positive decision.

The following day I went to Mr. Fuchs's office, thanked him for thinking of me for that position, and told him I accepted it. He instructed me to file an application with Director L. Khitrov for the P-5 post, the job vacated by Ivan. My application went in on April 9, 1986. Ivan Schwarts's last day at the UNO was June 30.

Before Ivan's departure, Mr. Fuchs told me to get ready to start in the new position of officer in charge as of July 1. Mr. Fuchs also set in motion the recruitment process to secure my replacement at the Legal Library. In keeping with the new hiring guidelines, he was looking for somebody from the inside to replace me. Then he told me to keep an eye on Amin and closely supervise his attendance and performance. He did not give me any further details, but I knew from my conversation with Karina what that was all about.

Meanwhile, Fuchs informed the Office of Legal Affairs about my impending promotion and position change, and the news spread very quickly around the thirty-fourth floor. John Scott, who had caused the appointment delay back in 1975, expressed his regret that I was leaving them and now congratulated me for my promotion. It felt good to see how Chris, Julio, and everybody else cared and wished me luck in my new position.

On June 30, I made an office-to-office good-bye tour, and then on July 1, I packed my belongings and moved to Ivan's former office. The office had a huge window facing the main entrance of the UNO. Opposite my desk, separating my office from Amin's room, was a semitransparent glass wall. As I started to put my things in order, Mr. Fuchs showed up to see how I was doing. He then took me on an introductory tour, although most people knew me already. Among those I met was Director Khitrov, who seemed very reserved. (I would find out that Khitrov had been supporting Amin as a replacement for Ivan while Fuchs and Wiezner were pushing for me.) In the Bureau of Document References we found Maureen Ratinsky, the one who had sent me the Christmas card with congratulations after the AALL Convention in New York.

For my replacement at the Legal Library, I had recommended Britt Kjolstadt, a native of Sweden, who has worked in the Bibliographies Section. Both Fuchs and the Russian director agreed with my recommendation. Britt did not have a law degree, but due to financial shortages, the UNO had to promote people from within. Just as Fuchs had done with me, I accompanied Britt, making introductions to people in the Legal Office. Then I left her with Chris and Julio while offering my help anytime she needed it.

On my new job, I started by reviewing the existing collections to determine what must be kept and what we needed to order. I touched base with all the section managers, calling them one by one into my office for a chat to familiarize myself with their responsibilities and assess whether they had any complaints or any ideas that would improve our work. In general, everybody was very cooperative, especially Maurine. From what she told me, I could read between the lines that Amin had been of little help, often avoiding responsibilities, coming in late, and taking long breaks. That was confirmation of the issues I had heard about from Karina Einola but that Fuchs had not mentioned.

When I invited Amin to my office and asked him the same questions that I asked the others, he assured me in an arrogant tone that he knew what he was doing. I told him I did not doubt that he did indeed know what he was doing, adding that it was for that reason I knew I could count on him and on his cooperation. After that, he stood up and left, assuming that we were done. I had been aware that I was going to have issues with him for at least two reasons: one, that he was resentful about not getting my job, and two, that I was a woman. (For a Sunni Muslim from the Sudan, it was demeaning to report to a woman.) I thought I should monitor his attendance and performance with special attention.

My next step was to review the performance reviews that my predecessors, James and Schwartz, had written about each of the thirty employees who were now reporting to me. I planned it so that when I left in March, I would have finished the evaluation report for each of them.

I had very little problem adjusting to the new job, but I was not happy with the kind of mostly administrative work I was doing. Regarding Amin, I had promised myself I would keep track of his attendance, performance, and discipline issues, but it was sometime before I decided to approach him. When I did, I reviewed with him the issues that he would need to correct if he did not want them reported in his performance evaluation. At that, he just stood up and left without saying a word. At least I was pleased that I could make a note that, on that day, I had given him a first warning.

Abruptly, at the beginning of August, Director Khitrov called me to his office and told me that, until my retirement, he wanted to transfer me to another P-5 position to the Technical Publications and Operations Section. I told him I could not accept the transfer because I was not qualified for that job, and we left the matter at that.

After I left his office, I wrote a memo to Undersecretary-General Wiezner reiterating the reasons why I could not accept the position that Director Khitrov was now offering me. In fact, Khitrov had already approved my transfer to that position, which had become available at the end of June.

Until I left on vacation, I had not received an answer to my memo, nor did I have an official notification about my promotion and salary increase. But before I left, I talked with Fuchs, and he explained that because of the US threat (made by Reagan) to cut their contribution to the UNO, all promotions had been frozen for six months. (In fact, the freeze lasted a full year.) With regard to the transfer requested by Director Khitrov, Fuchs told me not to worry about that, and I assumed he had probably been given some assurances by Undersecretary-General Wiezner. Actually, as far as I was concerned, I was more worried about my retirement than about these issues.

* * *

We left on our vacation to Austria, first flying to Vienna, where Ingrid and Gerold Herrmann greeted us at the airport. After, we drove to Badhoffgastein, a superb mountain ski resort and spa. There, we were immediately greeted by Lotte, the hotel manager, as Rodha Boyko had alerted her about our arrival and asked her to take good care of us.

At the hotel restaurant, the maître d' led us to a reserved table right by a window with a breathtaking view. Though Ingrid and Gerold left after four days, Rudi and I continued to be seated daily at the same round table meant for two couples, and Lotte stopped by frequently to make sure that everything was okay.

One day when we had no spa treatments scheduled, we took advantage of our "day off" to take a bus trip to Mount Grossglockner (Big Bell), the highest peak in Austria. The alpine road leading from the mountain township of Heilligenblut (Holy Blood) at the foot of the Mount Grossglockner to Salzburg is one of the most scenic and popular tourist attractions in Austria.

* * *

Back in New York, I found I was still in the dark about the outcome of the proposed transfer. Fuchs just told me not to worry and repeated his request that I keep an eye on Amin. I did, and continued to talk to Amin about his performance, but to no avail. While everybody was aware of Amin's issues, no one complained for fear that he might turn out to be their boss after I left.

At the opening of the General Assembly, the secretary-general pointed out that the UNO was facing the most severe financial crisis since its inception, due to the drastic cuts in American contributions that had been approved by Congress. He also mentioned that he was unwilling to run for a new mandate at the end of the year if the United States and the USSR did not make their arrears payments to the United Nations.

That policy clearly bore the mark of Ronald Reagan's uncompromising stand on foreign policy. Reagan thought that, while the United States made by far the biggest contribution to the United

Nations budget, its influence within the organization was steadily declining. While freezing the United States' contributions to the United Nations, Reagan requested the reduction of the number of Soviet diplomats to the organization. As Arkadi Shevchenko pointed out, those "diplomats" were in fact spies planted in the organization to foster Soviet interests.

* * *

Regarding Reagan's foreign policy, he felt no hesitation about withdrawing the United States from the SALT II agreement, accusing the Soviets of pact violations, and the president sent naval warships to the Black Sea in spite of Russian protests. He also authorized the bombing of Libya in retaliation for Libyan-sponsored terrorist attacks that had resulted in the deaths of several American citizens. Responding to Reagan's UN cutbacks, the secretary-general ordered the temporary freezing of any promotions within the organization. However, after the Security Council passed a positive resolution, Ronald Reagan subsequently agreed to pay all arrears contributions to the United Nations.

Besides Reagan's concern with the UNO contribution, his foreign policy was focused on diminishing the Kremlin's influence in the world. In his article "Who Broke the Evil Empire" published on May 30, 1994, in *National Review* (pages 46–50), Peter Schweizer revealed four important measures taken by Ronald Reagan that contributed to the weakening and fall of the Soviet empire and the ending of the Cold War. Part of them we knew from the news. The first measure regarded economic sanctions on Poland. The second measure was to abolish the technical help given to Moscow for the construction of the trans-Siberian oil pipeline. Third was convincing Saudi Arabia to increase its oil production to help decrease oil prices, which would cause a reduction in the Kremlin's oil revenue, income that was absolutely necessary for the financing of Michael Gorbachev's economic reforms. The fourth measure was building a powerful military program and promoting the Strategic Defense Initiative, known as Star Wars.

Being unable to compete technologically and financially with Reagan's program, Gorbachev proposed a summit in Reykjavik, Iceland. It was to Reagan's credit—in the opinion of the American journalist and political commentator Peggy Noonan, in her book *When Character Was King* (pages 292–295), where she stated that "the president refused to give up his Strategic Defense Initiative program when Gorbachev linked the arms reductions with America's giving up the SDI." Noonan observed, "However, Gorbachev wouldn't budge…Then Reagan sat back saying 'the meeting is over'…Gorbachev thought Reagan's vanity would make him accept a deal that the world would greet with the best reviews of his life… But Reagan was tougher than he was vain and he was most of all a patriot." In Noonan's view, that moment alone marked Reagan as the supreme architect of victory in the Cold War. Of course, in that respect, a lot of credit should also go to Pope John Paul II, the other outstanding personality of the twentieth century.

Moreover, one cannot overlook the failure of the Soviet empire's economic system, which was also the cause of the USSR's dissolution. (Gorbachev's economic policies proved to be cosmetic.) Unfortunately, the end of the Cold War did not bring down communists in the way that WWII annihilated Hitler's fascists. Moreover, the New World Order strengthened the neocommunists' status.

* * *

Meanwhile at the UNO, as of October 1986, I was finally appointed head of the References and Bibliography Section, a P-5 level position. My appointment was finalized following a memorandum from E. Wiezner, undersecretary-general of Conference Services to Library Director Khitrov. Soon after, I received an official note signed by Director Khitrov confirming the change of my position from the P-4 to the P-5 level, and my appointment as head of the References and Bibliography Section, starting October 1, 1986. But another note specified that my salary level would temporarily be maintained at the P-4 level because of lack of funds.

For now, I was glad that at least the appointment to my new position was confirmed, and Fuchs was gratified that the transfer requested by Khitrov had not materialized. My real problem, however, remained the prospect of my retirement, which was supposed to begin in about six months.

Then it occurred to me that the good news at the UN might augur well for me, and I decided to act. On a sunny October day, as I was walking across Central Park toward my office, I felt the impulse to get in touch with Julius, who had always brought me luck. As soon as I got to the office, I called to tell him briefly about my situation. Informing him that my mandatory retirement age was coming up at the end of the following March, I told him that I was not ready for retirement and that I wanted to find some way to remain active. Julius promised to be on the lookout and said he would let me know as soon as he found out about something that might interest me. He also told me that, in fact, he already knew about an opening at a legal library, but he was not sure whether that position had already been filled.

I felt relieved after that conversation, almost certain that Julius would work out something for me as he had done so many other times. And indeed, after only a few days, he called to let me know that the opening he had mentioned to me was at the United States Court of International Trade and that the position had not yet been filled. I knew that the chief justice of the court was Edward Re, whom I had met at the ASIL Convention in Washington, DC, and other places. Julius told me to call Mr. Lombardi, the chief court clerk, who—in Re's words—was the ultimate hiring and firing authority over there. I made a note of Mr. Lombardi's number and called him right away.

On the phone I introduced myself by telling him that Professor Julius Marke had referred me to him, and mentioned I was interested in the vacant librarian position. Mr. Lombardi was very polite, but the conversation was brief. Without further questions, he set up an appointment for an interview and gave me his address. I called Julius right away, delivering the good news that I already had an appointment with Mr. Lombardi. Julius was very happy for me and told me in passing that the court's library had given Mr. Lombardi many headaches over the years. That was not exactly very encouraging, but at that point any job was better for me than no job at all.

On the date and time of my appointment, I arrived at the Federal Court and went to Mr. Lombardi's fifth-floor office. Informing his assistant that Mr. Lombardi was expecting me, she called to let him know I was there, then showed me into a big room with an immense desk. When I entered, Mr. Lombardi stood up from behind the desk, invited me to sit down, and asked whether I would care for a cup of coffee. I said yes. While waiting for the coffee to come, he told me he was aware of my previous jobs at NYU and the UNO, and asked me a few questions about my former jobs. Then he went on to ask me about my personal background and about my life before and after coming to the States. Of course I was prepared to vent a lot of anger about my life in the communist system, but at the same time, I tried to be as reserved as possible. In fact, I knew that he brought up the subject not so much because he was particularly interested in my life but because he wanted to get an idea about my character, personality, credentials, and my way of thinking, to determine how qualified I was to assume the responsibilities of a leadership position.

I, in turn, had questions of my own about the benefits of the job and the activities I would be engaged in. Although I was reasonably familiar with the court operations from the article Judge Edward Re had sent me, I still wanted to know more. I found out that, if hired, the generous vacation time of six weeks given to me at the United Nations would be reduced to only two weeks in the first two years, which was standard for any newly hired federal employee. When the subject of money came up, I learned they would pay less than what I was making; that, however, did not concern me because any salary was preferable to the alternative of not being employed. In addition, I knew I could count on income generated by my UN pension.

From my point of view, the interview went quite well. Mr. Lombardi concluded by saying, "In case we make you an offer, before you accept it, please be aware that we would like you to stay on this job for at least a couple of years." Without batting an eye, I said I was prepared to stay on the job for as long as they wanted to keep me. At that, he laughed and asked me when I would like to start, quickly adding, "In case we decide to make you an offer." I said that my mandatory retirement date at the UNO was March 31 and that my preference would be to start in mid-April.

Before I left, Mr. Lombardi asked me another personal question, namely whether I was doing any sports. When I said I was going to the gym daily to swim laps, he commented that my exercising regimen explained my youthful demeanor and advised me to continue. It was obvious that, knowing that I was close to retirement, he had expected a very different person to show up at that interview. Before leaving, he mentioned, smiling, that regardless of his recommendation, it was the chief judge—as well as the other judges—who would have the final word. With that, we shook hands and said good-bye.

Calling Julius, I related how the interview had gone, noting that, in my estimation, I made a good impression on Mr. Lombardi. Julius cautioned that even though I would be taking a cut in salary if I took the job, the council of judges might opt for a junior person who would be paid even less, because federal funding was currently being cut back. Nevertheless, Julius encouraged me to be optimistic because he thought that with my credentials I had a very good shot at that position. I thanked him for his kind words.

*　*　*

In October, as is the tradition in the Christian Orthodox religion, I organized a *parastas* in my apartment, a memorial service and meal to commemorate one year since my father's death. I invited our closest friends who had met my father, along with the Reverend Viorel Sassu from our local Christian Orthodox church, who delivered a brief service, blessing the food offered in memory of my father.

*　*　*

Shortly after Thanksgiving, Cristine, Mr. Lombardi's secretary, called to set up an appointment for me to come to the court's Personnel Department to fill out some required forms. Nobody can imagine what a relief that phone call meant to me! Finally, gone was my dreadful fear of impending retirement. I was especially happy because, since the Federal Court had no mandatory retirement age at all, there was a good chance I could work as long as I wanted to.

On the date of my appointment at the Federal Court, Cristine introduced me to the head of the Personnel Department, who was already expecting me. Besides the standard hiring forms, I had to name two people as references. I gave the names and phone numbers of Professor Julius Marke, who was now teaching at Saint John's University, and John F. Scott, director of the Office of Legal Affairs and deputy legal counsel of the United Nations. My start date was set for April 13, in keeping with the preference that I had indicated to Mr. Lombardi during my interview.

* * *

That year, the new American ambassador to the UNO, Vernon Walters, hosted the Christmas party I attended at the American Mission. On Christmas Day, Rudi and I set off on a vacation trip to the world-renowned Mexican resort of Cancun, located north of Mexico's Caribbean coast, the Riviera Maya. In Cancun we signed up for a trip to Chichén Itzá, where we visited archeological sites that carried traces of the incredibly advanced ancient Mayan culture—a civilization that had spanned over three thousand years and excelled in mathematics, astronomy, and architecture. The highlight of the visit was the Kukulkan Pyramid, now declared one of the eight wonders of the world.

We also went to a Spanish-style corrida. At the sound of a trumpet, a beautiful, majestic, and full-of-life bull ran into the arena, only to be pulled out minutes later like a lifeless rag. Some may regard bullfights as a demonstration of pageantry, technique, and courage, but for us, that was not only the first but also the last bullfight we would ever see. Later I learned that Mexico had outlawed bullfights. Thank God for that!

1987

I returned to the office and started making plans to wrap up all my tasks prior to taking the remaining vacation time I was still entitled to. One of my final responsibilities was to analyze the performance of each person reporting to me. It was a thirteen-point evaluation with grades from A to E. After discussing the evaluations with each person separately, I forwarded them to the two directors. Of course, I had problems with Amin since I had to downgrade his report to correspond with his actual performance, noting that his attitude and attendance left a lot to be desired.

Soon after, Director Khitrov called me to his office and questioned Amin's less-than-flattering report because it contradicted the kind of reports he had previously received from Ivan. I was prepared with all documentation I had gathered to back up my report, which I showed him. Nevertheless, Director Khitrov suggested that I should change the report and make it less negative. I stood my ground. Since my life experience made me tough and resilient, I told him he could feel free to make any changes he wanted to the report and initial them, but that I, for one, would under no circumstances make changes to a document that I had endorsed with my signature. As I felt the situation becoming a little tense, I finally excused myself and left for my office.

When I mentioned to Fuchs how my conversation with Director Khitrov had gone, he was in full agreement with me. Finally, his wish to grade Amin correctly was happening. He was glad that I refused to sugarcoat Amin's performance report as Ivan had been doing for several years.

* * *

On March 8, Rudi and I started our South American vacation, with Uruguay and Argentina as our destinations. Our first stop was Montevideo, the capital and largest city of Uruguay, where the Spanish, Portuguese, Italian, and British influences were visible in the architecture. Montevideo, the main port, was a vibrant city which could boast a rich cultural life as well as beautiful beaches.

From Montevideo we made a one-day trip to Punta del Este, a beautiful Atlantic coast resort that reminded me of Saint Tropez on the French Riviera. There, I bought myself a nice dress that I intended to wear on my retirement day.

From there we flew to Buenos Aires, a city with a marked European flavor. We were impressed with Avenida 9 de Julio, the widest city in the world, with nine traffic lanes in each direction. It was a challenge to cross that street, as you almost had to run to get to the other side before the stoplight changed.

Another street we visited was where, according to legend, the tango was born. Later one evening we went to Casa Blanca to see a tango show with six pairs of dancers and the band of Leopoldo Frederico, a famous Argentine bandoneon player and composer. I shall never forget the virtuosity of those tango dancers. By the time the show was over, I felt enchanted.

Among other tourist sites we visited was the La Colletta, the cemetery where Evita Peron is buried. Our last stop was the famous Iguazu Falls, where we took a helicopter tour, dipping very close to the rainbow-creating waterfalls.

* * *

On March 20, I reported back to work. The vacation had recharged my batteries, and I was in good spirits, knowing that, instead of retirement, I could contemplate the challenges of a new job. The party that the UNO organized for my departure was one of the better ones I had attended there. Why, you may ask? Because present at the party were colleagues from two departments, the Office of Legal Affairs and the Dag Hammarskjold Library, as well as people from other departments and missions. In total, over two hundred people came. They allowed me to bring family and friends, so of course Rudi came, along with my friends Blanka Kudej and Ingrid Herrmann, who happened to be in New York at the time.

Fortunately, the organizers had anticipated the large attendance, selecting the ample Woodrow Wilson Hall for the party. Many of my colleagues volunteered to bring ethnic foods from their countries of origin; others contributed with sodas, desserts, and fruits. Seymour James honored me with his presence and, as my former boss, said a few words. But the first to speak was Undersecretary-General Carl August Fleischhauer, the legal counsel who spoke on behalf of the Office of Legal Affairs. He had nice words of praise: "Although Simone had to leave down to the Main Library, we still consider her as being part of the Office of Legal Affairs where she worked for eleven years."

Next to speak were Undersecretary-General Eugeniusz Wiezner, Director L. Khitrov, and Director Joseph Fuchs. They all wished me luck at the Federal Court. Then one of my colleagues, Fenote Salem from Ethiopia, handed me a present from my colleagues and a jumbo card with good wishes for my retirement. When I opened the box, I found inside a beautiful Lalique crystal apple. I thanked everybody for their kind words and the beautiful spread of food they had put together. I also expressed my gratitude for the valuable experience that I had gained during my twelve years with the organization. While some people were helping themselves to the food, drinks, and desserts, others were busy signing the card, writing brief personal messages wishing me happiness and success in my new life adventure.

Some also mailed me cards with good wishes for my retirement and my new job. For example. Seymour James wrote, "Simone, the party to honor your retirement was wonderful, surrounded by many friends, colleagues, and relatives. I watched you while you were talking and had been proud about your achievements. From now on remain the same, professionally dedicated and pleasant. I have been pleased to be there from the beginning to the end. Seymour 3-25-87."

Others, including my secretary Noemi and Maureen, also sent me cards with words of appreciation and expressing regret that I was leaving. Ernesto mentioned his "deep respect for your professional attitude which you brought with you in the position you held." Their appreciation, I suspect, was probably related to my firm attitude related to the difficulties with Amin.

Before I left, I received my last evaluation reports, covering my activities in the Legal Library and in the Reference and Bibliography Section. Joseph Fuchs gave me eleven As and two Bs (for my spoken and written English). He added, "Mrs. Kleckner was able to instill a renewed interest for an activity and professionalism which was lacking in the supervision of the Reference and Bibliography Department, Joseph Fuchs, March 17, 1987."

When the report reached Khitrov, he disputed the A that Joseph Fuchs had given me for item 7, referring to my relationship with coworkers and the readers. He made a note in section 5 of the report that the A could stay although it was obvious that I had difficulties with one employee.

I answered, expressing my opinion in section 6, a section reserved for staff member comments, as follows: "I agree with the remarks in section 5, only that the difficulties do not regard myself, having had the responsibility to supervise a difficult staff member. Simone Marie Kleckner, 31 March 1987."

* * *

In retrospect, the eleven years spent at the Legal Library were the best of my career because they allowed me to capitalize on my entire education, both the one I had in Romania and the one I acquired in the United States. A definite plus for me was my command of foreign languages, which had helped me both in my relationships with the readers and in the compilation of bibliographies. But above all, I had enjoyed my work, was dedicated to it, and was unsparing in my efforts to do well.

Another positive factor at the United Nations was the fact that I was surrounded by pleasant and friendly people. I was fortunate to meet the most qualified legal professionals in international law. Furthermore, I left with very nice memories about most of the bosses I'd had over the years, including Natalia Tyulina, Seymour James, and Joseph Fuchs.

Truth be told, I could not have possibly accomplished what I did without sacrificing a good deal of my personal life. In that respect, I was lucky to have a husband like Rudi, who was always supportive of my work and accomplishments.

On top of all that, I cannot overlook another perk of working for the UNO, namely that it offered me opportunities to come face-to-face with world leaders, such as King Juan Carlos and Queen Sofia of Spain, Pope John Paul II, who blessed me in the UNO rose garden, and Margaret Thatcher. It also gave me the chance to be present for speeches given by presidents Carter and Reagan. And at the American Mission, I'd had the pleasure and privilege of speaking with Jeane Kirkpatrick, whom I greatly admired both for her intellect and for her stance on foreign affairs.

From an administrative point of view, my last position as head of the Reference and Bibliography Section—with thirty employees reporting to me—was another valuable experience that would help me in my future job as library director at the Federal Court (although the difficulties I had had with Amin were there to haunt me until my last day on the job).

* * *

March 31 was my last day with the UNO. As it happened, I never benefited from the salary increase that was to come with my promotion from P-4 to P-5 employment levels. When I had the opportunity to see the memo with the names of the 125 employees promoted from P-4 to P-5, effective October 1, 1987, I noticed that my name was missing from the list. Obviously, the omission was not accidental.

I wrote a complaint directly to Secretary-General Javier Perez de Cuellar, explaining that I was entitled to the promotion and corresponding salary increase as head of the Reference and Bibliography Section, a position I held from October 1, 1986, to March 31, 1987. I thought it was worth my while to bring that to his attention, not so much for the extra money that would have been added to my paycheck, but also especially because the last average earnings were factored into the calculation of my pension income. My former colleague from the Legal Office, George Irving, also advised me to file a complaint with the Administrative Tribunal, which handles all employee grievances. It was quite a while before I was notified of a resolution.

It was not until 1990 that I received a note from Kofi A. Annan, the future secretary-general (who at the time was undersecretary-general in charge of the Personnel Department). In the note he wrote, among other things, "Dear Mrs. Kleckner, I am pleased to inform you that the organization has decided to promote you retroactively to the P-5 level from 1 October 1986 until the day of your retirement....May I take this opportunity to tell you that the decision to promote you, although belated, reflects the very high regard in which your excellent performance has always been held by the organization. Yours sincerely, KAA."

After the Administrative Tribunal reached a decision in my favor, my good friend George Irwin, who represented me in the proceedings, gave me a copy of my file. There I found a memo that Joseph Fuchs had sent to the Tribunal confirming my claim and reinforcing the fact that my appointment as head of the Reference and Bibliography Section included my promotion to P-5. His memo also pointed out that I fully deserved that promotion in view of my outstanding performance on that job.

In the same file I found a note dated May 27, 1986, that Amin wrote to Louis Pascal Negre, who at the time was heading the Personnel Department, asking for my replacement. Amin's note was also cc'd to Khitrov. Apparently, for some reason that remained a mystery to me, Khitrov sided with Amin. Apparently, Eugeniusz Wiezner, the undersecretary-general of Conferences Services, which includes the Dag Hammarskjold Library, foiled Amin's attempted action.

* * *

Since the end of decolonization and the Cold War, many authors have given their opinions about the urgent need for a revision of the United Nations Charter regarding the right to veto procedure. Many are in favor of changes that would align the charter with democratic principles. But as Edward McWhinney pointed out in his book *United Nations Law Making* (quoted previously), the Russians, on orders from the Kremlin, made sure that the request to reform article 27 (regarding the right to veto) never went past the Codification Division.

I am sorry to have to mention that over the years the organization's policy eroded public trust in the effectiveness of the authority vested in the Security Council "to maintain international peace and security." Peace is hampered by the difference of its permanent members' conception of ideologies, a fact that usually preempts solutions to conflicts or results in not taking any action at all.

Another case in point is the election in 2012 of the Sudanese president Omar al-Bashir to the Economic and Social Committee (ECOSOC) after the International Criminal Court (ICC) had already issued an arrest warrant (in 2009) for him for directing a campaign of mass killing, rape, and pillage against civilians in Darfur. In that respect, the director of the UN Watch agency, Hillel Neutral, stated that the Omar al-Bashir's election by 176 votes out of 192 countries was a "frightening decision that brought a severe prejudice to the credibility and reputation of the UNO." The fact that Omar al-Bashir had been reelected in 2013 is incomprehensible and unacceptable.

Reinforcing that view is the 2014 resolution of the Geneva Summit stating the appointment of representatives of countries that do not respect human rights to the UN Human Rights Council. This is incomprehensible.

I sincerely regret that the United Nations' policies are often not flattering, to the detriment of the organization.

C H A P T E R   6

US Court of International Trade (USCIT), 1987-1996

Thirteen turned out to be a lucky number for me. It was on November 13, 1965, when I received the passport to get out of the communist "heaven," and now on April 13, 1987, I started a new job with the United States Court of International Trade. I was very excited, considering the fact that at the age of sixty I got a prestigious job as director of the court's library or chief librarian with a two-week annual vacation. Although there will be nothing thrilling about how I managed to reorganize that library, however, this new position being part of my life, I can't overlook writing about some details of that episode and the people I worked with.

The new job required me to make a number of adjustments. First, I had to be at the office at 8:00 a.m. instead of 9:30 a.m. (the expected arrival time at the United Nations). In addition, while the United Nations was within fifty minutes' walking distance from my house, to get to the Federal Court I had to take the subway and wake up much earlier. After a while, though, Rudi suggested that he could take me to work in the mornings on the way to his own business.

On my first day I reported to the personnel office manager, who introduced herself as Mary-Jane. She showed me to the very large, pleasant, and airy library on the eighth floor. Then she introduced me to the team of people who were going to report to me. They were all very curious to see me. My predecessor had left at the end of 1986, and they had functioned without a boss for three months. I met Mary, a nice young woman; Ella and Myrna, who were middle-aged; and Herbert, a young, tall, and solid guy. Quite a difference in number from the many people I left at the UN!

Then Mary-Jane took me to meet some of the nine judges and their assistants. I could see from their expressions that, knowing I had retired from the United Nations, they were surprised to see someone who did not look at all like a retiree. That I looked younger than my years was due, at least partially, to the fact that I was exercising, swimming, and walking every single day. In addition, I had good genes from my Oltenia-region family.

Then I met with Chief Judge Edward Re. When I had met him before, outside the court, he had always seemed very exuberant. Now he was very pleasant but formal, which I guess his leadership position required. It made me laugh when I reflected on the way I had addressed him as "Dear Edward" when I had written him a note back in 1983. Of course, I had no idea, then, of the God-given opportunity that was in my future and that one day he would become my boss.

I was very impressed with the chambers, the judges' spacious and airy offices. They were quite a contrast to professors' offices in the academic world or to the offices of the bigshots at the UNO. Here, there was an aura of respect surrounding those judges, all of whom had been appointed for life by the president of the United States. Since they held appointed positions, they were either Democrats or Republicans, depending on which president had nominated them.

During my morning tour, I was introduced to the chief deputy clerk and Ralph, the financial manager, who would turn out, in the future, to be a very helpful and reliable person. I also met John from the Technical Department, where the judicial decisions were printed.

While I was chatting with them, the secretary of the clerk of the court called Mary-Jane to let us know that Mr. Joseph Lombardi was expecting me in his office at twelve o'clock. (Mary-Jane told me he was very particular about punctuality.)

We reached his office a few minutes before our twelve o'clock scheduled meeting. Mr. Lombardi greeted me with a warm "Welcome on board" and, rather than taking me to the court cafeteria, treated me to lunch at a neighborhood restaurant. Before our food came, Mr. Lombardi casually described my responsibilities, which would also include the maintenance of the collections in the judges' libraries. Then he got straight to the point, and with emphasis he told me that one of his main objectives was to improve communication within the library. (I knew from Julius that he had staff communication problems in the library.) He also mentioned that he was responsible for hiring and firing people and that he would not hesitate to fire somebody who caused problems. He did add, though, that he tried his best to avoid that, and mentioned that my administrative experience at the UNO was a guarantee that I would know how to handle staff problems.

I heard him out, and then I was the one to reassure him. I said I was planning to have separate talks with each staff member to know them and assess their personalities. In addition to human interactions, I said that I thought it was equally important to put the library on a sound and orderly organized basis to avoid useless conflicts. I saw that Mr. Lombardi was not particularly interested in what I said regarding organization: it appeared that, to his mind, managing human personalities was the only way to avoid human conflicts, while managing a well-structured organization had little or no impact. Seeing where he was coming from, I let it go and changed the subject. Before we returned to the court, Mr. Lombardi assured me I would have his full support in any issue—adding half-jokingly that his support was of course conditional upon his agreeing with my point of view.

From that very first morning when I met the judges and listened to Lombardi, I entered the world of federal civil service, which has an atmosphere quite different from the academic or international civil service world. There, I had dealt with international law, global politics, and conflicts, whereas here I would be concerned with the court's decisions on interpretation and application of US customs on foreign goods.

At the end of the day, on my way to the gym, I felt confident that, with Mr. Lombardi's support, I should have no problem, apart from the fact that there would be a much-earlier start of the workday. I knew I had to be punctual if I expected my people to be the same.

The following day, the first thing I did was to invite each staff member to my office for a chat, getting a feel for what they had on their minds. From Mary I learned she was of Irish descent but had been born in the States. She had no master's degree in library science but had had a lot of experience on the job. Before I was hired, she had been the de facto manager of the library, and for that reason she told me that she was a little behind in her work. I asked her to give me some statistic worksheets to get an idea of what questions the library received. She said there were none. On the whole, I did not think she was overly friendly, but even though she was somewhat reserved, I found her perfectly polite.

Next, I talked with Ella, who had come in late that day, blaming it on the subway. She was quick to mention that she was the only one there with a master's in library science from Columbia University. Then she told me that she had been born in Vilnius. She said her entire family died in Auschwitz, adding that she believed this was the reason some of her colleagues did not like her. I told her that those were personal matters, and it was only her job performance that counted at the office. To that she replied quite emphatically that all judges rated her work very highly, even if some of her colleagues did not share that opinion.

Then it was Myrna's turn. She was an elderly African American widow. Entering my office, she just stood by the door, ignoring my repeated invitations to take a seat. When I finally managed to convince her to sit down, she gave me a quick account of her responsibilities as if she wanted to get it over with and leave. Then she switched gears, taking time to emphasize that, as an old-timer at the library, she knew exactly what was going on. Being "a morning person" who always came to work early, she knew who was late most of the time, mentioning Ella as someone who was always late. She made her point emphatically, saying that those who were late most of the time were never reprimanded because the chief librarians were also often late themselves. I thanked her for bringing that to my attention and promised to keep an eye on that discipline issue. With a wave of her hand, she seemed to dismiss my remark, betraying skepticism that the situation would ever change.

The last one I talked to was Herb, a tall African American. He told me that his responsibilities were to receive the materials delivered three times a day by internal mail and then shelve them. He also distributed the mail meant for the judges' chambers. When I asked him whether he had any issue that he would like to bring up, he also complained about Ella, saying she was always relying on him to locate different publications, although—since she was someone with a master's degree—he thought it was her own responsibility to know all that stuff.

All those conversations were useful for me as they gave me a feel of what was going on in the library. From what I heard, I knew for sure that there were problems among the staff members and I had to find a solution to calm the atmosphere.

In addition, the very first day when I went to have lunch, I learned through the grapevine that the clerk of the court Lombardi was very demanding, always in control, and knew exactly what everybody was doing. Furthermore, I learned that most of my predecessors had used the job primarily as a stepping-stone to getting their law degrees, and as such, managing the library was of secondary importance. As I had realized from the conversations with my team members, I could see that Ella was somewhat unpopular there in spite of her having a master's degree. That explained why, before I came on board, it had been Mary rather than Ella who had been entrusted with the responsibilities of an interim boss. I suspected Mary had hoped she would be promoted to the position of library director. This is why she was somewhat stiff when talking to me.

When I returned from lunch, just a few days after I started on the job, I found a copy of *The Court Crier*, a monthly news bulletin, a source of information for everyone associated with the court. This issue included a comprehensive review of my background, including where I was born, when I came to the States, and how many foreign languages I spoke, with detailed references to my education, previous job experience, and professional affiliations. Even my Joseph L. Andrews Award was not overlooked.

After my first few adjustment days, it was time to start reviewing the collections with Herb. We went to the storage room, where floor-to-ceiling shelves were crammed with books, periodicals, and documents. I saw that free shelf space was at a premium, and Herb was dumping all new books wherever he could find some space. I said to myself it was no wonder Ella needed Herb's help whenever she had to locate one. Moreover, most document editions were old, the various issues of periodicals were not even bound together into annual volumes, and there was no consistent classification of the books' subject matter.

From my very first day, I had noticed that Herb's office door was always locked, which intrigued me. That morning I asked him to open it. When he unlocked the door and revealed what was inside, I was shocked. For a moment, I just stood still in the doorway. In front of me was a huge windowless room filled up with cardboard boxes, some stored on two levels. His desk was squeezed in behind the door. When I asked what was in those boxes, he said, "Well, what else but books and publications." He explained these were old books returned from chambers or newly arrived publications kept there for lack of storage space. I was mesmerized. I asked him why the old materials were not deleted from the catalogues and disposed of, and he had no answer for that. Along the same hallway were other locked rooms used, he told me, by other departments from other floors.

Talking with Mary, I found out that old publications could not be disposed of because they were considered federal property, paid for with federal money; hence, nobody would touch them. All of a sudden I now realized I was really confronted with a major problem.

Contrary to what Mr. Lombardi thought, a number of organizational issues affected the workflow and were the cause of much friction among employees. I was aware that now my own instincts for order would prove useful here. I would follow the organizational layout of the library used by Marcellia Simpson, my former boss at NYU. I decided my priority was to reorganize and optimize the storage space and get rid of useless materials; but for this I would need Lombardi's permission to discard federal-paid publications. (This was quite different from any private library.) Only after I had completed that task could I order new materials and have them classified and stored in proper order. A very big and time-consuming job!

As a result of my findings, I first asked Lombardi whether he could spend a few minutes with me discussing a number of issues. Thinking that I had come to report a staff crisis, he got a little tense. When I told him I was there to discuss organizational changes I had in mind, he was visibly relieved but also puzzled. I told him what I had found out and what I thought required immediate attention and remedial action. He said he found my observations legitimate, and he encouraged me to do exactly what I was hired for—that is, librarianship. I insisted that there was nothing much that I could do without him. Again, Mr. Lombardi seemed to wash his hands of the matter by saying he did not know what to do since he was not a librarian. That's when I spelled out that, among other things, I needed the approval of the clerk of the court to dispose of outdated federal property publications and to get more space by possibly acquiring two closed rooms on the eighth floor used by other departments. In addition, I insisted that I needed his approval for funds needed to buy shelves for the publications that were currently being stored in cardboard boxes or to bind annual publications together.

The more I talked, the more Mr. Lombardi frowned at me. Eventually, he said that prior to that day nobody had brought up the issue of discarding old publications, knowing they were federal property. I replied that, federal property or not, they had to be weeded out and withdrawn because they were no longer of use. I added that there was no point to keep new publications in cardboard boxes, which made it impossible for people to locate them. After a long silence and some pondering, he said he would talk with Ralph, the financial manager, to see whether we could liberate the two rooms on the eighth floor for the library and assess whether there was money in the budget to buy new shelves.

Due to the problems that I had brought to his attention, all of a sudden Mr. Lombardi was faced with issues that had never been raised before. Why? Because probably, as I had heard, some of my predecessors, having other preoccupations, tried to avoid discarding material, which meant getting approval and requiring extra work—first, making decisions about what was to be weeded out and, second, setting up withdrawing procedure itself. When I left, I was pleased that I had talked about all the problems that had obviously been avoided until then.

* * *

At about this time, the court was making preparations to attend the Federal Circuit Judicial Conference that was held every other November. Mr. Lombardi wanted me to attend, and one of the judges asked me to prepare a bibliography on a trade subject. I worked personally on the requested bibliography, which was included in the folder of materials that were handed out to conference participants.

Over the span of my years to come with the federal court, I would be asked—either for the conference or otherwise—to put together all kinds of documents, including bibliographies, legislative histories, legislative bills, or acts that were of interest to the court. Always, after each conference, the chief judge would send a note of thanks to each individual who had contributed to its success. I was the recipient of a number of such notes until 1994, the last year I attended a conference.

* * *

After returning from the initial conference, I decided that the solution for a better communication among library staff members was to have weekly meetings with them, to keep everyone apprised of my intentions. I explained what I planned to do and what was expected from each one of them (including myself) to achieve those goals. We discussed what would be the best use of the additional space, assuming we were able to get it. That way, everybody got to know exactly what was expected of him or her, and as always, I assured all of them that I would keep my office door open and always welcome their suggestions.

Also, I read the Employee Manual just to see whether there was anything else that I had to know. There I learned that any negative rating on the annual performance report had to be backed up with written proof. That requirement made me tell my staff that I would need written accounts of any disputes that might occur. (I believe that that requirement turned out to be a deterrent for avoiding disputes in the first place. However, incidents or disputes were still going on almost daily.)

One ridiculous incident, which I must describe, illustrates how disputes were arising and revealed to me the root or the pattern that caused many of them. One afternoon, Ella came to me complaining that somebody had taken her key to the Reference Desk drawer, located where she was sitting. I summoned everybody to my office and asked whether any of them had seen or taken that key. All answered in the negative and returned to their work. Then with Ella I went to the Reference Desk to see whether, somehow, the key had been misplaced. We first checked the drawer; the key was not inside. I also searched the top of the desk—and sure enough, the key was there, buried under a pile of papers. At that moment, Ella burst into a rage, saying she had checked that pile of papers before coming to my office and the key was not there. She claimed somebody had put it back during her absence while she was coming to see me.

As she became increasingly vocal on the subject, I invited her into my office. In the same loud voice, she continued ranting that everybody—and, in particular, Herb—was playing these pranks on her because they all were anti-Semites and envious because she was the only one with a graduate degree. I told her I was skeptical that anti-Semitism played a part in that incident—to which she replied, still in a loud voice, that I sided with those who were against her. And then came her important confession—that a number of times in the past she had seriously considered suing the court for discrimination. I kept silent and allowed her to vent her anger, after which I said I needed a written statement from her detailing everything she had told me. That had the desired effect. Immediately, she stopped her ranting, left my office, returning later with the document I had requested.

From now on I had to be Sherlock Holmes to find reasons for what was going on. There was a good chance that, indeed, someone played a prank on Ella to make her look ridiculous. I did not think there were anti-Semitic undertones to that incident, as she claimed; rather, I thought it was symptomatic of the way Ella managed to annoy all her coworkers with her relentless boasting about her graduate diploma. In any case, I could recognize her feelings. As one whose family had suffered so much under Hitler, I could understand being oversensitive and seeing everything through the prism of her personal experience.

I was sure Mr. Lombardi knew that Ella had seriously considered suing the court for discrimination, although he had not mentioned that to me. However, I remembered what Julius told me—that the court's library had given Mr. Lombardi many headaches over the years. I also recalled Lombardi's words that "I would not hesitate to fire somebody who did cause problems, but that I tried my best to avoid that." So now I knew that Ella's suing the court for discrimination was the crux of the matter, and it was what kept Lombardi annoyed.

My concern was to find out who was playing pranks on Ella. I knew that Myrna kept track of Ella's lack of punctuality in the mornings and did not speak to her. Because Myrna never budged from her desk, I suspected she might be the main troublemaker and might influence Herb to act. I asked myself how I could address that delicate issue, given that Myrna was African American and any complaints against her could be misinterpreted as racially biased.

While thinking what I had to include in my report to Mr. Lombardi as to how I intended to organize and update the library, including the electronic capabilities, it occurred to me that we should automate our accounts payable. This was Myrna's responsibility, and since Myrna was inexperienced with computers and software, I hoped she might ask for a transfer or take retirement (since she was already the right age). That, at least, seemed like a possible solution.

As for Ella, who had not reached retirement age yet, I decided to act as a shrink and try to convince her to forget about the past and enjoy the present, which was good to her. She had a good husband and son, she lived in the best country in the world, and she had a nice income and a safe job. In other words, she had every reason to be grateful for what the present had to offer. At the same time, I was thinking that another solution would be to hire a librarian with an MLS degree to replace Myrna; at least that might curb Ella's appetite for constantly boasting about her credentials, which irked everybody.

In my report I included all my requests to Mr. Lombardi. And since I knew they would require the allocation of additional funds, I was very careful to provide detailed justifications. In conclusion, I wrote that, in the event that I obtained everything I had requested, I estimated that I could complete the library reorganization within three years—that is, by 1990—and I would write regular progress reports.

When I was done with the report, I asked to see Mr. Lombardi. As usual, he invited me to take a seat in front of his desk while he listened to what I had to say. This time, instead of talking, I handed him my report, saying that *scripta manent*, to avoid any misinterpretation about the obligation I was assuming. Reading the report, he frowned a few times but made no comment. I watched his face while he read, knowing that my success depended on the persuasiveness of my written justifications. But it was not up to him alone; Mr. Lombardi, in turn, would have to be persuasive in presenting his report with my requests to the judges if he had any chance of getting approval for additional funds. When he finally finished reading, he said, "I see that you like to assume responsibilities." My answer was, "That's what I was hired to do and that's what I am paid for." He laughed.

Then came the big moment when I made my case regarding Myrna and Ella. I mentioned that, in my opinion, Myrna was an instigator in some of the conflicts. I also shared my thought that hiring another employee with an MLS degree would make Ella less inclined to show off her superior education, a habit that was so much resented by everybody. He heard what I was saying without any special comment. He closed by saying that he would see what could be done about hiring a new librarian.

Mr. Lombardi did recommend purchasing the shelves—a request that was subsequently approved by the judges. Subsequently, Ralph, with Herb's help, assessed the number and size of the shelves that would be required in each of the rooms. These included Herb's big room and the other two, already evacuated by other departments, which were now designated to be used by the library. Thus, I gained considerable space.

The shelves were finally delivered at the beginning of October when Herb, under my supervision, started to move the sets of books according to a predetermined, discussed plan. He also emptied the boxes and organized the materials accordingly.

On the six-month anniversary of my employment, I received my performance evaluation from Personnel. Contrary to the ones at the UNO, here the forms were more involved. We had to provide ratings in response to fifteen different questions, following up with a memo justifying each assessment—"unsatisfactory," "satisfactory," "very good," or "outstanding." I filled in the form, signed and dated it, and sent it to Mr. Lombardi. After a time, he called me to his office and handed me the report with no changes in my ratings. In his own comments, he rated my overall performance as outstanding. I was delighted.

In December 1987 I attended my first Christmas party at the court. Many judges approached me, asking how I liked my new job. I responded by saying the library was in the process of being reorganized and that our next task would be a review of the collections in the judges' chambers, which was also part of our responsibility.

Mr. Lombardi approved my application to take a few days off without pay, which I asked for because Rudi and I had made plans to spend the New Year in Puerto Vallarta, Mexico, together with Van and Pat Langley. Just before my vacation, however, there was another incident involving Herb and Ella, who complained that Herb was very rude to her. I called Herb to my office and reprimanded him for his behavior, but he responded in a tone that was, to me, completely unacceptable. I then put my complaint in writing and called Mr. Lombardi to request a meeting. That was the first time I had been pushed to such extremes. I had to brief him on the incident, stressing that in my view Myrna was inciting Herb, who otherwise was a good worker whom I would hate to lose. I think Mr. Lombardi finally understood the situation; he told me he would address the problem when I returned from vacation.

We flew to Puerto Vallarta on Mexico's Pacific coast, a resort with a colonial flair. The hotel was adjacent to a beautiful beach with fine sand, and the ocean water was almost the same temperature as the pool water. Removed from the issues I faced at my job, we managed to have a few very relaxing days in that beautiful resort.

1988

Back from Mexico, I received a note from Mr. Lombardi's secretary asking me to attend his meeting with Herb. During that meeting, I appreciated Mr. Lombardi's handling of the situation; he was calm and fair, but firm. Basically, he told Herb that he needed to change his attitude or else he would be required to hand in his resignation in keeping with the by-laws stipulated in the Employee Manual. Herb promised that he would be careful to avoid incidents in the future. Then Mr. Lombardi asked what my opinion was. I said Herb was a good worker, and he deserved a second chance to revise his attitude. (In time, Herb would prove that he was a man of his word, and he became a really reliable employee. Even now, as I write, he is still appreciated at the court.)

Then another problem followed: Ella's evaluation report came due. She gave herself very generous marks, and I knew I might have to adjust some of them downward. I did not expect her to be very happy about that, but I prepared all the necessary documentation to support my ratings. My main complaints about her were that she was obsessed with the idea that she was the only one with a library degree and that she felt discriminated against. As expected, when I called her to my office to discuss her performance report, I had to provide examples to justify each and every grade that I had lowered.

Finally, she signed the form and left. I was relieved to be able to send the forms back to Mr. Lombardi.

* * *

The time had come to send to Mr. Lombardi the first memo stating our accomplishments and comparing them to the previous year's overall report.

I also had to prepare for the annual Convention of the American Association of Legal Librarians (AALL) in Atlanta, Georgia, in June, because I was asked to contribute to a seminar on "Latin-American Legislation and Similar Legal Sources for Eastern European Countries." As usual, I met Julius and Blanka at the convention, and afterward I received a letter from Daniel L. Wade, foreign and international law librarian from Yale Law School, who wrote, "I want to thank you…and I want you to know that your presentation was greatly appreciated."

In February 1988, I received my second performance evaluation report for the entire year, in which Lombardi added two points with the overall rating of outstanding. When he called me to his office to review and sign the report, he again praised my initiatives and reiterated how pleased he was that things were going very smoothly at the library.

Soon after that satisfying meeting, I had another reward. Mr. Lombardi sent me via interoffice mail the copy of his memo dated March 16, 1988, which he had written to Chief Judge Edward Re. The memo said, among other things, "The purpose of this memorandum is to recommend for your approval the promotion of Mrs. Simone Marie Kleckner from grade JSP – 13/12 to JSP 14/1. It is difficult to describe my extreme pleasure and relief with Mrs. Kleckner as our librarian. In the short time she has been here, Mrs. Kleckner has significantly increased the efficiency and effectiveness of library operations and services. I have observed her to be a highly professional, dedicated, sind loyal member of the Clerk's Office staff. Needless to say, Ms. Kleckner received an overall rating of 'outstanding' on her last Employee Performance Appraisal." The chief judge approved Mr. Lombardi's request, and my next paycheck reflected the increase in my annual salary.

Good luck continued. A few days later, I heard that Myrna had given advance notice of her plans to retire at the end of April. She sent her notice to the deputy clerk of the court, bypassing me. I thought her decision to retire had a lot to do with my proposal to automate acquisitions and accounts payable, and the fact that she bypassed me definitely had a lot to do with the meeting that Mr. Lombardi had held with Herb in my presence. As far as I was concerned, her retirement was one less problem to deal with at the library.

Soon after, another one of my ideas to eliminate sources of friction at the library came to fruition when Mr. Lombardi called me to his office to let me know that he had the green light to hire a librarian with an MLS degree as a replacement for Myrna. I suggested to Mr. Lombardi that we approach Columbia University and recruit a candidate who was about to graduate in June. He gave me the go-ahead to do that. In fact, he said he preferred to recruit someone fresh out of college instead of somebody who was leaving another job, since you never knew whether a person had left voluntarily or had been forced out of their previous job.

* * *

In the meantime, I was not neglecting my international law meetings. Between April 19 and 20, I went to Washington, DC, to attend the annual meeting of the American Society of International Law. One of the subjects discussed was the emergence in 1988 of the worldwide web global information network and its potential as a source of reference and research.

Good news followed. As soon as I returned from Washington, DC, I found the three desktop PCs I had requested in a memo already installed in the office—one for Mary, one for the new employee who was to be hired to fill Myrna's position, and one for me. That was a really great surprise.

Then there was another nice surprise. Mr. Lombardi recommended to the chief judge that the library should be given a Special Achievements Award. In his recommendation he wrote, among other things, "During the past year, the staff of the library, in my opinion, has satisfied the requirements for this award and deserves a special recognition for their individual and collective efforts…The staff have provided substantial assistance under Simone's supervision with the completion of four library projects undertaken since 1987. In addition, I think that Simone, with her positive attitude and high professional standards is an excellent example to be followed by the staff." The chief judge approved.

That came at an auspicious time because boosting people's morale and self-confidence was the best way to improve performance. It gave everybody the feeling that their contribution counted and that each of them was performing a task that was important for the organization.

Toward the end of May, I attended the annual luncheon of the American Association of Foreign Law, and the following day I went to Columbia University to start the recruiting process for a position that had become available. I interviewed a number of potential candidates who gave me their résumés. The one who stood out was a young woman, Anna, of Armenian descent, but I gave our Personnel Department the names of three potential candidates. I also informed Mr. Lombardi about the results of my prescreening.

Meanwhile, we hired Wilfredo, who was Puerto Rican, giving him a desk next to Herb's. Wilfredo's task was to help Herb with the heavy mail for the library and chambers and to assist Ella with the filing of cataloging cards after new publications that I ordered were coming in.

Subsequently, I participated in the committee to interview the three candidates for Myrna's position. When a member of the committee asked Anna, who had been my favorite candidate, "If there was an employee conflict in your team, how would you handle that?" her answer was, "I would express my personal opinion about that, but I would go by whatever decision my boss reached about handling the situation." I think that answer tilted the balance in her favor. It apparently convinced Mr. Lombardi too that she was the right candidate. Anna started on the job on August 1, capping my efforts to fulfill my vision of reorganizing the library.

Before I departed on my next vacation, I gathered the entire team in my office to assign tasks during my absence. When I asked Ella to help Anna with the OCLC cataloging program, she agreed.

* * *

On a personal level, there were a few events worth mentioning, such as the baptizing of the two daughters of our friend Nicky Alimănişteanu. For the ceremony, Nicky selected me—together with Mica and Ahmed Ertegün and his brother Alexandru—to act as godparents. Mica had married Ahmet, as previously mentioned, who was the son of the Turkish ambassador in Washington, DC. After their marriage, Mica started an interior design company while Ahmet built his Atlantic Records empire, best known for its numerous recordings of rhythm and blues, rock 'n' roll, jazz, and hip-hop. He launched the Rolling Stones, Ray Charles, and many others.

On August 6, we flew to Munich, where we took care of some maintenance payments for Aimee's tomb. From Munich we drove to Badhoffgastein. Lotte, the manager, welcomed us, and we were soon joined by Rhoda and Rudy Boyko. As in the past, we enjoyed each other's company. From Badhoffgastein we drove to Frankfurt-am-Main, making one stopover in Amberg to visit Johann and Dorlee Schobel, the former administrator of my mother's estate at Radomir.

We visited Frankfurt, the city hall complex referred to as the Römer and the impressive cathedral (Dom), a sight no tourist can miss since its ninety-five-meter-high tower can be seen from far away. Among all the tourist attractions we visited, we were very impressed with the old Römerberg square lined with historical timber-framed buildings. The houses had been faithfully reconstructed according to the original plans, as if the dreadful night of bombing in March 1944 had never taken place.

Then we headed to the old, picturesque university town of Heidelberg. From there we drove to Stuttgart, where we met with Liky and Mitzy and her daughters, who had managed to leave Romania. While in Stuttgart we also met with my old friend Viorica and her husband, Radu Negru, who had escaped from Romania and come to see us. From Stuttgart we went to Paris to see my aunt Tancy, who was now in an assisted-living house, which the French call *maison de retraite*. Over there, she had her own studio apartment but took her meals in a common cafeteria. We returned to New York at the beginning of September.

* * *

Back in the office, though I wish it had been otherwise, I found that Ella had again been a troublemaker. She was supposed to mentor Anna and train her in the cataloguing business, but instead, as Anna complained to me, Ella was arrogant and unwilling to share her knowledge. Mary, who was just substituting for me, had not wanted to interfere. I called Ella to my office to get an explanation, but rather than explain, she told me she knew exactly why I had hired Anna—namely because I was planning to fire her. I decided to make her feel good by pointing out that her work was important and necessary for our success and that only as a team could we achieve our goal of putting the library on a sound basis. At the same time, as I had done many times in the past, I drew her attention to the air of arrogance that she assumed, pointing out that she must tone it down.

As what happened every year, the court organized a festive Christmas party to which all the judges and court employees were invited. During the Christmas season, I would find greeting cards on my desk both from members of my team and from many of the judges. This year, too, the chief judge sent me and my staff a greeting card that read, "Dear Simone, personally, and on behalf of all the judges of the court, it is with sincere pleasure that I express to each of you our best wishes for a joyous holiday season and a Happy New Year. It is also with great pleasure that I express our gratitude for your diligence and cooperation and your many contributions on behalf of this court. It is my hope, and that of my colleagues, that this New Year will bring many blessings and happiness to you and your families. With very good wishes, Edward D. Re, Chief Judge."

At home, we also celebrated Christmas Eve with Sorin, Tita, and a couple of friends, spending New Year's Eve with Van and Pat.

1989–1991

During the late spring of 1989, we were deeply saddened by the news that my aunt Tancy suddenly passed away on May 30. My cousin and her nephew, Matei Mirica, was not very close to my aunt; therefore, I was relieved that his former wife, Gaby, had been willing to take care of all the funeral arrangements prior to my arrival. Rudi and I flew to Paris without my mother because attending her sister's funeral was too emotional for her.

* * *

When I returned from Paris, I had to shake off my sadness and return immediately to my office obligations. Luckily, I had the full support of Mr. Lombardi, who turned out to be an excellent leader. He was rather demanding but very fair. Though very much in control, he was, at the same time, willing to delegate and to give a lot of autonomy to department heads. He never neglected to thank people for a job well done.

At the beginning of March 1989, I had sent him my second progress report detailing the goals I set for the library reorganization back in 1987 when I was hired, mentioning that we were right on target for fulfilling those goals.

As a result, Mr. Lombardi decided in October that the library should receive a Special Achievement Award with the name of each employee written in calligraphy. The award was nicely framed, and we hung it on a wall of our beautiful and spacious library hall. After the award was mentioned in the AALL review, we received many letters of congratulations from our professional peers. But what I liked most was a yellow sticker on the copy of Mr. Lombardi's recommendation, saying, "Simone, thank you. With God's will and other facts. Joe." That gave me more satisfaction than the formal notes or letters.

Finally, in March 1990, I sent Mr. Lombardi the last report informing him that the entire library reorganization had been completed as planned three years previously. However, we remained on a roll, pushing the library into the electronic era, and as usual, our efforts did not go unnoticed by him. In the two consecutive years that followed, we received another two achievement awards that we carefully hung next to the others. I think that not only my weekly meetings with my team had a lot to do with those achievements but also while being demanding on others, I was equally demanding on myself, which earned my people's respect and trust.

My entire career in the United States is clear proof that hard work and dedication are rewarded, and my experience at the court library was no exception. In March 1990, Mr. Lombardi wrote a memo to the chief judge recommending to award me "a quality step increase" ahead of term, which brought about an increase in my annual salary. When the award was publicized in the news bulletin of the Association of Legal Librarians, a lot of people I knew—as well as colleagues from previous jobs—called to congratulate me. It was especially Mr. Lombardi, one of the good people, who helped me overcome the problems I had found in the library when I started in 1987.

* * *

Because of my busy schedule at the library, I skipped the 1989 AALL Convention, but in 1990 I attended the convention, which was held in June in Minneapolis, Minnesota. There, I participated by giving a lecture on "US–Canada Free Trade Agreement: A Comprehensive Overview." The following year, I attended the convention again, this time in New Orleans. I took Rudi along because neither of us had been to New Orleans before and because we liked jazz. At that convention, I had a communication on the new Romanian trade legislation and took part in a seminar on the new trade legislations of East European countries. (Due to the end of the Cold War, new legislation was intended, but unfortunately it was never enacted because there was actually a change for the worse in the government in Bucharest; there the neocommunist took over the power, calling themselves democrats.) My friend Blanka also attended the convention, and she too had brought along her husband, Svatia. One evening, the four of us went to a restaurant with live jazz music in the French Quarter.

* * *

On another topic, the Romanian communist authorities finally approved the application that our nephew Dan and his wife, Dana, had made to immigrate to Israel. As we knew their intention to settle in the USA, we bought plane tickets for them to fly from Tel-Aviv to Vienna, where they would apply for an American refugee visa. Before their departure date, I had the brilliant idea of calling my friend Ingrid Herrmann in Vienna. I gave her the flight information and asked whether she could go to the airport to meet Dan and Dana. She did even more than what I had dared to ask her. She succeeded in contacting them in the Vienna airport, and through her they were able to get in touch with the UN Committee for Refugees. The committee provided Dan and Dana temporary accommodation for a few days, which was entirely due to the intervention of Gerold, Ingrid's husband, a UNO employee. Immediately, Rudi took the first flight to Vienna, met them at the hotel, and drove them to Treisskirche, where there was a triage camp for refugees. There, Dan and Dana were given refugee status in Austria.

Unfortunately, we could not help them come to the States because they were not first-degree relatives. They settled in Austria and eventually, after ten years, became Austrian citizens. Their two boys were both born in that country.

*　*　*

For our vacation we decided to go to Spain. Our first stop was Madrid. We visited all major tourist sites—such as the Royal Palace, Plaza Mayor, and the Reina Sofia Modern Art Gallery—but the highlight of our visit was the Prado Museum. Of course, this time we no longer ventured to any bullfights, although they say that the Ventas Arena—with a capacity of twenty-five thousand spectators—would have been worth seeing.

From Madrid we drove to Toledo, where it was necessary for us to walk up the hill to the town center, as the narrow and winding streets of this mediaeval little town were designed for donkey transportation, not cars. In the heart of the city is Toledo's cathedral, a place of great artistic achievement housing a magnificent collection of works by such artists as Goya, Raphael, and local hero El Greco.

In the Jewish quarter of town, there is an El Greco art gallery housed in the former home of this famous artist who lived and worked in Toledo. The streets of Toledo are very lively. Lots of little stores sell the famous Toledo swords and a range of other gifts that include anything having to do with Don Quixote and El Greco. These stores also offer Spanish shawls, lace, local produce and cheeses, painted tiles, walking sticks, knives—you name it.

From Toledo we headed to Cordoba. Arriving after 7:30 p.m., we were hungry and went straight to a restaurant. Arriving there, we found we were the only customers. It was not until we finished eating and were ready to leave that the restaurant started to fill with people. Among the many things to do in Cordoba is a visit to the mosque. The Arab influence can be seen in much of the architecture of this town that, after the Roman times, became the capital of the Islamic Emirate and then the Islamic Caliphate of Córdoba, which stretched over most of the Iberic Peninsula.

After traveling south to Sevilla, we then went on to Grenada, heading straight for the Alhambra Islamic Palace. The vast palace, fortress, and garden complex were all built for the last Muslim emirs in Spain. The Moors had planted the park with roses, oranges, and myrtles, enhanced by the sound of running water from several fountains and cascades. We spent almost the entire day there. I still remember the name of our very well-informed guide, Señor Pepe, who gave us a detailed history of the place.

The last stop on our Spanish tour was Marbella, on the Costa del Sol in the south of Spain, close to Gibraltar. We checked in at the beach-side Marbella Club Hotel, owned by Count Rudolf "Rudi" von Schonburg. Given the first name of the owner, my husband Rudi felt quite at home there.

We flew back to New York from the Marbella International Airport. Shortly after our return, we received a visit from Ioana Mirica, Liky's daughter, who visited with us in Avalon with all our friends. Later, with Rudi, we took a trip to Hilton Head Island near Savannah, Georgia. The island is a beautiful vacation spot with condominiums, hotels, restaurants, and lots of golf courses. There, we visited the place where the movie *Gone with the Wind* was shot.

* * *

I will never forget the weekend of September 16 at the house of our friend Nana Alimăneştianu in Southampton on Long Island. During the weekend, her husband, Mihai—who was in the African state of Chad on a work contract—called to let his wife know that he would be returning home in a few days. Three days later, on September 19, we heard on the evening news that a bomb had exploded on a charter flight operating from Brazzaville, Congo, via Chad, to Paris. The explosion occurred over the Sahara Desert, killing all passengers and crew. Knowing that Mihai was returning home from Chad, we made repeated calls to Nana to find out whether Mihai was on that flight, but the line was always busy. Eventually, we got through, and Nana's youngest son, Aki, answered the phone. He told us that he could not talk because he was expecting a phone call from the State Department. At that moment we realized that Mihai had been on that plane. President George H. Bush sent a team of investigators to the place where the plane went down. The president later announced that the extremist group the Islamic Jihad—a splinter group of Hezbollah of Libya—had claimed responsibility for the attack. After the State Department's confirmation that Mihai was on board that plane, a religious service took place at the Romanian Orthodox Church in Manhattan. Nana and Mica asked me to speak at the service, in remembrance of him. He being our good friend, it was very emotional.

* * *

Every year, as I have mentioned, I made arrangements with our Romanian Orthodox Church in Manhattan to hold a brief memorial service for the repose of the souls of the departed in my family at the end of the regular Sunday mass. I will describe this service, since it has a special meaning for my future activity.

Present at that day's Holy Liturgy was Dr. Ştefan Issărescu, the former husband of Princess Ileana, youngest sister of King Carol II. He approached me at the end of the service with a few customary comforting words and asked whether he could join us at home. Since we had invited a few of our closest friends to come to our apartment after the service for snacks and drinks, I figured I might as well invite him too. Little did I know, at the time, that two short years later Dr. Issărescu would be very much part of my life.

* * *

I will also mention that in the month of November an itinerant retrospective exhibition with works by the Romanian modernist sculptor Constantin Brâncuşi was displayed in Paris, Philadelphia, and New York. Our friends Ahmet and Mica Ertegün sponsored the New York exhibition and made arrangements for works by C. Brâncuşi to be loaned to the exhibition by the Craiova Museum of Art. (Craiova, the city of my childhood vacations and a place close to my heart, is the capital of the Romanian historical region of Oltenia, where Brâncuşi started his career before moving to Paris.)

* * *

On an altogether different note, while I had been struggling to reorganize the library in the last three years, important international events took place, due in great part to Ronald Reagan and Pope John Paul II. The Soviet Empire started to crumble; the Cold War was coming to an end.

Reagan's greatest merit was that he never hesitated to speak his mind. He called the Soviet Union the "Evil Empire;" and in June 1987, he challenged the Soviet leader in front of the West Berlin's Brandenburg Gate (Brandenburger Tor) with the now-famous words, "Mr. Gorbachev, tear down this wall." Reagan also forced the Soviets to abandon their request for the United States to give up their Strategic Defense Initiative (also known as Star Wars).

In Dr. Kissisnger's book *World Order* (page 311, 335), the author mentions that Ronald Reagan saw the Soviet weakness and American superiority…[and] his Cold War strategy was done in an optimistic way…by proscribing offensive systems and keeping defense systems as a hedge against violence. Also, in Dr. Kissisnger's other book *Diplomacy* (pages 765–767, 771–774), I found the following opinions: "He [Reagan] put forward a foreign policy doctrine of great coherence and considerable intellectual power…which demonstrates that a sense of direction and having the strength of one's conviction are the key ingredients of leadership." At the same time, at home, Reagan demonstrated "an uncanny talent for uniting the American people" by rejecting "Carter's guilt complex and promoting the notion that America was the greatest force for peace anywhere in the world."

Reagan promoted a policy of reducing the growth of government spending, reducing the federal income tax, and tightening the money supply in order to reduce inflation. Nevertheless, during his administration, the national debt surpassed one trillion dollars for the first time ever. (By comparison, now, under President Obama, it has reached $18 trillion.)

In his book *Pinheads and Patriots* (pages 84, 151), again Bill O'Reilly notes, "Mr. Reagan spent freely on defense, a strategy that caused the Soviet Union to go bankrupt. He slashed taxes, but the national debt surpassed 1 trillion for the first time ever...When Reagan left office in 1988, more Americans were working than at any other time."

And as a direct result of Reagan's foreign and defense policies, in 1989 the Berlin Wall fell, producing a domino effect that allowed the countries in Eastern and Central Europe to regain their independence one by one. These were events I never thought I would witness in my lifetime. Also, the Soviets had to withdraw their troops from Afghanistan, and on September 12, 1990, Germany was reunified. That was a glorious foreign policy, achieved without war but just through America's military power and presence.

When Reagan's second term ended, his vice president, George H. Bush, became his successor. The new president had excellent credentials, among them, that he was former director of the Central Intelligence Agency (CIA).

George H. Bush was undoubtedly a good man and a patriot, but unfortunately he seemed soft in trusting Gorbachev's reforms. The period that followed was one of chaotic transition as President Bush tried to accommodate the former Soviet Union in the world community.

He had the utopian vision that a new democratic Russia would emerge after the collapse of the Soviet Union, and he naively believed that, with the liberation of the former Soviet satellite states, communism would be on its way out.

Enter Nixon with an opposite opinion. In *The Presidents Club* (2012, pages 383–389, 391, 413), Nancy Gibbs and Michael Duffy write that while "President Bush was ignoring him…in 1991, Nixon had gone to Europe to check on M. Gorbachev's economic and political reforms. [Nixon found that they were] moving back wars and the Soviet Union [was] beyond salvation…He believed that it was time for H. Bush to understand that…and was astounded by Bush's lack of vigorous leadership (on this matter)."

The problem was that when the Cold War ended, it had not defeated communism in the same sense that Nazism had been defeated during WWII. Therefore, the former Soviet and satellite countries' bureaucrats remained in power under the name of "democrats" while former secret police officers reemerged and grabbed economic and political power. From among their ranks, a powerful and corrupt rich oligarchy emerged to control politics, business, and the media. This is why the East European countries, twenty-five years after the Cold War, still have not been able to revamp their economies to join the Western economic system. Besides, a new kind of despotism would develop in Vladimir Putin's Russia.

David Funderburk, the US ambassador to Romania, experienced directly the unfolding of harsh communist years from 1981–1985. In his book *Betrayal of America* (pages 29, 67–68, 70–72, 93), he addresses George H. Bush's policy of appeasement and compromise toward the communist regimes. Thus, in China, Bush rejected the use of sanctions, brushing aside human freedom as related to the Tiananmen Square massacre. In Russia, he granted trade benefits, recommending the "most favored nation" clause to help Gorbachev's *perestroika*, a fake type of communist.

I believe that it would have helped if President H. Bush had granted a conditional clause, as related to some internal reforms for democratic institutions and a market economy. However, granting an unconditional clause, to Russia or to the former satellite countries, that did not promote the expected real reforms.

Moreover, David Funderburk does not overlook that "on September 11, 1990, Bush addressed the Congress, presenting his vision of the formation of a New World Order, where East and West would cooperate freely, governed by the rule of law, with the USA and USSR being called upon to solve regional conflicts." The author believed that "the new global vision of the New World Order meant the end of American sovereignty" (pages 110–113).

As a result, later the neocommunists used this new global vision of the New World Order to "reinforce the inequities of the capitalist system they claimed to have overthrown," as Peter Georgescu remarked in his book *Constant Choices* (2013, page 86).

Personally, I think that Jeane Kirkpatrick would have been a stronger leader. She would have had an eye on the transformation of the Evil Empire with its satellites, and to maintain America's superiority, she would not have reduced the military budget the way George H. Bush did.

* * *

After the Cold War, with vivid interest, I followed the events in December 1989 in Romania. To understand what happened, I will have to distinguished between two real facts: a palace coup and a concomitant spontaneous popular street revolution. The palace coup was well planned in advance under Gorbachev's influence, resulting in the overthrow of the tyrant dictator Nicolae Ceauşescu, who was ultimately executed together with his wife on Christmas Day 1989, following a show trial. The spontaneous popular street revolution started with a series of riots, which was immediately hijacked by the orders of the members participating in the palace coup, namely the old communist *nomenclature* led by Ion Iliescu, Gorbachev's friend, together with the secret police, turning into *revolutionaries* overnight. They penetrated the new government structures and prevented the instauration of a real Western-type democracy. Then over one thousand young people, fighting for liberty, died in the wake of the revolution, and hundreds more died after the seizure of power by the new political structure.

Because all American TV channels had live transmission of the street fighting of late December 1989, I could see what was happening. I observed how the so-called *terrorists* (who were in fact members of the secret police) were indiscriminately shooting at the protesters. To this day, nobody has been convicted for those killings. I am still waiting!

Immediately, the neocommunist political organization, being called the National Salvation Front, seized power, replacing the outlawed communist party. The Front became the governing body in the first weeks of the revolution and subsequently became a political party, winning the 1990 election under the leadership of then-president Ion Iliescu, as I mentioned, Gorbachev's protégé. Understandably, Iliescu was not interested in rapid reforms that would have led to the creation of democratic institutions and a viable market economy, but tried to follow Gorbachev's *perestroika*.

Unfortunately, then, the former democratic traditional parties reemerging after forty-five years did not get any Western help or recognition. Instead, George H. Bush helped the neocommunist government by recommending the grant of the "most favored nation" clause.

* * *

The negative developments in Romania energized the Romanian exiles abroad to try to do something against the new neocommunist politicians. These changes affected my life personally.

In January 1990, another chapter of my activities started when Rudi and I received a phone call from our friend Cristine Valmy. She invited Rudi and me to come to her Manhattan apartment on January 22 to see what we could do to help Romania. Rudi and I accepted the invitation and found out that she had invited a handful of other mutual friends. She told us she had the idea of setting up an American-Romanian Committee (ARC) to help post-revolutionary Romania. Reflecting on the origins of the evil that had changed my life, I thought about my experience in Romania. That reemerged as a reminder of all that we had suffered. Therefore, Rudi and I agreed to join that committee and, in the spirit of anticommunism, pledged our help.

At that moment, I did not fully realize the extent of the activities that I was going to undertake—first between 1990 and 1998 in New York, when I lobbied in Congress for Romania, and subsequently between 1998 and 2000, when I served as an adviser to the Romanian president in Bucharest.

When I joined the committee, I was counting on the fact that I had access to a lot of information at the library where, every day, we received the *Congressional Record* and the *Federal Register*. It was part of my job at the court to scan those publications anyway, and in the process I could find out about the activities of the senators and House representatives regarding the East European countries. In our first meeting with Cristine, she was elected president of the committee, I was elected vice president, and Rudi became treasurer. Finally, we put together the bylaws of the committee.

As a federal employee, I thought it was appropriate to inform my boss about my work within the ARC. Mr. Lombardi advised me to write a letter to the Administrative Office of the United States Courts and ask whether there was any conflict of interest between holding my position with the court and serving as an ARC member. I received a reply specifying that "nothing in the materials you provided about the committee would appear to present a conflict with your employment by the court. I am not aware of any limitation on your association with this organization. M. J. Holmes, Assistant General Counsel." I gave Mr. Lombardi a copy of Mr. Holmes's letter, and from that point on I knew I could use my free time without restriction contributing to the work of the committee.

Rudi and I enjoyed our work within the committee and religiously attended all their meetings, but we had at one point divergent points of view: the issue was whether Romania should be granted "most favored nation" status by American authorities. Rudi and I were against the "most favored nation" clause, thinking that it would support Romania's neocommunist government that enjoyed Moscow's blessing. After a while, we withdrew from the ARC.

However, I was determined to continue my work in the direction of helping Romania. I got the idea to approach Dr. Ştefan Issărescu and suggest that together we should organize a committee. Toward the end of April 1991, we established the new political committee called the Ad Hoc Committee for the Organization of Romanian Democracy, with a constitution and bylaws. We were registered as a non-for-profit organization with the acronym ACORD.

The aim of the committee was to lobby Congress for Romania's transformation—after 1989 at the end of the Cold War—from a closed, totalitarian regime into an open society with a market economy. At the time, I was aware that Ion Iliescu, the newly Romanian president, a former Moscow-educated communist and Gorbachev's friend, lacked the necessary knowledge and mentality for a swift transition. Therefore, it seemed important for us to lobby to help promote institutional reforms, which Iliescu tried to obstruct. (The cosmetic reforms that he did propose were similar to those promoted by Gorbachev as part of his *perestroika* doctrine.)

Regarding the lobbying activity, ACORD sent many memos to the United States Congress and to the White House with background information about property rights that had been abusively nationalized starting in 1945. Our memos urged that those properties should be returned to their former owners and recounted the history related to the seizure of territories by the Soviet Union. The substance of ACORD's lobbying proved to be correct. The negative results of Iliescu's neocommunist regime—opposing liberalization of the economy toward a free market—can be seen even after twenty-five years. His leadership provided a favorable environment for corrupt, greedy politicians to enrich themselves—a practice which continued uninterrupted until 2014–2015 (when, finally, the judiciary power in Romania started to act against corruption).

Since the ACORD always provided reliable information, we earned a good reputation and the trust of many congressmen, who followed up most of our requests by proposing positive resolutions. Senators Jesse Helms, Dennis DeConcini, and Alfonse d'Amato—as well as Representatives Christopher Smith, Steny Hoyer, Frank Wolf, and David Funderburk—were among those who were most responsive. However, as I have said, I was disappointed when President George H. Bush signed the law granting Romania the "most favored nation" status with no preconditions. I regarded this as a favor to the neocommunist government rather than Romania's population. Preconditions would have forced the government to implement real reforms.

My activities within ACORD definitely changed my daily schedule, because now I was using almost every single moment of my free time writing memos addressed to different authorities. Eventually, Rudi bought me a personal computer so that, in the evenings, I could type the draft memos. (The computer at the office was federal property that I could not use for personal purposes.) After we had agreed on the text, I would give Rudi the master memo for duplication in his office; from there, he mailed the letters to congressional members or to the White House. That was my life while lobbying for Romania. I did it with Rudi's unwavering support and precious help.

Moreover, working for ACORD, I felt I could somehow take revenge to compensate for my former painful communist experiences. My desire to react now had no boundaries, and the commitment grew even bigger over the years. I was happy to give all my heart for this cause. Also, it occurred to me that maybe fate had not allowed me to leave Romania in the 1940s, wanting to give me, later in life, a mission to vindicate the past. This activity for ACORD became part of my life, and I would be driven to continue that work on a daily basis for years to come. I found my political purpose through ACORD (which is why I have written about it here in some depth).

* * *

For our summer vacation, this time we flew to Austria to visit our nephew Dan and his wife, Dana, who had asked me to be the godmother of their first son, the sweet Kevin Alexander. A local Christian Orthodox priest conducted the baptism ceremony in the open air. Besides the baby's parents, and Rudi and I, the only others present were our friends Ingrid, Gerold, and Christian Herrmann, who had been instrumental in helping Dan and Dana settle in Austria. My cousin Cristina Matei also came from Romania to see us. From the town of Kapfenberg where Dan and Dana lived, we traveled to the town of Graz, then continued to Vienna, where we spent a few pleasant days with the Herrmanns.

1992–1996

After we finished reorganization of the library in 1990, the routine workload was much more manageable, with every team member doing their assigned work. Of course, one of our responsibilities was to keep up with the latest technology, particularly adopting software that could assist us. I personally assumed a number of responsibilities, such as compiling bibliographies and verifying the documents of a host of events, including the United States–Canada Trade Agreement and the Punta del Este Conference (held in Uruguay under the auspices of the World Trade Organization). In 1993, I once again attended the annual AALL Convention held in Boston. As part of the program "How to Find the Law," focusing on new legislations in the East European countries, I did my part to provide information about the new Romanian laws.

All my annual performance reports from 1992 to 1995 were outstanding. Of course, that gave me a lot of satisfaction; but, again, I mention that even more valuable were the brief notes that Mr. Lombardi would write on the yellow stickers that he attached to reports he sent to me to sign. Typically, the notes said things such as, "Simone, thank you for another very good year. May there be many more…Pls. sign and send. Joe" On another one he attached to my 1994 report, he wrote, "Simone, thank you for another 'above and beyond' year. More challenges coming in 1995. Please sign. Joe."

I always admired and respected Mr. Lombardi because I thought he was a demanding but rational man who could be very friendly and understanding. That is why I have treasured all those little notes, which I kept in my file.

* * *

Starting in 1992 Mancy's health started to decline. The doctor said that her liver was enlarged. That was to be expected in view of the kind of food she had been forced to eat during her years in prison. She was admitted to a hospital for tests, and the doctor told us she needed permanent medical supervision. The hospital social worker gave us a list of recommended nursing homes, and we selected one closest to our house. That necessitated another change in our daily schedule. Now, in addition to my job, my responsibilities within ACORD, and the daily visits to the gym, we were going to see my mother every evening. Usually, she would not touch dinner until we (or, in our absence, Lydia Maghici) were with her. Returning home late in the evening, I would finally start doing the work at hand for ACORD or take care of other personal tasks such as writing the occasional articles that I was contributing to a Romanian weekly magazine.

*　*　*

In 1992 we went on a vacation to Greece. We flew to Athens, where we spent a few days visiting the city and the Acropolis. We also made a few one-day trips outside Athens, to Cape Sounion to visit the temple of Poseidon, and took a bus trip to Delphi.

From Athens we flew to the island of Crete. There we hooked up with our friend Chet, coming from London. We visited the capital of Crete, Knossos, the Saint Nicholas Church, and the pristine island of Iraklia. Next we visited the island of Santorini, the pearl of the Greek archipelago, known for its white-and-blue churches and houses, some of which are perched on the top of high cliffs and offer gorgeous views. Our next stop was Mykonos, a little town full of young people—therefore, with a lot of nightlife.

When we returned home, we found Mancy in relatively decent condition, but though we had hoped to take her home, that was still out of question. She had lost a lot of weight, and occasionally one of us had to spoon-feed her in bed. Her condition stabilized for a while, but at the beginning of summer I noticed she was having difficulty breathing. Then one morning in July the nursing home called to let us know she had been transferred to a hospital because her condition had worsened. The doctor told me that water had spread to the lungs, and he asked for my consent for surgery. This was a big risk for a woman who had turned ninety in May, but I decided to take a chance because she was more than uncomfortable, breathing with great difficulty. I could not bear to see her like that!

Incredibly, the three-hour operation was successful. After the anesthesia wore off, she was able to breathe normally, which made me think I had made the right decision. A week later, we took her back to the nursing home, where nobody had expected to see her again. But there, she started to refuse to open her mouth and eat. That lasted for a long while. I was prepared for the worst. Mancy died peacefully on July 18, 1993.

The wake and religious service were held at the Campbell Funeral Home in Manhattan. Among those who came to pay their respects were Her Royal Romanian Highness Princess Maria, two judges from the court, colleagues from NYU and the United Nations, as well as family members and friends.

The morticians at the funeral home did a wonderful job on her, as she looked really beautiful. I almost expected her to wake up, smile, and thank those present who had come to pay their respects and bid her a last farewell. We buried her in the vault that she had selected and bought at Woodbridge Cemetery in New Jersey.

Evidently, Mancy left a vacuum in our lives. She certainly remains in our hearts and minds as we look back at her long life. She had started in an environment of affluence and elegance. Managing the Radomir estate, she had displayed an extraordinary organizational spirit inherited from her grandfather Vasile Mirica. Then she endured incredible misery during thirteen years in thirteen communist political prisons. Finally she ended up in New York, where, as always, she relied on nobody but herself and proudly maintained her independence, both financially and spiritually. May God rest her soul in peace!

* * *

Returning to ACORD's activity, I have to add that besides the lobbying aspects, the committee supported—together with the Romanian community—the wish to reinstall its former monarchy. Our King

238

Michael, exiled in Geneva, was a man who had been respected, and he had been the one in power while the country had democratic institutions and a market economy. (His government was based on the 1923 Constitution, observing the principle of separation of powers in state and the guaranty of property.) Our thinking was that the king's presence would have been a shortcut to getting Romania back on the democratic track. However, the problem was that, after half a century of communism, most of the citizens knew little or nothing about our former monarchy.

Nevertheless, the Romanian community decided to invite the royal family to New York. I was elected to a special committee for that purpose. I did it with Rudi's help, even though he was not part of the committee. The gala event took place at the Waldorf Astoria Hotel, followed by events at other locations, including churches, for a whole week. In the end we considered the royal family's visit a success, which made us feel well rewarded for our effort.

On Easter day in April of 1992, following forty-five years in exile, His Majesty King Michael set foot on Romanian soil for the first time. (I want to give some details here, since the story relates to an event that occurred back in 1977.) The king attended a religious service at a church in downtown Bucharest, where one of the hundreds of thousands of citizens who greeted him was my uncle General Constantin Anton, aged ninety-nine. On that occasion my uncle had the opportunity to personally greet and shake hands with His Majesty. That was the way the prediction that was made back in 1977 by Urania Comăneanu—who had fortune-telling talents—was ultimately fulfilled, but in a different way. It was 1977 when my uncle expressed his hope that the monarchy would be reinstated.

On the same day in New York, King Michael's three daughters—Princesses Margareta, Sofia, and Maria, together with Dr. Ştefan Issărescu—were our guests for dinner. After the extraordinary reception given to King Michael by the population of Bucharest, now we all hoped that a monarchy would indeed be reinstated in Romania. With that hope in mind, ACORD organized both a meeting of the royal family with the Romanian community in 1993 and 1995 at the plaza and at the Waldorf Astoria Hotels.

And with the same hope in our hearts, in August 1992 we went to Washington, DC, to greet the delegation of the Romanian Democratic Convention (CDR). This was an electoral alliance of several political parties that seemed to be positioned to win the presidential election and uproot the leftist president Ion Iliescu. However, as it turned out, to our disappointment, President Iliescu was reelected for another four-year term.

* * *

During that summer of 1993, for our vacation, we went with Chet to Austria, in Salzburg, then spent a few nights in Badgastein, followed by Graz. Here we visited again Dan, Dana, and their adorable son Kevin. From Austria we went to the Czech Republic and the city of Prague, nicely renovated after the end of the communist era. We also went to the Karlovy Vary, known also as Carlsbad, where my father and Mancy had stayed when my father attended a penal law conference. In Carlsbad we saw a Russian Orthodox church and the statue of Karl Marx that had not yet been removed (even after their "velvet revolution").

* * *

I cannot omit mentioning my encounter with Lady Margaret Thatcher, which occurred soon after we were back in New York. It occurred when I attended a dinner at the Waldorf Astoria Hotel, hosted by the Legal Center for the Public Interest, in honor of Margaret Thatcher, Great Britain's prime minister, who was to make the speech and then take a few questions from the audience. As I was frustrated with the situation in post-revolution Romania, I stood up and asked her whether, at that time, her attitude toward Romania was any different from that of Winston Churchill. (Back in 1944, he had granted Stalin 90 percent influence over Romania in exchange for Britain's 90 percent influence over Greece.) Mrs. Thatcher did not seem to like my question. Visibly irked, she answered that from a recent meeting with Romania's ambassador Mircea Malița, she understood that things were quite well in Romania. I shook my head, betraying my skepticism. Visibly displeased, she said, "If you disagree with my answer, feel free to write to me," and she moved on to another subject.

I did write her a letter with a comprehensive account of the unsatisfactory state of things in Romania under the regime of the neocommunist president Ion Iliescu. Later, on October 6, 1993, I received a letter from the House of Lords, signed by Clare Lowtherde, informing me that Lady Thatcher appreciated that I had taken the trouble to give her an account of what was going on in Romania, but for the time being she was unable to reply to me personally because she was busy launching the first volume of her memoirs. Well, at least I tried. While she could not deny what was going on in Romania, I hoped she would pay closer attention to what was going on in that part of the world.

*　*　*

Though Romania was always on my mind, I was equally concerned with events at home, where in 1994 Bill Clinton was elected as the forty-second president of the United States, former governor of Arkansas, and described as a "new Democrat."

Of course, I paid close attention to the Clinton presidency because it was during his two terms I hoped that Romania would make the long-overdue leap from communism to democracy and ensure the nation's security from Russian expansionist policies. Clinton appealed to Americans because his campaign focused on domestic policy as opposed to George H. Bush's mostly foreign-policy approach.

But as soon as Bill Clinton became president, I was disappointed to hear about all kinds of scandals related to him and his wife, Hillary Clinton. First was the Whitewater Development Corporation real estate investments scandal involving their associates Jim and Susan McDougal. Also, there was the Travelgate scandal, in May 1993, when seven employees of the White House Travel Office were fired.

Then it was revealed that Bill Clinton had extramarital affairs with Gennifer Flowers and Paula Jones. Subsequently, on July 20, 1993, Deputy White House Counsel Vincent Foster committed suicide under very suspicious circumstances. His death was ruled a suicide but remains a subject of conspiracy theories. But it was the sexual relationship between Bill Clinton and the twenty-two-year-old White House intern Monica Lewinsky that made most waves. I recall the TV newscasts referring to the scandal, which eventually led to the impeachment of President Clinton by the US House of Representatives (though he was eventually acquitted of all charges of perjury and obstruction of justice).

About this scandal, Bill O'Reilly, in *A Bold Fresh Piece of Humanity* (page 199), observes that "The whole sordid mess seriously damaged the country, but few actually realized what was really going on. While we Americans were wallowing in voyeurism, al Qaeda was killing people overseas and planning greater massacres."

Part of Clinton's domestic policy had to do with his administration's relation to the Association of Community Organizations for Reform Now (ACORN). I will dwell on it since it will prove to have a roll in American politics. Thus, ACORN's background started with the 1960's New Left as explained by S. Kurtz in his book *The Radical-in-Chief Barak Obama and the Untold Story of American Socialism* (pages 31, 39. 60, 131, 197–198). In a nutshell, after the collapse of the SDS (Students for a Democratic Society, which I encountered at Columbia University), that organization was absorbed in 1970 by the New American Movement (NAM) and in 1982 merged with Harrington's DSOC to form the new Harrington-led Democratic Socialists of America (DSA). Harrington's overall strategy was to force a "realignment" by pulling the Democratic Party sharply to the left when most DSAers were committed to electoral politics within the Democratic Party. As S. Kurtz describes (in pages 161–162), Volunteers in Service of America (VISTA) was captured by the left under President Carter. (The leftists collapsed under Ronald Reagan, breaking its networks.) However, later they resurfaced again during President Clinton's administration, when VISTA grants were directly distributed to various networks, including the Association of Community Organizations for Reform Now (ACORN).

M. Vadum picks up the topic, in *Subversion, Inc.* (pages 183–184, 188), informing us that in 1993 Bill Clinton and ACORN were old friends while he was Arkansas's attorney general and the organization endorsed him when he ran for governor. During his presidency, ACORN used its influence within its administration, based on the 1977 Community Reinvestment Act (passed by President Carter), to meet credit needs of low-income citizens, opening the door to community organizers. The most-ACORN-friendly Clinton administration official was the secretary of Housing and Urban Development, Henry Cisneros, who supported giving unsecured loans to people who had difficulty repaying them. These loans increased considerably from 1992 to 1999; as a result, it is ACORN that contributed to the outburst of the financial crisis in 2008 during the presidency of George W. Bush.

I learned another Clinton issue from Dick Morris and Eileen McGunn's book *Because He Could* (2004, pages 229–230), regarding the Chinese contributing to Bill Clinton's campaign at the same time that the president was approving technology transfers to China. (This was after satellite communication technology had been decontrolled.) Clinton's policy allowed China to purchase sophisticated antijamming and encryption for its military satellite system. That was very troubling, especially given China's record of reselling nuclear and missile information elsewhere.

The good news for Bill Clinton was that in 1996 midterm, Republican Newt Gingrich came on board. Following Gingrich's suggestion, Clinton approved dropping the capital gain taxes, which contributed enormously to both the annual surplus budget and the reduction of the federal debt. In addition, due to the president's reduction of the expenses of a strong military, after his last term came to an end, the US finances were in good shape. This occurred, however, at a time of growing jihadism (which also did continue to grow during George W. Bush's presidency).

* * *

In connection with Clinton's foreign policy, it was no surprise that as former governor he did not have much experience in this matter. From *The Presidents Club* (pages 7, 10, 416–419, 410, 421) I found out that "Clinton came to see how…he could use former president's experience as an arm of his foreign policy. Therefore, he found in

Nixon a welcome tutor and a helpful confessor." Nixon was also in touch with "Strobe Talbott, Clinton's new point man on the former Soviet Union…, Nixon told him he intended to visit Russia and Talbott told Nixon…that the administration supported his upcoming trip…Then Nixon made it clear he was keen to help the Yeltsin reformers." On his return from Moscow, Nixon and Clinton "discussed Russia and the Chinese economy as well as defense spending at home…Clinton genuinely appreciated Nixon's help. After Nixon died Clinton said…'I wish I could pick up the phone and ask him what he thinks we ought to do about this' [or that]."

Former President Richard Nixon died on April 22, 1994. Four living presidents—Ford, Carter, Reagan, and George H. Bush—attended his funeral. They expressed words of appreciation for his foreign policies. Nixon had changed the "containment" foreign policy concept with "détente and linkage" as a procedure to bring home the POWs from the long-lasting Vietnam War. After Watergate, Nixon wrote many books and shared his anticommunist views with future presidents, some having appreciated his political suggestions.

*　*　*

Due to my ACORD activity, Clinton's position toward NATO was for me of special interest because of the lobbying I was doing on behalf of Romania's admission into NATO. Dr. Kissinger, in his book *Diplomacy* (pages 823–825), explains the position of the Central and Eastern European countries after the Cold War: "Without ties to Western Europe and Atlantic institutions the former Soviet satellite states in Central and Eastern Europe would become a no man's land between Germany and Russia." And he referred to President Clinton's position on NATO enlargement and admission, by writing that "President Clinton has used the occasion of a NATO summit in January 1994 to offer an alternative (to NATO membership) calling it 'Partnership for Peace' by inviting all the successor states of the Soviet Union and former Eastern European satellite countries to join what amounts to a vague system of collective security…[by] equating the victims of Soviet and Russian imperialism with its perpetrators…

The 'Partnership for Peace' is not a way station into NATO…but an alternative to it."

In any event, the expectation was that all countries had to abide by NATO and EU's conditions for admission.

However, regarding Romania, President Iliescu's leadership had initially avoided real reforms; unfortunately, President Clinton approved an unconditional "most favored nation" clause, which meant he was not helping to impose institutional reforms or to decrease corruption. Unfortunately, Bill Clinton followed President George H. Bush's policy of appeasement instead of requesting changes.

Here, I cannot omit quoting Adrian Karanycky, who explains very well what happened, in reality, in former satellite states after the Cold War was over because it had had far-reaching consequences for the East and also for the West. Thus, he points out in his article "How the East Was Lost" (published in the *National Review* on June 27, 1994) that "there has been no country in the former Soviet bloc in which ex-Communists have failed to enhance their political influence…They have retained or reasserted power in the face of democratic and anticommunist challenges especially in Moldova, Romania and Ukraine. Yet the startling political comeback…excites little concern in the United States and Western Europe…Communists were lying low over the last two years…now they feel much more self-assured; they are on the offensive."

Then the author analyzes the motives: "First, the West vastly underestimated the psychological damage inflicted by decades of Communist rule that destroyed the ideas of voluntarism, self-help, and cooperation. Second, it is now clear that the old *nomenklatura* never relinquished its influence over politics and economics, especially in the former Soviet Union, through a tightly controlled process of privatization accompanied by rampant corruption, which seemed to discredit capitalism and economic reforms. Thirdly, we underestimated the intense solidarity of ex-Communists."

And he continued, "Moreover, in view of the situation in the former Soviet countries, the U.S. Congress erred when they approved cuts and then the total elimination of the funds available for the *National Endowment for Democracy*. Furthermore, the budgets for

Radio Free Europe, Voice of America, and *Radio Liberty* were also decreased before being cut off altogether."

That well describes the situation in East European countries, including Romania. And in my opinion, those radio stations could have played a very critical part in providing better information to the public and accelerating democratic reforms.

Still about Bill Clinton, from another angle, in 1998 he intended to change the policy toward Iraq bombing Saddam's WMDs capabilities, and later he struggled with jihadism. If Clinton had kept a strong military, maybe this would have spared the United States from facing future terrorism. In *World Order* (page 316), H. Kissinger opines, "Jihadism spread and assaulted Western values particularly those of the United States...Before Clinton's UN speech an international group of extremists, including an American citizen, bombed the World Trade Center in N.Y....[however] the challenge brock into open on September 11, 2001," under President W. Bush's administration.

*   *   *

Going on with my own life, I was very pleased to receive an invitation from the United Nations Office of Legal Affairs to attend the reception in honor of Mr. Carl-August Fleischhauer, who was leaving his prestigious job as undersecretary-general—the chief legal counsel of that office—for another even more prestigious job as judge at the International Court of Justice at the Hague. The reception was held on the top floor of Dag Hammarskjöld Library on January 31, 1994. It was a real pleasure to be able to congratulate him, wish him good luck, and also to have an opportunity to see my former colleagues with whom I had spent eleven very happy years of my life. In fact, the Legal Office continued to invite me to their Christmas party for a few more years until those who knew me also retired.

A happy event! At the beginning of summer, we received the visit from my unforgettable good friend Ioana Crătunescu, now Raush. I was delighted to be with her again for a while, and we made arrangements to see each other during the summer in Europe. Then our nephew Dan, his wife, Dana, and their son Kevin visited us.

After all our guests had left, in the month of July, I attended another AALL Convention in Seattle, Washington, where I made a presentation about the General Agreement on Tariffs and Trade (GATT), as well as the North American Free Trade Agreement (NAFTA), regulating trade relations among the United States, Canada, and Mexico.

That July also marked one year since my mother, Mancy, had left us; we organized a *parastas* in her memory. The following month, on August 4, 1994, our very close friend Sorin Anagnoste died, which filled our hearts with grief. We shall never forget him, and we will treasure memories of our friendship for the rest of our lives. *C'est la vie!*

* * *

In September we left on our annual vacation. That year we flew to Paris from where we traveled to the Loire valley. Then we flew to Venice, where we met with Chet and Ioana Crătunescu-Raush, who came by train from Milan. We spent a wonderful week in Venice enjoying their company. Then Ioana left for Milan while Chet, Rudi, and I continued our trip to Vicenza, Verona, and Padova. Our next stop was Sicily, where we visited the Siracusa coliseum. We returned to Rome for a few days, staying just long enough to refresh our memories about our 1966 experiences there. Finally, we flew home.

* * *

Back in New York we were happy to find out that the Republicans now controlled both the Senate and the House. We were also delighted to find out that David Fundeburk, the former US ambassador to Romania, had been elected as North Carolina's representative in the House. Now I was contented that Romania had finally a voice in Congress, as Fundeburk had firsthand knowledge of how much the people had suffered during Ceausescu's regime and was familiar with the situation in post-revolution Romania during the presidency of Ion Iliescu, an ex-communist.

Due to ACORD's lobbying, some senators and House representatives answered our notifications with statements in the *Congressional Record* or with letters addressed to the Bucharest government (but without real support from President Clinton). Likewise, little, if anything, had been accomplished in Romania, nor in the Republic of Moldova.

A crisis occurred in the Republic of Moldova on May 19, 1992, in the Transnitria region on the left bank of the river Nistru or Diester. I mentioned this incident since it is similar to what became an issue of the separatists in 2014 in Eastern Ukraine.

Thus, the Cossacks started a rebellion meant to force the independence of an unrecognized Transnistrian Republic. That conflict was obviously instigated by the Russians, who were interested in keeping their Fourteenth Army there, despite OCSE's request for its withdrawal.

As a result, ACORD wrote numerous memos to Congress and to President Clinton pointing out that the presence of the Russian Fourteenth Army hundreds of miles from the present Russian boundaries was a security threat for Moldova, Ukraine, and Romania. The involvement of the Soviet Fourteenth Army in Transnistria at that time delayed the admission into NATO of both Moldova and the Ukraine.

Later, when I had an opportunity to talk personally with Senator Dennis DeConcini about Transnistria, he told me that President Clinton ignored this crisis because he was too busy with the war in Bosnia and Kosovo, which also coincided with the Monica Lewinski crisis. The Transnistria crisis has never been resolved even now in 2016.

In fact, today's Russia, under Vladimir Putin, is applying the same policy of aggression, by supporting the pro-Russian rebels in Eastern Ukraine.

Moreover, President Clinton approved again for Romania a permanent status to the "most favored nation" clause, although Senator Alfonse D'Amato and Representatives Cristopher Smith and David Funderburk wanted to renew the clause on a conditional basis until there was tangible progress being made in different areas, especially concerning respect for private property. However, Clinton explained that he took that action "to promote the market economy and the transition to democracy." That was exactly what was not happening in Romania. He disregarded the fact that after WWII, when the USSR disappeared, the communists remained in Russia and in Eastern Europe and wanted American help through MFN status but did not bother to initiate reforms.

* * *

As I have already mentioned, ACORD organized a meeting of the royal family in 1995 with the Romanian community. A special request was made on that occasion: HRH Princess Margareta, King Michael's eldest daughter, asked me if ACORD could contribute to the organization of the marriage of Princess Marie, her sister, in September in New York.

* * *

The year 1995 marked the tenth year since the death of my father, and we decided to commemorate his death with a special memorial service in the Romanian town of Craiova, the cradle of his ancestry. But first we flew to Austria because Dan and Dana had asked us again to serve as godparents at the baptism of their second son. They called him Rudolf Sebastian and immediately nicknamed him Little Rudi to distinguish him from his great-uncle, Big Rudi.

During that visit to Austria, we fulfilled a desire I had had for a long time—to visit the town of Wels, where my longtime governess, Haagi, once lived (about which I wrote a lot in my first volume). We went to the address Kaiser Joseph Plaz 46, an address that I knew by heart. It was composed of a relatively small square, with a little park and a statue of Emperor Franz Joseph in the middle. At number 46 was a big gate leading to an inner courtyard with many doors all around. In the courtyard, an elderly lady asked us whom we were looking for. When I told her we wanted to see where Betty Haager had lived, the lady pointed to one of the doors, adding that Betty had died a few years before at quite an advanced age. The elderly lady was curious to know who we were. When I told her that Mrs. Haager (whom I called Haagi) had been my governess in Romania and that I basically grew up with her, the elderly lady's eyes lit up, and she exclaimed, "Oh my God, you must be Moni," and told me she had heard a lot from Haagi about a little girl with that name. When I confirmed that I was that person indeed, she said that Haagi always mentioned how much she loved me and how difficult it had been for her to part with me. For me those were really heartwarming words, because Haagi was very special to me. From Haagi's house we went to the cemetery of the town of Wels, located Haagi's grave, and put a bouquet of flowers on it.

From Austria we made a detour to Munich to visit Aimée's grave, and then we continued to Stuttgart to see Viorica, Mitzy, and Liky.

Finally, we arrived in Bucharest; from there we traveled to the town of Craiova, where, as planned, we organized the memorial service for my father. We had a lot of help from relatives of people who had worked for us at our former Genune estate. Being in the area, we could not resist the temptation to revisit the places where our family estates had once been.

What did I find? At Mancy's Radomir estate, almost all the buildings had been destroyed (with the exception of a big barn). My maternal grandmother Manini's Bârca estate had been transformed into an agricultural machine station, now abandoned. Of my father's Genune estate, nothing existed anymore: it was just open land under a blue sky.

It was very disheartening to see that everything built by a few generations of hardworking people had been stolen or destroyed. Gone were the stately houses, the beautiful flower gardens and orchards, the vineyards, and of course, the farming equipment. Instead, we found barren fields taken over by weeds, a few grazing grounds, or the rundown structures of the former collective farms coercively created by the communists. In fact, the only thing the communists were able to accomplish in the name of their utopian ideology was to replace prosperity with poverty.

Arriving in Craiova, we visited the local art museum. To our great surprise, there we found a sculpted bust of my mother that had been made in 1940 by a somewhat famous Romanian sculptor, Militza Pătrașcu, a pupil of Constantin Brâncuși. A little metal plaque identified the sculpture as the *Head of Artemis*. (The Greek goddess Artemis was the equivalent of the Roman Diana.) Apparently, the museum had no idea whose bust it actually was, and for lack of a better name, they had called it *Head of Artemis*. When we revisited the museum in 1996, we would find my mother's name, Clemenţa M. Radian, engraved on the little metal plaque under the bust.

Back in Bucharest we went to the Consular Relations Department of the Ministry of Foreign Affairs, where we found that our application to get back our Romanian citizenship had been approved on September 23, 1995.

Also in Bucharest we met with the highly esteemed conservative Romanian politician Corneliu Coposu, who had spent many years in the communist political prisons. I asked Mr. Coposu's opinion about the 1996 presidential elections in Romania, reminding him that ACORD was a pro-monarchy organization. During that meeting, Mr. Coposu told me, "Mrs. Simone, monarchy-backing parties have only a 12 percent chance to win the elections. Instead, you should support Mr. Emil Constantinescu, the candidate of the Romanian Democratic Convention, because, if elected president, he intends to bring back the monarchy." I received the same advice from Ana Blandiana, a poet and former dissident turned politician.

Following their advice, I called Professor Constantinescu, who agreed to see Rudi and me the following day at the headquarters of his Democratic Foundation. During that meeting, Mr. Constantinescu said it would be very useful if we could organize a New York visit for him to meet the Romanian community in New York. We promised to pursue that idea, pending the approval of the other ACORD members who were supporting the monarchy.

Returning to New York, we first informed Dr. Ştefan Issărescu about Professor Constantinescu's request. Dr. Issărescu and the other members were not very happy at all about supporting Constantinescu, although they held Mr. Coposu in high regard and valued his opinions. However, they had to give in since there was no other alternative.

* * *

For the time being, we were very busy organizing the royal wedding for September 16, which turned out to be a success. As a result, the next day Rudi and I were invited to visit the royal family as their way of thanking us for organizing the wedding. It was then when Rudi was asked to be part of the queen's escort, which was due to visit Romania in October. He replied that he would be very honored to join and would come to Bucharest.

Taking advantage of that occasion, and of our return to Romania in October, I had Rudi deliver Newt Gingrich's *Contract with America* to Professor Emil Constantinescu. I suggested that he should adapt it for the campaign. Later, in December, I was very pleasantly surprised when we found out from the Romanian press that Professor Constantinescu had indeed launched his own contract with Romania. I was so excited that I picked up the phone and called Professor Constantinescu to congratulate him. He thanked me and said, "Don't forget that the idea was all yours," adding that he was planning to travel to New York in February 1996.

During the month of December, as in previous years, I attended the court's two Christmas parties and also the party at the UNO, where my former colleagues were kind enough to invite me.

1996

This year was a very eventful one. ACORD prepared for Professor Constantinescu's February trip to the States. He travelled to Washington, DC, where, on ACORD's suggestion and with the approval of the Senate of the University of Bucharest, he granted the diploma and title of doctor honoris causa to David Funderburk, the former US ambassador to Romania. It was also on that occasion that Professor Constantinescu had the opportunity to see Hon. Benjamin Gilman, the senior Republican US representative from New York, who came to the event, giving Professor Constantinescu the opportunity to discuss with him Romania's current situation.

In New York, I was able to arrange, on short notice, a meeting between Professor Emil Constantinescu and Boutros Boutros-Ghali, the UN secretary-general. The following day, we organized a meeting at the Waldorf Astoria Hotel in Manhattan, where the Romanian presidential candidate had a chance to meet and answer questions from members of the Romanian diaspora and the local press. All those present were very pleased with Professor Constantinescu's answers to all questions.

Back in Bucharest, Professor Constantinescu sent a nice thank-you letter by fax and mentioned that, should he be elected president in November, all ACORD members were invited to his inauguration.

* * *

In our turn, we invited David and Betty Funderburk to a reception that ACORD organized in collaboration with the Romanian Doctors' Association in New York to express our gratitude for everything Mr. Funderburk had done for Romania while serving as US ambassador to Romania and as a US representative from North Carolina in Congress.

This was followed, soon after, by an outstanding event. We received an invitation from Her Royal Highness Princess Margareta to attend her wedding to Mr. Radu Duda in Lausanne on September 21, 1996.

* * *

All of a sudden, I was faced with several scheduling conflicts. Together with Chet, we had planned, a long time ago, a trip to the Far East in October. Now that trip was sandwiched between Princess Margareta's wedding and a possible November trip to Bucharest (if our candidate Emil Constantinescu won the presidential elections and we attended his inauguration). To be able to make all those trips, I would need to take at least a four-week leave of absence in addition to the four paid vacation weeks that I was entitled to. As I knew that Mr. Lombardi was planning to retire, I thought it would be wise to approach him right away with my vacation request to avoid seeking the approval for such a long absence from whoever replaced him.

Immediately, I went to his office with my vacation request in hand and explained to him the reasons why I needed to leave the office for such a long time. To my surprise, Mr. Lombardi said that I should address my vacation request to the new clerk of the court, which was exactly what I had wanted to avoid. If my vacation request was rejected, all my plans would be up in the air. I left disappointed.

As I was heading back to my office, all of a sudden I had a brilliant idea. Though I knew the clerk would not approve my vacation time, I realized I did not need his permission to retire. Reaching my desk, I started to type a memo to Joseph Lombardi. The date was August 19, 1996. I wrote that, when he interviewed me for my job back in November 1986, he had told me that, as a precondition my being hired, I had to stay on the job for at least two years. I had more than fulfilled that condition. In fact, I had stayed on the job for nearly ten years, during which time I had accomplished all the goals I set for myself in connection with the library. I had solved the space problem, I had brought all collections up to date, I had automated all manual functions, and I had resolved personnel issues, restoring peace among my team members. All of that had required time and hard work, although (I added) I was well aware that none of my accomplishments would have been possible without his support. I also mentioned that, while his support was critical, I appreciated that he did not micromanage me but, rather, gave me full authority to solve the issues at hand in the best interest of the library. In conclusion, I wrote that I intended to retire on September 30, and since we were both retiring on that date, I wished him all the best for long, happy, and healthy retirement years.

The very next day, Mr. Lombardi replied to my memo with flattering words of appreciation for my work and achievements. In his words, it was "divine intervention" that had sent me here, and in his view I had brought the library from the Middle Ages to the Space Era. In his memo he praised my personal qualities, noting that I had never settled for mediocre results. In conclusion, he wrote, "May God keep you and Rudi in His care and give you good health and happiness during all the years that you have ahead of you. You will be missed."

When my retirement notice became official, the chief judge in action wrote to me the following: "Dear Simone, you always demonstrated a superb knowledge regarding the court's library administration. We were lucky to benefit from your services. I am sorry to hear about you're leaving us, but I am happy that you decided to offer yourself more time for personal enjoyable activities. I wish you many healthy and happy years. God bless you. GC."

* * *

Using the vacation time that was still due to me, Rudi and I soon left for Switzerland to attend Princess Margareta's wedding. On September 19, we boarded a plane to Vienna, where we rented a car and drove on to Versoix, Switzerland. The following day, on September 20, 1996, we went directly to Saint Ghrasim Orthodox Church in Lausanne, where Rudi was to be an usher to the wedding ceremony. About four hundred guests were present, including representatives of most constitutional monarchies in Europe. The religious service was conducted in four languages—Romanian, Greek, English, and French. After the photo session, all guests headed for the reception at the Miles Polo Club. In the evening, there was a champagne banquet at Villa Serena, where we again congratulated the newlyweds. Then we said our good-byes and drove back to Innsbruck, Austria.

We chose to stop at the Ambras Castle and discovered the original portrait of the Romanian king Vlad the Impaler (Vlad Tepeş), also known as Dracula. It was hung in the Armour Hall of the castle. (It is widely assumed that Bram Stoker based his novel *Dracula* upon the historical figure of Vlad Tepeş.) While in Austria, we also spent a few days in Kapfenberg with Dan, Dana, and our lovely godsons Kevin and little Rudi.

* * *

We returned to New York in time to attend the party the court organized on September 30 to celebrate the retirement of Joseph Lombardi and me. In addition to the judges and their assistants—as well as all our coworkers—I also invited my former bosses Professor Julius Marke from NYU and Seymour James from the UNO. There were many speeches, some for Lombardi and some for me. In addition to the speeches made by my boss Lombardi and three other judges, to my surprise Julius Marke and Seymour James also spoke about my participation in their organizations. At the end, in a brief speech, I thanked those present for attending and those who had said nice words of praise about me. I also expressed my gratitude to my adoptive country for the opportunities it offered me to further my education at two of the most prestigious American universities and to have a very rewarding career.

* * *

Looking back, I can see that my years of employment as library director at the United States Court of International Trade (USCIT) were very rewarding. For one thing, as a federal worker, I was fortunate to meet distinguished judges who had been appointed by different American presidents. Then I had earned another ten years of active employment, which would be reflected in my retirement income. Also, my work accomplishments had given me a lot of satisfaction. I had been able to reorganize and modernize the library, bringing it into the electronic age, while dramatically improving the morale and relationships among coworkers. I felt I was, thus, leaving behind a happy group of people, which reflected positively on their work ethics and efficiency.

A lot of credit for what I was able to accomplish certainly goes to my boss Joseph Lombardi, whose management skills were superior. He treated people with a lot of respect, putting a great deal of trust in them and skillfully delegating authority. An efficient problem-solver himself, he also trusted our ability to solve our own problems without endless debates. I will always remember him as a great gentleman and manager.

* * *

October 1, 1996, was the first day in my life (including my childhood) when I was not held to any fixed schedule. Now I was free—able to read, to dedicate more time to the ACORD organization, or to travel. In fact, by October 10 Rudi and I were enjoying that freedom, boarding a plane to Los Angeles, a flight scheduled long before. As usual, we met with our friend Chet and also our friends Patricia and Fred Kuri. With them, we made a trip to Pasadena, where we visited the splendid Huntington Botanical Gardens bequeathed by the railway magnate Henry Edward Huntington. We also saw the Getty Museum, designed by the famous American architect Richard Meier.

From Los Angeles we continued to the Far East, our first stopover being in Singapore. This was followed by a trip to the seaside resort of Bali, Indonesia, and from there on to Bangkok, Thailand. We also flew to Hong Kong. Our last stopover was in the former Portuguese colony of Macao.

* * *

Upon our returning home, the chief judge invited me to his office and handed me a testimonial presented to me by the Administrative Office of the United States, signed by Ralph Mecham, dated September 30, 1996, on the occasion of my retirement, "in recognition of faithful and devoted service to the Federal Judiciary."

Also during that visit, the chief judge asked me who in my opinion was best qualified to fill the position that I had vacated. In an explanatory memo I recommended Anna, whom I thought was best qualified for the job. With that, I fulfilled my last duty to the library. During the years that followed, I would receive many invitations to visit my former workplace, and it was always a pleasure to be there and meet with judges and my old colleagues.

* * *

With more free time at my disposal, I was watching more TV news reports than I had in the past. I was somewhat disappointed with the liberal leaning of the major network stations—ABC, CBS, and especially NBC. In 1980 billionaire Ted Turner founded the CNN cable news channel, which was also biased, as its news presentations were often incomplete and taken out of context. The only conservative voice in the media at the time was Rush Limbaugh's radio talk show in the morning. Rush was very candid and never hesitated to be very blunt about the state of affairs in this country.

Then, in 1996, a miracle happened in the TV world. The Australian billionaire Rupert Murdock founded the cable news channel Fox News and appointed Roger Ailes as its president and CEO. Fox News went on the air in October 1996 with "fair and balanced"

news and commentaries that, for a change, were finally from a patri-
otic and conservative perspective. What a breath of fresh air after the
cable news monopoly of CNN—what Roger Ailes once called the
Clinton News Network. Over the years, Fox News gained an increasingly large audience to become the number one cable news channel
with a much bigger audience than CNN. I am convinced that the
liberal media has a detrimental influence on American public opinion, and in that respect Fox News has fulfilled the critical task of
counterbalancing that influence.

* * *

The other miracle of the year was the election in November 1996 of
Emil Constantinescu as the first democratic president of Romania.
The results of the elections generated hope that the new president would finally push for the real democratic reforms that most
Romanians were hoping for, and which his predecessor, Ion Iliescu,
had failed to deliver. Answering the new president's invitation, several ACORD members, including Dr. Issărescu, myself, and Rudi,
travelled to Bucharest to attend the inauguration ceremonies. As I
listened to the president's inauguration speech, it seemed to me that
it lacked the enthusiasm he had displayed in America. To my surprise
he made only scant references to the fundamental changes he had
promised during his American visit.

I owe my readers a last explanation. While in Bucharest, I met
my friend Ion Lungu (known as Nelu), who was a former colleague
from the last job I held in Romania (which was recommended by
my friend Mario Navarra on a bus). Nelu told me that our former
director from DSAPC, Mr. Octavian Ţurcanu, had heard about my
visit and would very much like to see me. I expressed my doubt that
he would remember me, but Nelu assured me that Mr. Ţurcanu did
remember me, and gave me his phone number. I called. When I told
him who I was, he exclaimed in a very friendly voice, "Ah, Simone,
I am so happy to hear from you, and I would be even happier if we
could see each other after all these years! I can't wait to hear stories
from the time you worked for the UN." I was amazed, and asked
him, "How do you know that I worked for the UNO?" His answer

was, "Of course I knew, because the Ministry of Foreign Affairs asked me to give them a reference about you." On the spot, I accepted his invitation to stop by his house that afternoon. We had a pleasant chat about the not-so-good old days.

Finally, after twenty years I understood the real reason why my employment with the UNO had been delayed for two months. Since I was a naturalized American, the UN Personnel Office had contacted the Romanian Foreign Ministry to ask for references related to my last job in Romania and to find out whether I had defected or left the country legally.

When I left in 1965, I thought that I had cut off all ties to my old communist country. However, as it turned out, the UNO did not hesitate to ask for references from a communist government about an individual (me) who had been dubbed by that government as an "enemy of the people." It seemed incredible that somebody from the communist regime, which I had left behind, turned out to be instrumental in the process of my being hired at the UNO. Thank God he was a decent man who knew everything about my past, including my mother's imprisonment, yet he still gave the UNO good references. God should rest him in peace! He died shortly after we met.

As soon as I arrived in New York, I called Seymour James to share the incredible news with him. He confirmed to me that indeed the UNO policy was not to hire people who had defected from the "communist paradise." Again, that UNO policy seemed quite incredible to me. Recently while I was revising this volume, I called Seymour on the phone to wish him a happy birthday on October 12, 2015. He is now ninety-three and was happy to hear me and that I did not forget him. He also remembered Rudi, wishing him good health.

* * *

While in Bucharest, I contacted the American Bar Association to get information about the Central and East European Legal Initiative (CEELI), which was made up of legal experts from fourteen countries, including Romania. It had been set up to assist local governments with the implementation of the required post-communist legal reforms. Mr. Bosco, who was then head of CEELI, gave me two draft laws in Romanian and told me that he was ready and willing to work with the new Romanian democratic government to speed up the reforms in the nation's legal system. Of course, I was eager to share those documents with the newly elected Romanian president. Therefore, I called his chief of staff and asked whether he could schedule a meeting with the president before my departure from Bucharest.

The surprise came exactly on the day of my departure for New York, when the president's chief of staff told me that the president would like to see me. On my way to the airport, I stopped at the presidential palace. Arriving at the Cotroceni Palace, I found out the reason the president wanted to see me. He told me right away that Romania needed the assistance of ACORD in lobbying the US Congress in support of Romania's admission into NATO within the first "wave." I took that opportunity to tell the president that Romania's admission into NATO was conditional upon real democratic reforms and on progress toward a market economy, which, under the previous president, left a lot to be desired.

It was then that I handed the president the two draft laws given by Mr. Bosco, suggesting that his government could use them as guidelines in the interest of saving time. And, indeed, time was of the essence because the next NATO summit was to start in Madrid on July 1997. That was just six short months away.

After all my years living in the United States, I had a pretty good idea about the dynamics of a market economy and the sanctity of private property. I knew that viable economic development was only possible with minimal government control and with the help of tax incentives that would attract domestic and foreign investors. I also knew that a country with a nonpolitical judiciary was needed, along with a solid middle class that could create small businesses and generate a lot of national wealth.

Also, I knew that all the above desiderata were hard to implement after almost fifty years of totalitarianism, where the existing mentality supported a state-controlled economy. Moreover, there was the fact that while the population had voted overwhelmingly for the president, his government did not hold a majority in parliament. He would have a tough job ahead of him. He needed to be strong to implement a new vision. He also needed an efficient prime minister and competent, convinced advisers who would share his vision of a new democracy and economy.

Furthermore, to move the country in the right direction, he would need to address the population as often as possible in order to keep citizens informed about the reforms that were under way. He would need their support. The positive aspect, I thought, was that over the past half century, the population had become accustomed to having a strong president who imposed his agenda.

Upon departing, Rudi and I wished the president success and hoped he would be as strong as necessary!

After that meeting, we were in a big hurry to catch our 3:30 p.m. flight to New York.

CHAPTER 7

USA-ROMANIA, 1996-2014

After I retired, my ACORD responsibilities still prompted me to keep abreast of international affairs. At center stage was news regarding developments in the Romanian neocommunist government and ongoing analyses of the American foreign and domestic policies. As I have said, communism first opened my eyes to politics, and that became my passion and primary interest.

Soon after I arrived in New York, in accordance with the Romanian president's instructions, I travelled to Washington, DC, to lobby on behalf of Romania. Our objective was to ensure that Romania would gain admission into NATO with the "first wave" of former Soviet Satellites from Central and Eastern Europe that was scheduled for 1997.

With the help of Representative David Funderburk, I was received by Representatives Christopher Smith and Frank Wolf, who were closely monitoring Romania's progress toward democracy. Representative Wolf expressed his view that Romania would not have enough time to implement the comprehensive legal and economic reforms that were required before the 1997 NATO summit in Madrid. In his opinion that goal was unrealistic and underlined the necessity for the president to concentrate his energy pushing for the required reforms, this being the best way to position Romania for the next wave of NATO admissions a year later. In addition, Representative Wolf suggested that one of Romania's priorities must be the restructuring of the former Securitate (the feared communist secret service), which had been only superficially reorganized into the Romanian Information Service (SRI) and a Foreign Information Service (SIE).

I promptly conveyed Representative Frank Wolf's suggestions to the president. I was hoping that one extra year would be enough time for the Romanian government and parliament to meet the conditions required for its NATO admission, and I also saw it as an outstanding way to motivate these institutions to act. I thought that the two draft laws offered by CEELI, which I handed to the president, would be instrumental to speed up the legislative reform process, as well as the cooperation with CEELI for further legislation.

Unfortunately, genuine reforms were not adopted, and most of the old Securitate structures were preserved. Moreover, the actual changes were, for the most part, just cosmetic. As Frank Wolf had predicted, Romania was not admitted to NATO in 1997.

* * *

Meanwhile, in an ACORD meeting I was appointed the president of the organization effective March 1997. I promptly informed both the Romanian royal family and President Emil Constantinescu about my new function within the organization.

After the 1997 NATO summit, I continued to lobby on behalf of Romania by sending out letters and memos to congressional members showing that real reforms had not materialized. It was my hope that Congress would intervene to expedite those reforms.

One such a memo had special significance: ACORD took the initiative of writing a letter to Senator Alfonse D'Amato urgently appealing for his support of fair property legislation. It was obvious that the Romanian Parliament was dragging its feet when it came to adopting satisfactory legislation regarding the return of nationalized private properties to their former owners. In the ACORD letter dated May 14, 1998, I explained in detail how the left wing parties, which have a substantial number of former communist *nomenklatura* members, pushed in parliament for unreasonable tenant rights and rent control. Specifically, they supported the idea of giving tenants ten to fifteen years or even lifetime occupancy rights while imposing severe limitation on the owner's right to rent the property at market value. Without such a change, tenants could pay the same ridiculously low rents that they had previously been paying to the state. In other words, the new owners had to pay property taxes that reflected the market value of their property while being denied the right to charge fair market value rents to cover their tax and maintenance expenses. I urged Senator D'Amato to advise the Romanian authorities to adopt legislation that would be fair both to owners and to their existing tenants.

* * *

President Constantinescu came to New York at the beginning of June 1998 to attend a United Nations special session. During that visit, he also attended a Q&A meeting with the Romanian community in Manhattan's Carnegie Hall, where I was asked to serve as moderator. After the meeting, while I was talking to President Constantinescu, he offered me a position as his chief of staff. I told him I would consider his offer and would inform him about my decision during the summer when I planned to make a trip to Romania.

* * *

Arriving in Bucharest in July, I received an invitation to meet with the president. Before that meeting, I was asked to bring Rudi along, which seemed to me kind of peculiar. When Rudi and I were in the president's office, Constantinescu handed me a letter with the US Congress letterhead and asked me whether I knew who had provided the information included in that letter. As I skimmed through the letter, which was addressed to the president of Romania, I saw that it was signed by Senator Alfonse D'Amato and Representative Christopher Smith, who at the time served as the president and the vice president, respectively, of the Congressional Commission on Cooperation and Security in Europe (CSCE), also known as the 1975 Helsinki Commission (OSCE). I immediately realized that their letter was in response to our (above-mentioned) memo regarding property legislation in Romania. I told the president that ACORD had provided that information to Senator D'Amato. The president folded back the letter and put it in his pocket. His body language somehow betrayed that he was somewhat annoyed with having the Americans lecturing him.

Given that incident, I was surprised that, even so, the president asked me to work for him in some advisory capacity, though not as chief of staff. Moreover, he wanted me to start immediately—the following day, if possible—saying that he would sign an order to that effect. (At that point I understood why he had wanted Rudi to be present at the meeting, as the president wanted us to make an immediate decision.) I was taken aback and told the president that we needed some time in New York to prepare for a longer absence but that we would let him know when we could be available. Constantinescu agreed, and we said good-bye.

*　*　*

Back home, I first reread the letter I sent to Senator D'Amato, being now satisfied that our lobbying had had an impact in Romania while also helping congressional representatives better understand what was really happening over there.

Due to the effect of that ACORD memo, it occurred to me that I should write a book for the Romanian public. I wanted them to know what we had done on behalf of Romania and the Republic of Moldova. As I am a workaholic, I immediately started to get myself organized for this project, which resulted in writing a book entitled *From Exile: Lobbying for Romania in the USA, 1990–1998*, published in Bucharest in 2006. In the book I explained that the goal of the ACORD Committee was to address issues facing post-revolution Romania, where the communist system had collapsed but former communists had remained in power. ACORD's aim was to slough off the legacies of state control to achieve faster economic growth and promote democracy.

I showed ACORD'S lobbying on the following matters:

1. Need to counteract President Ion Iliescu's reluctance to promote real reforms, including restitution of private property and respect for the rule of law
2. Need to expedite those required reforms for Romania's admission into NATO and the EU
3. CSCE's need to put pressure on the Russians to withdraw their troops from the Transnistria region of the former Soviet Republic of Moldova

Also, my book included the responses of the American authorities to our actions. All the lobby activity could have been averted, in part, if the West had not been in a hurry to declare that the Cold War was over and that a New World Order had been achieved. (This illusory belief has helped keep former communists in power to this day.)

In my book I gave details about the three visits of the Romanian royal family to New York (only two of which were organized by ACORD), as well as about the meetings of the presidential candidate Emil Constantinescu with the Romanian Diaspora.

* * *

Throughout my ACORD activity, while I acknowledged with gratitude the enormous help received from US congressmen, I expressed my dissatisfaction with President Bill Clinton's approach in matters that would be, in the future, strategically important in Europe. In spite of many memoranda sent to President Clinton, he ignored the danger posed by a sizable Russian military contingent in the Transnistria region of Moldova, where Russia intended to establish an independent state.

(I would like to note that the 2014–2015 events provoked by the Russian Federation to support the Russian separatist in Eastern Ukraine are similar to the 1992 events in Transnistria. With that situation in mind, I do not think that the Russian Federation will withdraw from Eastern Ukraine, where there have been over six thousand deaths already.)

* * *

While I kept busy with the book writing project, I was torn by the decision to either continue lobbying through ACORD or to work for the Romanian president. In the end, I decided to do the latter on a pro bono basis, because I hoped to make a difference in my native country. However, since I was not on the presidential payroll, they were unable to provide me with housing. For that reason, Rudi and I bought an apartment in Bucharest, moving there in August of 1999.

I shall not go into any detail regarding my eighteen months as a personal advisor to the Romanian presidency. However, I must mention the day of July 17, 2000, when President Emil Constantinescu addressed the nation on TV during the evening primetime making public his decision not to run for reelection. This was unheard of! That announcement occurred just a few days after I came back from my campaigning on his behalf for his second term. It was both a very unexpected and quick decision on his part. Later, he acknowledged the pressure that had been put on him, admitting that members of the Securitate had defeated him! No wonder the former communists and the Securitate remained strong! I think it all goes back to WWII when only Nazi Germany was defeated by war. Communist Russia had not suffered defeat through war. It collapsed economically due also to Ronald Reagan's economic measures. There was never a Nuremberg trial to condemn communism as Nazism had been condemned. Now these were the results!

The president's withdrawal from the election race was a big disappointment for everybody, especially since he made the announcement only three months before the elections, leaving little time for an effective right-of-center campaign.

On July 17, all the hope I had placed on the results of the November 1996 elections melted away like a drop of ice in boiling water. As expected, the left Social Democratic Party took advantage of the situation and again grabbed power, electing Ion Iliescu as president again. With the corrupted former communist *nomenklatura* in power, Romania was deprived of the opportunity to prosper economically, as it had been before 1945, and to be admitted into NATO.

In spite of my disappointment with the president, whom I had previously supported, I thought it was a privilege to work in the Cotroceni presidential palace, a place rich in history that had once been the residence of Prince Ferdinand and Princess Maria (niece of England's Queen Victoria, and who, as queen, was instrumental in creating Great Romania in 1918). In addition, I remain thankful for the friendship shown to me by my former colleagues in the Romanian presidential staff. And in appreciation for my services, in December 2000 President Emil Constantinescu awarded me the medal for the Order of Faithful Service, Captain Grade, for which I am also very grateful.

Despite what I accomplished within ACORD, unfortunately the situation in Romania did not evolve as I had envisaged. But as the renowned French microbiologist Louis Pasteur once said, "Il faut être en droit de se dire: j'ai fait ce que j'ai pu!" which means "I should have the right to tell myself that I did whatever I could," and that gave me satisfaction. With that feeling in my heart, I finished my active work for Romania.

* * *

In January 2001, Rudi and I returned to New York after eighteen months in Bucharest. Soon thereafter, we traveled to Florida to see our dear aunt Ida. It was during that visit that we bought an apartment for ourselves in Palm Beach, Florida. We continued our regular visits to Aunt Ida for the next four years, up to the time of her death in April 2005, when she was almost one hundred years old. To the end, her mind remained sharp. She had always been like a caring mother to us, and we shall always keep her and her family in our minds and hearts with love and gratitude.

Since we kept our apartment in Bucharest, after 2001 we divided our time between Bucharest, New York, and Florida.

* * *

It is in Florida that I had time to read President Constantinescu's book entitled *A Time to Build, A Time to Destroy*. Somewhere in the book, he referred to a private conversation that I had with him in

New York back in 2001. That intrigued me, and I decided to answer. My response, in fact, turned into a book in which I provided an in-depth analysis of the president's entire mandate between 1996 and 2000. Appropriately entitled *A Provoked Confession*, the book was published in Bucharest in 2004.

After that book was published, I resumed writing the one about my activity within ACORD, entitled *From Exile: Lobbying for Romania in the USA between 1990 and 1998*, a project I had put on hold during my time in Bucharest. That book, published in 2006, was the last I wrote documenting Romanian politics.

Unexpectedly, the crowning moment of my lobbying activity through ACORD, and the respective receptions for the royal family, came on June 9, 2008. That was when former Romanian king Michael I personally awarded me the medal for Loyalty as part of a ceremony at the Elisabeta Palace in Bucharest. This reward made me very happy and proud because it was based on hard work done with conviction.

A couple of years later, I embarked upon the writing of the current memoir.

I will say a final word about Romania. Corruption was rampant in post-1990 Romania, and the progress in the fight against corruption mandated by the EU began very slowly. But in 2014, an anticorruption effort was launched with a vengeance. To date, nearly 1,200 public figures have been convicted so far, and likely more are to follow. Romania's business environment rating holds forty-second place out of eighty-two, according to the 2015 *Economist*. I hope that with proper leadership, and with a free-market orientation minus the corruption, the country can again become foremost among welcoming business environments.

Encouraging news came on November 16, 2014, when Mr. Klaus Iohannis, the former mayor of the beautiful city of Sibiu in Southern Transylvania, was elected to be the next president of Romania. He was sworn in on December 21, 2014. He is a totally different breed of politician, one who wants to see Romania rid of corruption. However, until the 2016 parliamentary elections, the president has to deal with a parliamentary majority from the opposition.

* * *

For the American presidential elections in 2000, Rudi and I cast our ballots at the American Embassy in Bucharest in favor to George W. Bush, who became the forty-third president of the United States. President Bush had to face two unusual circumstances: the 9/11 jihadist terrorist attack and the 2008 financial crisis.

Regarding 9/11, H. Kissinger opines in *World Order* (page 316 -317), "Jihadism spread and assaulted Western values particularly those of the United States…[and] the challenge brought into the open with the attacks on September 11, 2001."

On September 11, 2001, Rudi and I were still in Romania. Arriving home at about three o'clock in the afternoon, I turned on the TV set and saw an airplane crashing into one of the World Trade Center buildings. I could not believe my eyes. I thought I was watching a movie until I heard the news reports. This was the infamous day when al-Qaeda launched coordinated attacks in New York City and Washington, DC. The apocalyptic images we saw on TV will forever remain etched in our memories.

Of course, we all waited to see how President Bush would react to the deadliest terrorist attacks on American soil when thousands of people were killed. I felt protected when President Bush signed the Patriot Act to empower law enforcement and intelligence agencies to prevent future attacks on the United States. However, some in the media immediately pointed out that the act was infringing on the civil liberties of the American citizens.

President Bush adopted the doctrine of "preemptive strikes" believing that the United States had the right to act against terrorists and those countries giving aid to terrorist groups before they would attack again. That policy led to both the October 7, 2001, invasion of Afghanistan and the president's decision to deal with Saddam Hussein, who gave aid to terrorist groups. Case in point was Iraq, as pointed out in Bush's book *Decision Points* (pages 228–229) as follows: Saddam "didn't just pursue weapons of mass destruction, but used them…I could only imagine the destruction possible if an enemy dictator passes his WMD to terrorists…that seemed like a frightening real possibility."

The president tried diplomatic measures within the UN Security Council, where Saddam Hussein had already defied sixteen Security Council resolutions and the seventeenth Resolution 1441, on November 8, 2002. In his book about the United Nations, Gabriel Pleşea (in pages 132–135, 148) underlines that Hans Blix, one of the inspectors, had recognized the insufficiency and inconsistency of documentation that Saddam Hussein forwarded to the inspectors; further, on February 6, 2003, Secretary of State Colin Powell had a presentation at the UN General Assembly about satellite images that seemed to indicate WMD movements in Iraq: further, the United States introduced a second resolution on February 24 which was opposed by France and Russia; and, finally, President Bush gave Saddam forty-eight hours to leave Iraq with his sons, which he didn't. It was only then, on March 20, 2003, the Operation Iraqi Freedom began to remove Saddam from power.

The war became a controversial issue over its legality regarding collective security. The United Nations Charter approves the *use of force* for a member state only if it first gets the authorization of the United Nations Security Council. Case in point, the United States had been denied to use force—by France and Russia through their veto power, to advance their own interests. As a result, many scholars supported the idea that the war was illegal.

John Yoo's book *Point of Attack* (2014) deals with this issue, having an opinion related to "reality" (page 78, 80–81). His view point is that "the veto reserved for the United States, Russia, China, France and the UK biases the international system against taking any action" and that "collective security…has become increasingly divorced from the reality of…new international challenges—such as the threat of Jihadism…in an age when rogue states can threaten millions of innocent civilians with instantaneous destruction…It is the international system, including the U.N. Charter, which has to keep up with reality."

Conversely, Ralph Zacklin, my friend and former colleague at the UN Office of Legal Affairs, in his book *The United Nations Secretariat and the Use of Force in a Unipolar World. Power vs. Principles* (2010, pages 157–158), opines that "the combination of an (USA) illegal war and occupation…completely undermined the values of law and justice in the name of which the war had been carried out."

In closing this controversy, Bill O'Reilly, the Fox News commentator, in *A Bold Fresh Piece of Humanity* (2008, pages 194–196), justly considered that "Bush rose to the occasion and was looking out for us by aggressively bringing the fight to our enemies."

With regard to C. Powell's presentation at the United Nations about Saddam Hussein's WMDs, President Bush has been accused of lying about their existence, although Saddam had a long history of a weapon program, demonstrated by the existence of multiple UN resolutions on this matter.

To support the probable existence of those WMDs is Karl Rove's book *Courage and Consequences, My Life as a Conservative in the Fight* (pages 210, 339), where he reproduces the opinion of "General James R. Clapper Jr. that indeed the WMD intelligence might not have been so wrong" and "General Georges Sada, deputy chief of Saddam Hussein's air force, who claimed that Iraq moved weapons of mass destruction into Syria before the war."

However, the most compelling account and a real eye-opener on this subject I found in Defense Secretary Donald Rumsfeld's book *Known and Unknown, A Memoir* (2011, pages 447–448). Here he mentions his own intervention in February 2003, at a National Security Council meeting, when he spoke on Khurmal (a place suspected to hide WMD), saying, "If we were ever going to hit the facility and have a favorable result, we would have to do it at the same time, or preferably just before Powell spoke, since he would be telling the world that we knew about the (location of the) WMD facility… Ironically, had Powell not objected to an attack on the Khurmal site before he gave his presentation to the UN, we might have been able to gather the conclusive evidence of an active WMD facility that he said existed in the UN speech." If Rumsfeld's advice had been followed, most probably the lie/accusation would not have substance.

On the whole, Bill O'Reilly's position in *A Bold Fresh Piece of Humanity* (2008, pages 194–196) was that Collin Powel's presentation on the "WMD intelligence turned out to be wrong, but there is a big difference between a mistake and a lie."

In the end, with additional troops and a new strategy, after the 2007 surge and before President W. Bush left office, Iraq was in an acceptable shape. Then Iraqis were fighting al-Qaeda together with the US Military as Dick and Liz Cheney underscore in their book *Exceptional* (2015, page 112).

Unfortunately, President Obama worked against the US achievements in the area, by ordering the premature withdrawal of the American military. And this was when al-Qaeda's spin-off, ISIS, appeared in the Middle East.

The second important challenge that President Bush had to deal with was the 2008 economic crisis. As I explained in chapter 2, I believe that the roots of this crisis started in the 1960s, with the establishment of the National Welfare Rights Organization, NWRO, by the Marxist theorists Richard Cloward and Frances Fox Piven, who were seeking a socialist transformation of the United States. Further, in chapter 5, I mentioned how ACORN, a community organizer association formed in 1970 by Wade Rathke, favored low-income lending. And, in chapter 6, I pointed out that Henry Cisneros, the secretary of Housing and Urban Development in the Clinton administration, was the most ACORN friendly, when lending had been intensified. As a result, due to ACORN's lobbying, Congress imposed low-income lending quotas on Fannie Mae and Freddie Mac, spreading the practice of subprime lending. In his book *Decision Points* (pages 448, 455, 457–459, 464–465), President W. Bush underlines that "Fannie Mae and Freddy Mac, private companies with Congressional charters and lax regulations, fueled the market for mortgage-backed securities…When, in early August Freddie and Fannie announced huge quarterly losses…I decided that the only way to prevent a disaster was to take Freddie and Fannie into Government conservatorship. As a result W. Bush signed the Troubled Asset Relief Program (TARP)," which "sent an unmistakable signal that we would not let the American financial system fail…I abandoned free-market principles to save the free-market." In a nutshell this is how the crisis developed from the '60s and broke out in 2008.

On a different note, to President W. Bush's credit, on March 29, 2004, Romania was admitted into NATO, although not on its own reform merits but on its geopolitical situation. And later in 2007 Romania was admitted into the European Union. Both admissions were a stroke of luck for the country.

Furthermore, I have to stress the fact that in 2005, on the sixtieth anniversary of the Yalta Conference, President W. Bush stated that this conference was one of the most unfair in history. It was at Yalta that the liberty of the Central and Eastern European countries was sacrificed by the United States, the United Kingdom, and the Soviets. Personally, I was longing to hear such a statement—and finally, George W. Bush said it.

* * *

Rudi and I were in New York for the 2008 presidential elections between Republican senator John McCain, for whom we voted, and Democrat Barrack Obama, Illinois senator, little known nationally, whose campaign was all about promising "change." I, for one, had never heard of Mr. Obama before he announced his candidacy. Nevertheless, he won and became the forty-fourth president of the United States. I think, the media, with the exception of Fox News, failed to reveal details about Mr. Obama's biography that could have shed light on his background.

Only after the election did I hear some details regarding the newly elected president on Mr. Hannity's Fox News program about his close relationship to Reverend Wright. And also about his close association with Bill Ayers, who during the '60s was a communist revolutionary who founded the Weather Underground Group to conduct a campaign of bombing public buildings. In addition, from Matthew Vadum's book *Subversion, Inc.* (pages 15, 35–36), I found out that Bill Ayers, after being acquitted of criminal charges on a legal technicality, was a professor at the University of Illinois at Chicago, and his wife, Bernardine Dohrn, professor at the Northwestern University.

From Sean Hannity's book *Conservative Victory, Defeating Obama's Radical Agenda* (2010, pages 88–94), I got details about

Obama's $800 billion-plus Stimulus Bill or his signature legislation, the Affordable Care Act (also known as Obamacare).

As time passed by, I came to see the meaning of Mr. Obama's campaign "changes." They were meant to replace the American "equal justice" for all, with the "social justice" brand to equalize everybody's economic social status.

From my Romanian experience, I knew that such a policy decreases everybody's income and everybody became poor, with the exception of those in power. Therefore, I found very interesting Bill O'Reilly's assessment in *Pinheads and Patriots* (2010, pages 128–129, 231) about Obama's socialist vision and the redistribution of wealth in America, by writing, "Certainly, the president is trying to change the country by imposing his version of social justice…and yes, has intruded into private sector in the areas of health and finance."

About Mr. Obama's personality and his Marxist convictions as a community organizer, I found Wayne Allyn Root's article "On Barack Obama" most important, because he knew him personally as his former classmate (Snopes.com, September 19, 2012, 2 p.

I am quoting what he revealed: "Barak Hussein Obama is not… incompetent. On the contrary, he is brilliant. He knows exactly what he is doing…following the Cloward-Piven strategy that outlines the path to socialize America by overwhelming the system with government spending and entitlement demands…to destroy the United States from within and turn it into a Socialist/Marxist state with a permanent majority that desperately needs government for survival." Root said it all.

The Cloward-Piven strategy, seeking a socialist transformation of the United States, comes as no surprise for me, neither the fact that they have been Barak Obama's ideological mentor.

Further, regarding Obama's conviction in community organizing, M. Vadum's book *Subversion, Inc.* (pages 44, 49, 53–60, 104, 353) mostly concentrates on ACORN and indirectly on Obama. Besides ACORN's financial activity, I found out about its electoral activity, called Project Vote. Its mission was to mobilize low-income and minority people to register to vote. Barak Obama himself worked for Project Vote, running in 1992 a highly successful voter drive in

Chicago, praised by Cloward-Piven. ACORN's national political action committee had endorsed him in the 2008 election.

Also, from Vadum's book I learned that B. Obama was a member of an Illinois socialist party called the New Party, created with the help of the Marxist organization Democratic Socialists of America (DSA).

Likewise, the author writes that ACORN received substantive contributions from important organizations or people, including George Soros, the preeminent funder of left-wing activism in America (pages 202, 365–376).

And finally (pages 53, 332, 370), I was happy to read that in 2010 ACORN and its 370 networks had to file for bankruptcy after having become a political liability in 2008. But Vadum then warns that ACORN might in the future resurface under new names.

Barak Obama had the help of his attorney general, Erik Holder. Holder's activity has been described by Christian J. Adams, a former lawyer in the Justice Department during Eric Holder's leadership, who recounts in his book *Injustice, Exposing the Racial Agenda of the Obama Justice Department* (2011) "how…the DOJ's Civil Rights Division, has degenerated into a politicized fiefdom for far-left militants.

In their book *Erik Holder's Justice Department* (pages 9, 14, 16–18, 201), John Fund and Hans von Spakovsky explained that Erik Holder "politicized the Justice Department to an unprecedented degree…to carry out the political objectives of Barack Obama and to implement his radical ideology."

In November 2012 Rudi and I voted for Mitt Romney. When we heard the results, we were not only extremely disappointed but also very surprised at the outcome: incredibly, Barak Obama had been reelected to a second four-year term in spite of a poor first-term record.

I cannot overlook Obama's domestic policy, with an increased national debt reaching an unprecedented level of $18 trillion and growing bigger by the day, economic depression, high unemployment, the eroded middle class, with the expansion of those depending on government entitlements, etc.

Neither can I overlook his foreign policy failures. Among others, I mention the eleventh anniversary of the 9/11 attacks, when the American Consulate of Benghazi, Libya, came under attack from terrorist groups that killed four Americans, including our ambassador to Libya. Or the 2015 Vienna negotiation with Iran, making Iran only stronger.

Finally, under W. Bush the country had to face two unexpected challenges. He kept the country safe and will be remembered as a good president. Under Barak H. Obama, he tried to change the country, believing that something is truly wrong with America and he has to fix it.

* * *

When Rudi and I arrived in the USA on a sunny day, April 27, 1966, the country was a big power, and we thanked God that this blessed land adopted us. It gave us the "right to life, liberty, and the pursuit of happiness." It gave us the opportunity to study and freely practice our religion. We regained freedom!

Unfortunately, since our arrival in the '60s, a number of factors have challenged the country. For one, the Vietnam War contributed to important changes in the people's mentality.

Another event that I think had a significant negative impact on American society was the increase of drug consumption and the landmark decision *Roe v. Wade*, when the United States Supreme Court legalized abortion in the first trimester of pregnancy. This ruling probably started the sexual revolution trend. In connection with this, I appreciated Ralph Reed's book *Awakening*, in which he captures the fact that four out of ten children are born out of wedlock.

* * *

In parallel with the above trends, I cannot avoid mentioning the ideological phenomenon of "political correctness." It actually started in the '60s as a natural consequence of the existence in the United States of a multitude of cultures, traditions, and religions. Conceptually, political correctness meant avoiding forms of expression or actions perceived to offend or marginalize certain groups of people, especially in matters of race and sex orientation. That was noble in its original intent, but—in the '80s especially—universities and the media pushed this trend, in my view, to absurd extremes.

* * *

With regard to capitalism, for us it turned out to be a fertile ground where Rudi was able to develop his own electrical contractor business. He became successful based on his work in a free-market, competitive environment, despite opponents of capitalism claiming that the system does not look out for people. No doubt, the United States became the wealthiest nation through capitalism.

I found an excellent description of the essence of capitalism in *America the Beautiful* by Ben and Candy Carson 2012. They wrote, "What exactly is capitalism? It is an economic system in which individuals or corporate groups have the right to make private decisions and to acquire private property and capital goods based on their own work and competition in a free market" (page 65).

And incidentally, I found the best recipe to help America emerge from the difficult situation it found itself in 2015, in the book *Things that Matter*, by the distinguished political analyst Dr. Charles Krauthammer, a Pulitzer Prize winner. Dr. Krauthammer recognizes "America's role as hegemon…(Because) we have the most dynamic, innovative, technologically advanced economy in the world.…We have in our power to release huge domestic petroleum reserves by dropping the ban on off shore and Arctic drilling…to continue our dominant role in the world by keeping our economic house in order…(but) 'Don't do what we are doing now.'"

Back to reality. I am concerned about the 2016 elections, recalling author Vadum's contention that ACORN might be resurfacing under new names with its former fraudulent electoral activity.

About the quality of the candidate, I quote again Bill O'Reilly because I share his view. He wrote in *Who's Looking Out For You?* (pages 66–67), "Of all the active politicians in America, I consider Mrs. Clinton to be the most dangerous…she will promise massive government spending to cure all social ills." Bill had been right then after the Whitewater event. But now from Vadum's book I know about Hillary Clinton's ties to ACORN "in her early days in Arkansas," a fact which might become an issue if she is nominated as the democratic candidate in 2016. In addition, Hillary has important character and competence issues. As secretary of state, Mrs. Clinton failed to prevent the Benghazi attack by ignoring the ambassador's repeated requests to beef up the security of the Benghazi compound. Then, as her e-mails reveal, she lied to the American people about the nature of the attack. Another issue is in connection with the use of a private server for her e-mails during her tenure as secretary of state, or the cash activity of the Clinton Foundation, which reveals serious character flaws not only of Hillary Clinton but also of the Clinton couple. In that respect, I think that Peter Schweitzer's book *Clinton Cash* (2015) makes an in-depth analysis of the huge contributions to the Clinton Foundation in exchange of favors, raising huge questions about the Clintons' character.

All I can wish and hope for the United States is that, in the 2016, a strong Congress will emerge and that a strong and skilled president will be elected to bring back America's economic and military power, indispensable in the world to protect us all and defend our freedom. I believe that without a strong American military and a strong NATO, our civilized era in America and Europe will vanish away.

* * *

Now I come to the end of my memoirs. Retracing my steps in two worlds, I reached the point when I can look back and say that I had a warm, loving family, received a good education, and I am truly grateful and thankful for that. In fact, my education was the only asset I had when I ventured from Romania into a wider world. I had a very difficult twenty years under the social-communist system, where I was considered an "enemy of the people." Then finally I enjoyed freedom in America. Through hard work and perseverance, I was able to reach the goal I had pursued ever since I arrived—that is, a professional career, which helped me to occupy prestigious positions.

* * *

We all go through life being mostly concerned with the daily chores or with some longer projects, which gives us less time to contemplate the past. Before writing my memoirs, I never kept track of the turning points and pinnacles of my life through the years, nor did I wonder why fate had put me through the social-communist trial.

Then, while writing, I have not only found out more about myself; I have also brought to the surface unrecognized feelings and almost-forgotten events, arising from deep down in my conscience, where they were fading away. While writing, the recollections passed before my eyes all over again as if I were seeing a movie.

Also, this is when I realized how fate directed my life when I connected the dots between what I wanted or prayed for to happen and how certain people came my way and helped me, either immediately or even ahead of time, with issues I could not have anticipated beforehand.

On cue, some examples of incidents were when Professor Oroveanu, knocking at the classroom door during my last exam at the Law Faculty in Bucharest, whispered about the presence of a young communist group in the room who intended to obstruct my getting my diploma and how due to that unexpected warning, I had been able to avoid the group and in the end passed that last exam and got my diploma; or just when after my eviction as an "enemy of the people" from the Ministry of Transportation, my cousin Cristina incidentally met in the street, my friend Sandu Missirliu, who got me a job within a few days; or just when I was eager to find a way toward a professional career in the USA, at George Kendall's dinner, his wife seated me next to an Egyptian lady who gave me the necessary information how to reach my desired goal, etc.

All these, and many other such incidents, were answers to my prayers when fate smiled on me, putting me in touch with the right people, who guided or directed me when I needed it most!

Ultimately, while writing, I understood that I had first to suffer in Romania, to sink further and further in a despair of no return, so that later I could appreciate the freedom that came my way in the USA.

Lastly, I would like to mention the fact that after the end of the Cold War, due to my firsthand experience of terror of the social-Marxist ideology in the old country, politics became my passion, giving me the incentive to act against evil in Romania after 1990. I did not fully succeed in all my endeavors, whether through ACORD or otherwise, but to my inner satisfaction, I can say I tried.

Also, by writing my life's story, I came to see that my biggest personal satisfaction stems from my work and accomplishments, and I discovered that my political heritage has been a part of who I became and am, remaining always interested in the future of my two beloved countries, Romania and America.

* * *

Before closing my story, I have to recall one of my childhood memories to convey its value. When I was three years old and lived in a house in Bucharest, there was a door leading to a room that was kind of off-limits for me. One day, I was very curious to discover what was behind that door. I opened the door and tripped, making a loud noise. As it turned out, that door led to my parents' bedroom, and my mom was sleeping there. The noise woke her up, and she got quite upset. She took me by the hand and placed me in a corner between an armoire and the wall, saying, "You shall stand here for five minutes as a punishment to remember not to do that again." The image of that armoire, made out of orange wood with darker veins, stuck in my memory.

After 1995, during one of my visits to Bucharest, I went to visit Sanda, a distant cousin from my mother's family side. She is still living in her house, and I asked her why the communists had not evacuated her as they had done to my family and so many others. She told me that, in her case, they placed families in separate rooms of the house, and for years they had to share all common-use facilities, including the kitchen and bathrooms. As we were talking, she offered to give me a tour of the house to show me what it looked like after she managed to move those strangers out.

When we entered the master bedroom, I was in shock. The orange armoire from my mother's bedroom was there. Seeing my reaction, Sanda told me that my mother had given her the armoire as a present because that piece of furniture was too bulky to be transported to Craiova (where my mother moved for a while after her divorce).

I hardly heard Sanda's explanation. Mesmerized, I went to the side of the armoire that faced the wall and kneeled down, assuming the height of a three-year-old, to see once again that orange-colored wood with darker veins that were so vividly etched in my memory. In that moment, all my lifelong experience seemed to vanish into the air; once again, I was back in another world, the punished three-year-old girl waiting for my mom to extend her hand and take me out of there. Of course, my cousin Sanda had no idea what caused my unexpected emotional reaction.

Well, memories haunt us throughout our lives, and they were what compelled me to write these two volumes of personal memoirs together with the political analysis, because politics shaped my existence between liberty lost and liberty regained.

And now good-bye. Enjoy your own life!

Bibliography

Adams, Christian J. *Injustice, Exposing the Racial Agenda of the Obama Justice Department.* Washington, DC: Regnery Pub., 2011. 281 p.

Bădin, Andrei. *Noel Bernard.* Jurnalul National, Bucureşti, Decembrie 23, 2007. 5 p.

Borchgrave, Arnaud de, *Global Peace Index; Iceland ranks first, Afghanistan last, US is No. 110.* (http.//www.newsmax/deBorch-grave-Global-Peace-Index-Iceland/ 2013/ 06/ 17/ id/510).

Brown, Floyd G., *Slick Willie, Why America Cannot Trust Bill Clinton.* Annapolis, MD, 1993. 114 p.

Bush, George W., *Decision Points.*, New York, Crown Pub., 2010. 497 p.

Carson, Ben with Candy Carson. *America the Beautiful, Rediscovering What Made This Nation Great.* Zondervan, 2012. 205 p.

Chafets, Zev, *Roger Ailes, Off camera.* NY, Pinguin Sentinel, 2013. 258 p.

Cheney, Dick and Liz Cheney, *Exceptional, Why the World Needs a Powerful America.* New York, Threshold Editions, 2015. 324 p.

Constantinescu, Emil, *Timpul dărămării, timpul zidirii.* Bucureşti, Universalia, 2002. 4 v.

Fund, John and Hans von Spakovsky, *Obama's Enforcer Erik Holder's Justice Department*. New York, Harper Collins, 2014. 256 p.

Funderburk, David B., *Betrayal of America; Bush's Appeasement of Communist Dictators Betrays American principles*. Larry Mcdonald Foundation, 1991. 152 p.

Funderburk, David B, *Pinstripes and Reds an American Ambassador Caught between the State Department and the Romanian Communists, 1981–1985*. Washington, DC, Selous Foundation Press, 1987. 225 p.

Georgescu, Peter with David Dorsey, *The Constant Choices; An Everyday Journey from Evil toward Good*. Austin, Texas, Greenleaf BookGroup Press, 2013. 309 p.

Gibbs, Nancy and Michael Duffy, *The Presidents Club; Inside the World's Most Exclusive Fraternity*. New York, Simon & Schuster, 2012. 639 p.

Hannity, Sean, *Conservative Victory, Defeating Obama's Radical Agenda*. New York, Harper, 2010. 248 p.

Hannity, Sean, *Deliver Us from Evil. Defeating Terrorism, Despotism and Liberalism*. New York, Regan Books, Harper Collins, 2004. 338 p.

Huckabee, Mike, *Simple Government*. New York, Sentinel-Penguin, 2011. 228 p.

Institute of Jewish Affairs, *World Jewish Congress*, NY, February 1952. 3 p.

Ioanid, Radu, *The Ransom of the Jews,* Chicago, Ivan R. Dee, 2005. 217 p.

Karanycky Adrian, *"How the East Was Lost"* New York, National Review June 27, 1994. p. 5–6.

Kiehr, Harvey, John Earl Haynes and F. I. Firsov, *The Secret World of American Communism*. New Haven, Yale University Press, 1995. 348 p.

Kissinger, Henry, *Diplomacy,* NY, Simon & Schuster, 1994, 912 p.

Kissinger, Henry, *World Order*. New York, Penguin Press, 2014. 420 p.

Kleckner, Simone M., *Din exil lobby în SUA pentru România. 1990–1998*. București, Ziua, 2006. 423 p.

Kleckner, Simone M., *O mărturie provocată, 1995–2000*. Bucureşti, Themis Cart, 2004. 398 p.

Kleckner, Simone M., *Pe urmele mele in două lumi, România- SUA* Bucuresti, Curtea Veche, 2013-2014. 2 v.

Kleckner, Simone M. and Blanka Kudej, *International Legal Bibliography*. New York, Oceana, 1983. 99 p. + 57 p.

Krauthammer, Charles, *Things That Matter, Three Decades of Passions, Pastimes and Politics*. New York, Crown Pub., Penguin Random House, 2013. 387 p.

Kurtz, Stanley, *Radical-in-Chief: Barack Obama and the Untold Story of American Socialism*. New York, Threshold ed., 2010. 485 p.

McWhinney Edward, *United Nations Law Making*. Paris, Holmes-Meier Pub., 1984. 274 p.

Morris, Dick and Eileen McGann, *Because He Could*, New York, Regnery Books., 2004. 303 p.

O'Reilly, Bill, *A Bold Fresh Piece of Humanity*, New York, Broadway Books, 2008. 256 p.

O'Reilly, Bill, *Culture Warrior*, New York, Broadway Bks. 2006. 219 p.

O'Reilly, Bill, *The O'Reilly Factor*, New York, Broadway Books, 2000. 214 p.

O'Reilly, Bill, *Pinheads and Patriots, Where You Stand in the Age of Obama*. New York, Harper-Collins, 2010. 255 p.

O'Reilly, Bill, *Who's Looking Out for You?* New York, Broadway Books. 2003. 235 p.

O'Reilly, Bill and Martin Dugard, *Killing Kennedy, End of Camelot*. New York, Holt, 2012. 325 p.

O'Reilly, Bill and Martin Dugard, *Killing Reagan, The Violent Assault that Changed a President*. New York, Holt, 2015. 306 p.

Orescu, Şerban, *Ceauşismul, România între anii 1965–1989*, Bucureşti, Albatros, 2006. 314 p.

Pacepa, Ion Mihai, *Red horizons, chronicles of a communist spy chief*. Washington, Regnery Gateway, 1987. 446 p.

The Penal Code of the Romanian Socialist Republic. Translation with an introduction by, Simone M. Kleckner, S.Hackensack, N.J., 1976. 143 p. (NYU American Series of Foreign Penal Codes, 20)

Pleşea, Gabriel, *Un reporter român la Naţiunile Unite: corespondenţe de la sediul din New York al Organizaţiei Mondiale (perioada 1994–2011)*, Bucureşti, Vestala, 2012. 238 p.

Reed, Ralph, Awekening. *How America Can Turn from Economic and Moral Destruction Back to Greatness.* Brentwood, Tenn. 2014. 255 p.

Root, Wayne Allyn, *On Barack Obama.* Snopes.com, 19 September 2012. 2 p.

Rove, Karl, *Courage and Consequences: My Life as a Conservative in the Fight.* New York, Threshold Editions, 2010. 596 p.

Rumsfeld, Donald, *Known and Unknown: A Memoir.* New York, Sentinel, Penguin Group, 2011. 815 p.

Schweitzer, Peter, *Clinton Cash: The Untold Story of How and Why Foreign Governments and Businesses Helped Make Bill and Hillary Rich.* New York, Harper Collins. p. 245.

Schweitzer, Peter, *Who Broke the Evil Empire? Winning the Cold War.* National Review, May 30, 1994. p. 46–49

Shevchenko, Arkady N., *Breaking with Moscow.* New York, Knopf, 1985. 378 p.

Sowell, Thomas, *Intellectuals and Society,* New York, Basic Books, 2009. 398 p.

Sowell, Thomas, *Intellectuals and Race.* N. Y, Basic Books, 2013. 184 p.

Thatcher, Margaret, *Statecraft, Strategies for a Changing World.* NY, Harper–Collins, 2002. 486 p.

Vadum, Matthew, *Subversion, Inc.* Washington, DC, World Net Daily, 2011. 436 p.

Yoo, John, *Point of Attack—Preventive War, International Law, and Global Warfare.* New York, Oxford University Press, 2014. 259 p.

Zacklin, Ralph, *The United Nations Secretariat and the Use of Force in a Unipolar World. Power vs. Principles.* Cambridge University Press, 2010. 163 p.

Photos

Family and Friends

With my parents, JFK airport, 1972

With my father, George Vrăbiescu, New York, 1979

Rudi Kleckner, 1970

Ida Fass, Rudi Kleckner, Florida, 1982

Rudi Kleckner, Ioana Herescu, Ion Vorvoreanu, London, 1970

Pamela Richards

Aimée Tyllo

Sorin Anagnoste

Chester Frank, Simone M. Kleckner, New York, 1982

My Graduations, at
the United Nations and Friends
1969–1985

Leonarda "Lee" Wielavsky

Columbia University, MLS graduation, June 3, 1969

Van Langley

New York University, LLM graduation, June 1973

Professor Julius Marke and Blanka Kudej
in my apartment, New York, 1973

Tanţi Busuiocescu

With my mother and Cellica Neamţu, New York, 1974

Sandu Missirliu

At my desk at the UN Legal Library, 1977

Seymour James

With my assistants, Darrell Stewart and Ingeborg
in the UN Legal Library, July 1983

Natalia Tyulina, Director of the UN-DHL, 1970-1978

Ingrid Herrmann

Jeanne Kirkpatrick, US Ambassador to the UN

At the American Association of Law Libraries
Seminar in Detroit, June 1982, with Tom Reynolds,
Blanka Kudej, and Claire Germaine

International and Foreign Law presentation in the
United Nations auditorium, October 26, 1982, with
Blanka Kudej and Seymour James (moderator)

At the International and Commercial Law Seminar offered by the American Society of International Law, Washington, DC

Joseph L. Andrews award ceremony at the AALL Convention, San Diego, July 4, 1984, with Blanka Kudej and Anthony Grech

UN Retirement, 1987

At my desk as chief reference and bibliography
section of the DHL, 1987

At my UN retirement with Seymour James, March 25, 1987

At my UN retirement with Undersecretary-General Carl-
August Fleischhauer the Legal Counsel, March 25, 1987

At my UN retirement with Director Joseph
Fuchs (USA), March 25, 1987

At my retirement with Director Lengvard
Khitrov (USSR), March 25, 1987

At my UN retirement with Undersecretary-General for
Conference Services Eugeniusz Wyzner (Poland), March 25, 1987

US Court of International Trade
1987-1996

At the US Court of International Trade Annual Award
Ceremony with Chief Judge Edward Re, April 28, 1990

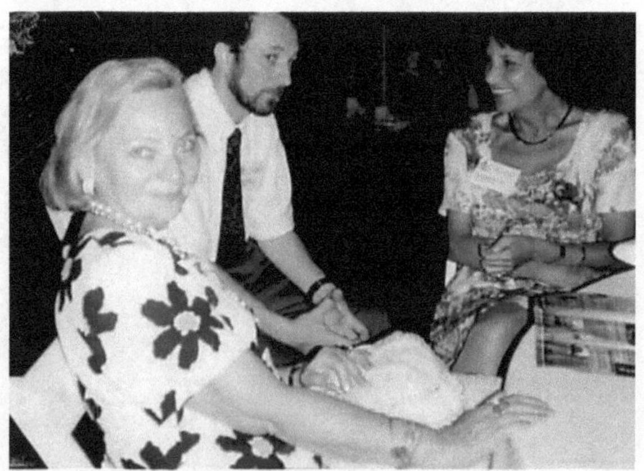

At the annual AALL Convention with Blauka Kudej
and Radu Popa, Minneapolis, June 17, 1990

At my retirement from the court with Rudi Kleckner,
Joseph Lombardi Clerk, Judge G. Carman, and
Professor Julius Marke, September 30, 1996

At my retirement at the court with Judge Thomas Aquilino, Judge
Dominic DiCarlo, Judge Nicolas Tsoucalas, September 30, 1996

With Professor Julius Marke and Rudi
Kleckner, September 30, 1996

With library staff, Herbert Crenshaw, Rosemarie DiCristo,
Ella Lidsky, Mary Finnegan-Hurley, and Anna Djirdjirian

Romanian Activity

Reception of the Romanian Royal Family at the Waldorf
Astoria Hotel, HM Queen Ana, HM King Michael, Simone
M. Kleckner, Bishop Nathanael Popp, April 26, 1991

At the Romanian Presidency Decoration Ceremony with
President Emil Constantinescu, December 11, 2000

Simone M. Kleckner

Rudi Kleckner

My mother, Mancy Radian, New York, 1991

About the Author

Simone Marie Kleckner was born in Bucharest, Romania, where she grew up. In Romania, she graduated from Bucharest Notre Dame de Sion Lyceum and the Central School for Girls in 1944. Simone earned a Juris Diploma at the University of Bucharest School of Law in 1949. She left for the United States of America in 1966. She has a Master's degree in library science from Columbia University and a master's degree in International Public Law from New York University. Simone Marie has always been interested in politics. She was the copresident and president of the Ad Hoc Committee for the Organization of Democracy in Romania (ACORD); the Personal Advisor to the Romanian President, E. Constantinescu, Bucharest, 1999–2000. Simone has written two Romanian documentaries, *O mărturie provocată* (*A Provoked Confession*) Bucharest, Themis, 2004, and *Din exil: lobby în SUA pentru România, 1990–1998* (*From Exile: Lobbying for Romania in the USA*, Bucharest, Ziua, 2006, and her memoirs entitled *Pe urmele mele în două lumi, România-SUA* (*Retracing My Steps in Two Worlds—Romania USA*), Bucharest, Curtea Veche, 2013–2014 in two volumes. In the United States, she has published various library and legal articles. Simone currently lives in South Palm Beach, Florida, with her husband, Rudolf.